CRITICAL THEORY, PUBLIC POLICY, AND PLANNING PRACTICE

SUNY Series in
POLITICAL THEORY: CONTEMPORARY ISSUES

Philip Green, Editor

CRITICAL THEORY, PUBLIC POLICY, AND PLANNING PRACTICE

Toward a Critical Pragmatism

John Forester

STATE UNIVERSITY OF NEW YORK PRESS

Published by
State University of New York Press, Albany

For information, address State University of New York
Press, State University Plaza, Albany, NY 12246

Production by Ruth Fisher
Marketing by Terry Swierzowski

Library of Congress Cataloging-in-Publication Data

Forester, John, 1948–
    Critical theory, public policy, and planning practice / John
Forester.
        p.   cm.
    Includes bibliographical references and index.
        ISBN 0–7914–1445–0 (acid-free). — ISBN 0–7914–1446–9 (pbk. :
acid-free)
        1. Policy sciences.   I. Title.
    H97.F667   1993
    320'.6—dc20
                                                                            92–1633
                                                                            CIP

10 9 8 7 6 5 4 3 2 1

For Jack Dyckman,
C. West Churchman,
and Martin Krieger,
teachers who knew
that boundaries join

543. Can I not say: a cry, a laugh, are full of meaning?
And that means, roughly, much can be gathered from them.

546. In this way I should like to say the words "Oh, *let* him come!"
are charged with my desire. And words can be wrung from
us,—like a cry. Words can be *hard* to say: such, for example,
as are used to effect a renunciation, or to confess a weak-
ness. (Words are also deeds.)

Ludwig Wittgenstein
Philosophical Investigations

CONTENTS

Preface   ix

1   Toward A Critical Pragmatism:
    The Contemporary Relevance, Promises,
    and Problems of Critical Theory   1

2   Understanding Planning Practice:
    An Empirical, Practical, and Normative Account   15

3   The Micropolitics of Planning and Policy Practices:
    Questioning and Organizing Attention   37

4   Practical Rationality: From Bounded Rationality
    to the Critique of Ideology in Practice   67

5   The Geography of Practice and the Terrain
    of Resistance   83

6   Challenges of Organization and Mobilization:
    Examples from Community-Labor Coalitions   107

7   Toward a Critical Sociology of Public Policy:
    Probing Policy-shaped Contra-Dictions in the
    Communicative Infrastructure of Society   135

Notes   163
Bibliography   179
Indexes   201

PREFACE

Hindsight has advantages over foresight at times, and writing a preface is surely one of those times. For each of the chapters that follow began as a hunch.[1] After ten years of hunches, some portion of which bore fruit, I have tried to gather together the results that have not already, for the most part, appeared in my *Planning in the Face of Power*. This book, accordingly, explores the implications of critical social theory for our understanding of planning, administrative, and policy analytic practice.

When I originally wrote the chapters of this book, I did not know what the results would be, and I certainly was not sure that the results would complement one another as systematically as these chapters do. What follows, then, is a stock-taking of an evolving line of research exploring a critical pragmatism. These essays present no last word, but they do present beginnings and openings that suggest the fruitfulness of critical social theory for research exploring diverse arenas of professional practice.

This book works, essentially, with a few relatively simple ideas. It asks, "What if social interaction were understood neither as resource exchange (microeconomics) nor as incessant strategizing (the war of all against all), but rather as a practical matter of making sense together in a politically complex world?" Planning and public policy analysis would then become processes of envisioning and attending to possible futures, shaping public attention to public possibilities. Public policy itself, by patterning social interaction, could then be seen to shape not only the distribution of "who gets what," but the more subtle constitution of ways we learn about and can attend to our concerns, interests, and needs.

So these chapters propose a critical sociology of public policy, planning, and policy analytic practice. Their treatment of critical theory is unconventional (sociological and not epistemological), particularly given the increasingly philosophical turn of critical theory in recent years. The theoretical preoccupations in the chapters that follow concern social action rather than textual interpretation—their interesting affinities notwithstanding.

The fashionable term "postmodern" is not used here, but insofar as it refers to rendering problematic instrumental rationality and associated models of social engineering, this book is thoroughly postmodern. In those terms, of course, the great bulk of 20th-century philosophy has been devoted to the "crises" of modernity and the challenges and enigmas of postmodern epistemology—following Husserl and Heidegger (and Derrida), Peirce and Dewey (and Rorty), Austin and Wittgenstein (and many others).

This book recalls attention to a central sociological concern: the understanding of social interaction, its vulnerabilities and contingent accomplishments in a political world. Accordingly, these essays deal less with problems of institutional politics—as in "theories of the state" and discussions of "politics and markets"—than they do with the micropolitics and microsociology of public policy and planning processes. These chapters provide a theoretical complement to my more practically pitched *Planning in the Face of Power* (University of California, 1989).

Finally, because this book explores the implications of Habermas's theory of communicative action for the analysis of public policy and planning practice, I want to write clearly and explicitly: the widely misunderstood notion of the "ideal speech situation" plays almost no role in this book. It plays almost no significant role—widespread assumptions in the secondary literature notwithstanding—in Habermas's sociology either. What matters here, instead, are the practical and institutional contingencies, the political vulnerabilities, of communicative action, not the abstract principles that might characterize anything resembling an inevitably counterfactual fiction of "ideal speech." It is the idea of the vulnerable precariousness of our speaking and acting together, and not the assumption of the holiness of ideal speech, that animates Habermas's fresh and strikingly fertile analysis of the practical-rhetorical structure of communicative action—an analysis that can in turn animate a powerful, critical sociology of public policy, administration, and planning practice. So one distinctive contribution of this book may be to show that a Habermasian critical *sociology* can be enormously rich even as—or, indeed, because—it in no way relies upon assumptions of "ideal speech situations." We need, again, to explore the contingencies, the fragility and vulnerability, of dialogue and social interaction, not only the ideals of dialogic or communicative action.

In the last several years I have looked more and more closely at the politics and ethics of planners' and so-called public managers' everyday talk—in negotiations, in staff meetings, in first-person accounts and profiles of their practice. That work integrates Habermasian and neo-Aristotelian concerns; focusing largely on the character of practical judgment, professional rhetoric, and the micropolitics of practice, it will appear in a future book, and it is not included here (e.g., Forester 1987a, 1987b; 1992a, 1992b).

For a great deal of assistance, criticism, and support, thanks go to friends and colleagues within several fields of the social sciences and professional disciplines. Without the persistent encouragement of Shimon Neustein, Howell Baum, Charles Hoch, Jim Mayo, Kieran Donaghy, Cathy Campbell, Annette Sassi, Patsy Healey, Ray Kemp, Frank Fischer, and John O'Neill, many of these essays would not have been written. Many of these arguments have benefited from the comments of Guy Adams, Sy Adler, Mats Alvesson, Stephen Blum, Richard Bolan, Rob Burlage, Dudley Burton, Pierre Clavel, Robert Denhardt, Jack Dyckman, John Friedmann, William Goldsmith, Linda Gondim, Ralph Hummel, Judith Innes, James Killingsworth, Richard Klosterman, Robert Kraushaar, Seymour Mandelbaum, Dieter Misgeld, Claus Offe, James O'Connor, Jay White, and Hugh Wilmott. For more recent editorial suggestions, thanks go to Brian Jacobs, Dennis Merryfield, and Robert Letcher. For help with typing and timing and more, before and after the days of word processing, thanks go, too, to Jackie Fox, Diana Wiegand, Jan Routledge, and Nancy Hutter. Finally, much more than thanks go to Betty, Kate, and Daniel for their patience and wry humor.

1

Toward A Critical Pragmatism:
The Contemporary Relevance, Promises,
and Problems of Critical Theory

What is the contemporary relevance of critical theory for the study of public administration, planning, and public policy? To begin to answer this question, we can explore six closely related areas of inquiry: (1) methodological approaches; (2) the analysis of practice; (3) the political analysis of rationality; (4) the examination of action and learning; (5) the "double structure" of organizing and organizational behavior; and (6) the analysis of policy initiatives. By surveying these thematic areas briefly, this chapter introduces the main lines of argument and the research implications of the chapters that follow.[1]

1. Methodological Approaches

Theories do not provide answers to problems; people do. But a theory can provide a framework for analysis. We do not need to make a falsely forced choice here between the most recently debated functions of adequate social theory—to explain behavior or to understand the significance of action. Theories are also coherent accounts that serve as reminders. Powerful theories redirect us toward problems and issues we might otherwise have ignored—or

1

from which we have been ideologically or methodologically distracted.

In all these varied ways critical theory is relevant to our grappling with the methodological problems of assessing planning, policy, and administrative issues. The legacy of critical theory, and particularly Habermas's more recent work, challenges us to devise methods of investigation that are: (1) empirically sound and descriptively powerful; (2) interpretively plausible and phenomenologically meaningful; and yet (3) critically pitched, ethically insightful, as well (Fay 1976, 1987; Bernstein 1976, 1983). Further, critical theory also challenges us to overcome the troubling disjunction between actor-focused and institution-focused ("micro" and "macro") research strategies (Giddens 1984). That much is easy to say but very difficult to carry out in practice.

These challenges work not only against the grain of those who claim that the behavioral sciences alone will give us explanatory power while interpretive studies will produce only (perjoratively!) "stories," but also against the grain of those who insist that the assessment of social facts will simply never allow us to develop the basis for systematic social criticism. These debates are neither settled, nor foolish. But neither do they need to paralyze research efforts.

Critical theory brings us right into—and then through—the middle of these debates about interpretation and the problematic radical distinction between facts and values. Habermas's theory of communicative action enables us to study meaningful action as it is systemically staged and structured. In the staging of communicative action, we are confronted with the causal influences of institutional context and history. In the enactment and utterances of communicative action, we are confronted with the actors' own theorizing, interpretations, articulations of self and other. Thus in the study of organizations, for example, we can assess not only the meaningful and carefully contextuated character of members' actions, but the institutionally resisting or maintaining character of those actions as well. Likewise, in the study of planners' or policy analysts' work, as chapter 2 argues, we can study the situated, performative qualities of their conversations and texts and realize how far broader institutional and structural questions of power, class, culture, ethnicity, and control manifest themselves in daily speech, writing, and gesture.[2]

Yet even if we could better integrate micro- and macroanalyses, assess meaningful action as pragmatically communicative performances in institutional contexts, would we have progressed an inch toward the goal of social and political criticism? Perhaps and perhaps not. If, for example, we could understand more powerfully how particular actions *betray* their own professions (both institutional and rhetorical professions), would not this be important, social scientifically and politically? Would the fact of such betrayal be either a descriptive or normative proposition or both at once? If, to be more concrete, we can show how self-professedly democratic institutions (say local planning agencies) selectively include and exclude members of the public they are supposed to serve, is the resulting account "factual" or "evaluative" or indeed both? Surely the answers to these questions hold that the simple distinction between factual and evaluative propositions is no longer tenable. But that is virtually trivial good news. The problems of articulating political criticism in a systematic sociological sense remain.

Here we can simply note three possible research strategies. The first strategy involves, but hardly relies upon, the terribly misunderstood Habermasian notion of "the ideal speech situation," a counterfactual anticipation we make, Habermas argues, whenever we seek mutual understanding.[3] The "ideal speech situation" is one characterized by the absence of coercion and the presence of the force of better argument alone; it characterizes Habermas's idea of discourse, the form of argumentation we presuppose we are able to step into, he argues, *when we seek to step aside* from the flow of action and (suppose that we could, in principle) *check* a problematic claim. Putting ideal speech aside, then, we might explore instead the actual social and political conditions of "checking," of political voice, and thus too of possible autonomy, even if we, again, do *not* hold those conditions up to the standards of any "ideal speech situation." Think here, for example, of doctor-patient interactions. We might expect that interaction to be characterized by complex relations of inequality, and we might accept that in large part because, or to the extent that, patients can enter the interaction willingly, with access to information, with the ability to seek independent third-party opinions, free of blind faith, and so forth. Our acceptance of certain inequalities of power and resources often depends, particularly in liberal democratic contexts, on an evaluative condition: the patient's ample ability to check, to test, to explore the conditions of his or her patienthood. Here Habermas's work alerts us to the possibilities of actors' contingent difficulties of having actual "recourse to discourse." This evaluative strategy orients us toward the always tenuous conditions of (roughly speaking) "informed consent." This approach is suggestive, but it faces difficulties quickly. How are we to assess the no doubt imperfect conditions of checking we will find? Which reflect domination, and which reflect instead the forces of necessity?

The second and third normative strategies are different versions of one another. Both direct our research attention toward the always vulnerable and precarious intersubjectivity of social actors. From one angle, we can investigate this social capacity to act from the standpoint of (as Habermas puts it) "the colonization of the lifeworld." With this second strategy, employing Habermas's "system-lifeworld analysis," we assess the ways that institutional pressures work through the media of power and money, bureaucratization and commodification, to preempt or encroach upon autonomous or even tradition-appropriating social action. Here we might see, for example, how routine notions of planners presumptively identify and preempt indigenous ideas of community and territory from community members. Here we attempt to explore the struggles over, the dialectics of, social rationalization at a level of administrative organization, planning processes, and public policy making (Fraser 1989).

From another angle, we can explore the contingencies of ordinary social interaction and assess how organizational and institutional contexts render "making sense together" problematic and politically vulnerable. With this third strategy, whatever we may lose in institutional generality, we gain in the analysis of the very conditions of interaction itself. In the analysis of planning, for example, here we can see how subtly the everyday claims of planners can have political effects upon community members, empowering or disempowering, educating or miseducating, organizing or disorganizing them (Forester 1985, 1989; O'Neill 1989). In both the second and third strategies, we have normative analysis in its most sociological clothes.

Critical theory does not solve these problems, but it poses them powerfully for us. It brings us yet closer to developing a framework of social research that neither ignores normative problems nor shunts aside interpretive and phenomenological issues. With critical theory, we have a research framework that confronts us with the challenge to assess the vulnerabilities of our basic capacities to act with one another, to act meaningfully together, and to protect and nourish forms of social cooperation, forms of sociality. We are given the beginnings of a framework with which to integrate critical ethnographic and more structural and historical work.

But what issues might such a research framework illuminate for us in our analysis of public administration, planning, and public policy? Let us review several "areas of application" briefly.

2. The Analysis of Practice

Studies of practice in public policy, planning, and public administration are often social-psychological in character, paying somewhat peripheral attention to questions of politics. In the insightful and interesting work of Donald Schön and Howell Baum, for example, we learn a good deal about individual practitioners but wonder about the political significance of their actions (Schön 1983, 1991; Baum 1983, 1987, 1990). In the work of Andreas Faludi, we have a renewed Popperian approach that focuses largely upon issues of justification in its concern with decision-centered action (Faludi 1987).

By contrast, critical theory gives us a rich sociological formulation—of communicative action—that allows us to explore the political implications of practice in powerful ways. Practice is intentional and purposive, to be sure. As intentional, it is phenomenologically accessible to us: we can investigate the ways that practitioners formulate and come to reformulate problems as they explore them (indeed as Schön's analysis does). As purposive, that practice is partially instrumental to be sure; it makes sense for us to ask what particular actors are after and how they may think strategically about reaching they ends they seek. But practice is far more than that. The ends that planners and political actors seek are far more diverse than they know at any one time, and the close analysis of any flow of conversation will demonstrate as much. The analysis of communicative action allows us to look closely at the "how" and the "what" of practice, at the phrasing of talk, for example, to see how practitioners read their political environments in skilled ways to reproduce political relationships even as they satisfy a complex host of "goals," values, commitments, obligations, and senses of self and others.

We can assess practice not simply as the achievement of goals, but more subtly too, as chapter 3 shows, as the practical, communicative organizing (or dis-organizing) of others' attention to relevant and significant issues at hand. Such attention-direction is behaviorally observable, phenomenologically powerful, and deeply political at the same time. Recall E. E. Schattschneider's dictum (Schattschneider 1960; Lukes 1974) that all "organization is the mobilization of bias." But organizations do not mobilize bias in the abstract; their members do that as they select some issues as appropriate to address and others as inappropriate, as they serve some clients and not others who may need services, as they attend to some problems and put others aside. This formulation of ordinary practice suggests normative results: any organizing of others' attention is simultaneously a structuring of their neglect as well (Bruner 1990).

This analysis allows us to link planning and administrative practice directly to the exercise of influence and power. Most obviously, the ability to shape others' attention generalizes the form of power commonly discussed as "agenda-setting." Less obviously, but perhaps more importantly, recognizing the attention-organizing character of practice raises crucial questions about the organization, administration, and planning of democratic participation in a modern polity (Krumholz and Forester 1990). Following the normative directions discussed briefly above, this understanding of practice suggests a distinctively counterhegemonic or democratizing role for planning and administrative actors: the exposure of issues that political-economic structures otherwise would bury from public view, the opening and raising of questions that otherwise would be kept out of public discussion, the nurturance of hope rather than the perpetuation of a modern cynicism under conditions of great complexity and interdependence.[4]

Note that this formulation of planning and administrative practice is purposive but not reductively instrumental. It is phenomenologically sensitive—to the shaping and reading of action as meaningful—but it does not treat meaning making as a disembodied and apolitical activity. It is political and interested, too, without automatically being cast functionally in the service of one class interest or another. But this notion of practice leads to a closely related problem, that of rationality. If we are to consider practice as the situated, practical, politically charged organizing of attention, when can we call that activity "rational," and when not? For if we cannot make sense of the rationality of such practice, our very formulation of practical activity will be suspect.

3. The Political Analysis of Rationality

The situated, attention-organizing formulation of practice leads to an intriguing reformulation of our notions of administrative and planning rationality. Thirty years ago, the equation of rationality with optimization was broken by Herbert Simon's ideas about bounded rationality (Simon 1957). Simon argued that the real constraints of decision makers' own information-processing abilities led those decision makers not to optimize but to "satisfice," to meet lowered expectations, expectations that could then be satisfied rather than optimized, given that the ideal conditions of perfect information were not to be met. In planning and administrative theory, such "bounded" rationality has long appeared to be virtually natural: "Of course we can't really optimize! We have to 'satisfice' instead" (Friedmann 1987; Denhardt 1981).

Chapter 4 argues that the theory of communicative action leads us to a powerful extension of Simon's account, an extension that recognizes both politics and structural, systematic distortions of decision making and cooperative action. Simon's powerful attack on the optimizing model focused on a particular category of constraint: constraints that were both *necessarily* present and independent of contingent political-economic *structures*. By considering administrative practice now as communicative interaction rather than as the cognitive activity of decision making, we can explore further questions about the bounded nature of rational action. Shouldn't we distinguish necessary from unnecessary bounds upon such interactions? Shouldn't we distinguish structural from nonstructural bounds?

Just as Simon argued that the satisficing model of bounded rationality called for distinctively different strategies of action than the optimizing model did, so a Habermasian reformulation of bounded rationality points to yet further, and indeed politically richer, strategies too. We need not carry through this line of argument here, for that argument has been developed elsewhere (Forester 1989, chapters 3 and 4). Yet note that the response to "bounds" upon action that are both socially unnecessary and structurally based must be a response that challenges or seeks to alter present social structures, a response that challenges any perceived "necessity" or "natural" or reified character of such constraints. Here we have the link between a tradition of ideology critique and political action and a previously altogether depoliticized understanding of administrative and planning rationality.

4. The Examination of Interaction and Learning

The analysis of communicative action also points us toward a rich and multilayered formulation of social interaction. When we speak, we do not send messages as senders electronically linked to receivers. We perform speech acts in socially rule-structured contexts in which we seek to make meaning and in which we interpret the meanings of others' speech (and gesture) in turn. So we know that a simple "hello" is not so simple: depending on context, inflection, tone, and history, for example, what is heard literally as an utterance of greeting may be instead an affectless, if not curt, acknowledgement of one's presence (from a harried clerk), a grudging act of obedience to rules (from a child), a soft expression of desire (from a lover), or a sarcastic comment upon an obligation betrayed (from a housemate kept waiting too long for one's arrival).

When we assess the structure of speech acts, we find a curious "double structure" that communication theorists have long noted: speakers simultaneously *enact relationships* with one another as they *speak about* whatever they do. Habermas suggests that speakers seeking mutual understanding—even if they only ask for the salt at the dinner table—ordinarily make four pragmatic claims upon their listeners, claims: (1) to the truth of what's referred to (there *is* salt on the table to be passed); (2) to the legitimacy of the norms invoked in the context (having prefaced my request, for example, with "please," I am now entitled as a full participant at the dinner table, to receive the salt); (3) to the trustworthy expression of self by the speaker (no, I'm not kidding); and (4) to the meaningful character of the words, gestures, or tokens used (perhaps a whispered "please" and a point of a finger toward the salt so that another conversation will not be interrupted).

This pragmatic analysis of claims making suggests effects upon listeners under ordinary conditions just as it tells us something about what we do when we speak. So we can now explore how claims to the truth of states of affairs may alter listeners' *beliefs* about what is so; how claims to legitimacy may alter their *consent* and deference to norms; how our expressive claims may alter listeners' *trust*; and how claims to have formulated meaning coherently may alter listeners' basic *mode of attention paid* to the issue at hand.

This analysis in turn suggests a provocative extension of theories of power that focus upon the mobilization of bias and agenda-setting. For now, as chapter 5 shows, we can assess administrative and planning action as it shapes what others know, the norms and rules they may take to be legitimate, the expectations of others they internalize, and the frameworks in which they come to pose issues. This suggests how, in speaking practically, administrators and planners shape quite pragmatically (and politically!) the ways that other citizens learn or fail to learn.

Significantly too, this analysis of the structure of pragmatic interaction suggests the nature of doubt faced by participants in

administrative and planning processes, when claims making may
be contested or challenged. Doubts about truth claims raise uncertainties, but doubts about legitimacy, expressive, or meaning-con-
stituting claims raise not uncertainties but ambiguities. This
result is important for two reasons. First, uncertainty and ambiguity appear to call for quite different practical responses. Facing
uncertainty, we need information. Facing ambiguity, we need
practical, perhaps authoritative, judgment. Second, in administrative and planning contexts, questions of ambiguity (what do they
really *want*?) are likely to be reduced to those of uncertainty (shall
we devise a questionnaire to see what they really *do* want?). The
resulting call for more information (and perhaps more information-processing equipment) may then only further obscure the
political and social judgments that must inevitably be made. If this
argument is half-right, then the reduction of ambiguity to uncertainty may have subtle and perverse depoliticizing effects.

5. The "Double Structure" of Organizing and Organizational Behavior

We can turn now to the study of organizations and organizing
practices. The analyses of communicative action, dimensions of
social learning and doubt, and the link between the organizing of
attention and the play of political power have instructive implications for our understanding of formal and informal organizations.

Most importantly, the double structure of communicative
interaction has a powerful organizational analogue. Political organizers must pay attention simultaneously to the goals they wish to
achieve *and* to the ways in which their actions—their speech, gestures, pronouncements, expressions—reconstitute their own identities, shape their reputations, and thus further enable or undercut their future abilities to act. The same is true more generally of
organizational continuity. Organizations do not survive by themselves, for they are reproduced by their members. Organizations
have both productive and reproductive elements, if not functions.
Whether we have in mind a city hall bureaucracy, a labor union, or
an environmental advocacy organization, as organization members
act purposively to accomplish their ends, so do they reproduce, for
better or worse, in more and less skilled ways, the very social relations that may sustain their organizations in the first place. Dealing with the problems at hand raise productive or instrumental

issues; maintaining or building "the membership" raises reproductive issues.

The structural features of the pragmatics of communicative action have their organizational counterparts too. But now we can explore the organizational repertoires of skills and knowledge that actors draw upon to pitch their claims rhetorically as they seek to shape others' beliefs, consent, trust, and formulations of issues. We can expect that organizational action will draw upon these elements in quite variable ways. Here the examination of advocacy and oppositional organizations can be instructive.

In chapter 6 we consider the experience of organizers' efforts to build community-labor coalitions concerned with industrial pollutants and workers' and community members' "right to know" about industries' use of toxic chemicals. In such cases, we can see immediately the organizers' attempts to frame issues selectively and to educate the public about information suppressed by powerful corporate actors. At the same time, we can see the careful attempts by the organizers to constitute their own organizations: to build their "selves," their reputations, through expressions of solidarity with the interests of others, to build their legitimacy through coalitions with respected others in the community. The "double structure" of speech, as Habermas put it, has a direct organizational analogue: organizations concern themselves with goals, substance, and content to be sure, but as they do so, they must also continually renew themselves, work to maintain relationships, work to maintain reputation and identity.

This balancing act has two central risks, of course. First, a narrow concern with instrumental outcomes can weaken an organization's ability to maintain itself. For example, voluntary organizations typically go through cycles in which task performance drives out attention to recruitment, burnout of the shrinking core members begins to set in, and a crisis of identity ("Can we continue this?") ensues. Second, a narrow concern with organizational maintenance and reputation, conversely, can drive out attention to task performance and instrumental production. Thus we have the stereotype of career bureaucrats who are risk averse, risking so little in the way of reputation, political and professional support, and trust of other actors that only the most routinized and non-controversial tasks can be achieved.

A critical theory of organizational behavior and organizing leads to many more questions than it answers. In particular we must explore the strategies organizations and their members use to reproduce beliefs, consent, trust, and attention in highly politicized contexts. These questions lead immediately to those of the maintenance and vulnerability of hegemonic power.

A critical account of organizing leads us directly to a dialectics of power and resistance: power exists as a social relationship reproduced by concrete actions. Power, too, has its limits, its vulnerabilities. If we can investigate how the reproduction of power, as hegemonic patterns of attention, for example, can be itself vulnerable, we would be able then to inform possibilities of resistance to various forms of domination.[5] Furthermore, if policy making shapes our political future, in part by restructuring the political and administrative organization of schools, hospitals, relief services, banks, regulatory agencies, and so on, then the theory of communicative action should inform our understanding of the political significance of various policy proposals and alternatives.

6. The Analysis of Policy Initiatives

We have too little cogent sociology of public policy today (Bell 1976; Alford and Friedland 1985). We have instead two forms of policy analysis, incrementalist and utilitarian, which severely constrain our vision.

The incrementalist analysis focuses on the negotiations involved in the formulation and implementation of public policy. As policy is being formulated, advocates of various interests lobby and exert influence to shape the (typically legislative) proposals being considered (Wildavsky 1979). As policy, once legislated, then mandates administrative and organizational action, a new round of negotiations takes place. Given limited resources of time, expertise, knowledge, and the established organizational interests at hand, how now is a broad policy directive actually to be carried out in practice (Lipsky 1980)? The utilitarian line of policy analysis is best typified by the widespread interest in variations of cost-benefit analysis as a foundation for the examination of alternative policy proposals (Tribe 1972; Paris and Reynolds 1983).

In each case, policy initiatives are treated as tools, as instrumental strategies to reach ends. The incrementalist asks how compromises are made along the way so that the original ends are displaced; the utilitarian asks how, whether, and which ends have been reached. Yet neither approach—helpful as both of these may indeed be—helps us to understand how policy making and policy implementation reshape the lived worlds of actors, restructure social worlds in ways that alter actors' opportunities, capacities to act, and self-conceptions too. Here critical theory can help us in intriguing ways.

Habermas's social theory poses problems of social learning at two levels of analysis. Following but drastically reformulating Marx on a societal level, Habermas argues that societies learn in both technical-instrumental (productive) and moral-practical (reproductive) dimensions. The former echoes the development of forces of production; the latter echoes the development of social relations of production. At the level of action, however, we learn in the dimensions in which we act communicatively: those of making and testing claims about states of affairs in the world, about appropriate and legitimate social relationships, about personal and social identities, and about ways of framing issues at hand.[6]

We must ask, though, how the particular claims of social and political actors can ever be established or even routinized in enduring social and political structures. How can we connect the interactions of claims-making actors to the structural learning embodied in developing institutions? How, alternatively, can an institutional pronouncement be challenged and reformulated so that institutional developments are redirected?

We can answer these questions if we explore the nature of the social infrastructure that mediates: (1) between enacted truth claims and the social stock of knowledge; (2) between particular legitimacy claims and political patterns of authority; (3) between our expressive claims and social patterns of identity and membership; and (4) between particular claims formulating the significance of problems and the socioeconomic institutions that allocate social attention. As such mediating institutions (the knowledge industries, courts, and legislatures, and cultural organizations, for example) change, so do they affect the social levels they mediate between: structural learning and actors' developing beliefs, patterns of consent, relations of solidarity, and investments of attention.

This analysis leads to wide-ranging but closely integrated questions in the examination of public policy. We can now explore how particular policy proposals promise to alter this socially mediating infrastructure, this mid-level range of institutions that links the lived worlds of actors to the broader structures of society. For example, with the onset of policies promoting environmental deregulation, not only will corporate actors be instrumentally given greater autonomy of action, but public *knowledge* of private action is likely to suffer, false claims to public safety and corporate vigilance are likely to manipulate public trust, and issues of profitability are likely to preempt public attention to those of public health and alternative possibilities of public investment and control. Here a critical communications theory can integrate a structural analysis of institutional change with a phenomenological analysis of the ever-vulnerable and shifting lived worlds of social actors.[7]

Concluding Notes

These introductory claims have been abstract, promissory, and broad rather than deep. The chapters that follow seek to show how a critical communications theory of society might inform our methods of social research and our analyses of administrative practice, rationality, interaction, organization, and public policy analysis.

Whether these claims can be extended and built upon rather than revised altogether only subsequent research efforts will show. The attempt to "apply" critical theory to issues of planning and administrative practice is still in its early stages.

Habermas's work has been provocative, controversial, ambitiously pitched, and consistently metatheoretical: it provides a framework rather than a series of particular explanations; it poses systematic questions rather than sets of hypotheses to test; it seeks to integrate styles of analysis and research approaches in fresh ways. It shapes our inquiries rather than providing operational tools with which we might manipulate data. It brings us insistently to the intersection of concerns with action, rationality, politics, structural change, and history—and then leaves us to carry out more concrete analyses, to investigate concrete cases, to try to marry ethnographic analysis with social structural accounts, and to do so without taking a pledge of normative agnosticism (Forester 1992a).

The glass of critical theory is surely half-empty: we are still missing a good deal of guidance about the most fruitful ways to carry out empirical, historically situated, phenomenologically cogent, normatively insightful analyses. Here surely the balance must now shift from necessarily abstract methodological analyses toward the effort to assess specific cases, concrete attempts to work out the implications of a critical communications framework in particular cases, specific analytical experiences on the basis of which our collective research abilities and judgments will develop. But the glass is also half full: the theory of communicative action represents certainly the most systematic rethinking of action theory in the context of societal rationalization that is available today. That it draws not only from the classical sources of Marx, Weber, Durkheim, and Mead, but depends heavily too, if more implicitly, on the work of Wittgenstein and Austin, Gadamer, and Apel, makes the work both more challenging and more daunting. As a result, a critical theory of public administration, public policy, and planning is likely to be provocative and instructive, but remain marginalized too. Both its insistent attention to a dialectics of power and resistance and the very theoretical reach it demands will provide counterweights against the pressures to absorb it into more conventional theories of public administration and public policy.

Critical theory remains, these chapters will argue, a rich source of insights, a source of challenge to social and political analysis, and a reminder of the structured vulnerabilities and contingencies of social action throughout society. Critical theory reminds us, too, of our continuing need to explore the contingencies of power and our possibilities to organize a just and good life in the diverse settings in which we live.

2

Understanding Planning Practice:
An Empirical, Practical, and Normative Account

Introduction

This chapter explores one small part of planning education, research, and theory: understanding what planners actually do in their day to day work. The chapter is not immediately about urban fiscal crises, inflation, the history of class struggles, utopian communities, causal models, or democratic theory—however important and perhaps inseparable these topics may be. The first part considers the requirements for an adequate account of planning practice. The second section considers the contributions and limitations of four conventional accounts of what planners do. The third part then suggests an alternative and arguably more powerful account of what planners actually do. Section four, finally, suggests practical research questions that flow from the analysis of planning as communicative action that organizes or disorganizes citizens' attention to possibilities of public action.

Requirements for Theory of Planning Practice

Since planning is a value-laden activity whose success or failure has consequences for the society encompassing it, any theory of

planning must meet broader requirements than those demanded
of theories in the natural or physical sciences. Not only must an
adequate account of planning practice be *empirically fitting*, it
must also be both *practically appropriate* to the settings in which
planners work and *ethically illuminating*, helping planners and
citizens understand and assess the ethical and political consequences of various possibilities of action, policy, or intervention.
Such is the argument with which Richard Bernstein concludes his
Restructuring of Social and Political Theory:

> In the final analysis we are not confronted with exclusive
> choices: *either* empirical theory *or* interpretive theory *or* criti-
> cal theory. Rather there is an internal dialectic in the
> restructuring of social and political theory: when we work
> through any one of these moments, we discover how the oth-
> ers were implicated. An adequate social and political theory
> must be *empirical, interpretive, and critical*. (Bernstein 1976,
> 235)

This chapter attempts to provide a preliminary account of
planning practice, and thus a research framework, that does justice to Bernstein's demands. In particular, by treating planning as
inherently political and communicative, a critical theory of planning practice can: (1) be grounded in an empirical analysis of what
planners do intentionally and unintentionally; (2) be sensitive to
the practical situations which planners face and seek to interpret
and understand; and (3) be discriminatingly critical of the extent
to which planners counter (or perpetuate) unnecessary political
distortions of problem formulations, analyses of options, or broader
planning agendas.

To begin, then, what does it mean to hold that a planning
theory (or the results of planning research!) ought to be empirical,
"interpretive" or practically fitting, and "critical" or ethically illuminating? To be empirically grounded, an account of planning
practice must fit the experiences of real planning practice. Data
must be available—in principle, if it is not already collected—that
could substantiate or weaken the account. Given a suggestion that
planning practice in metropolitan planning departments can be
described (and ought to be understood) as technical problem-solving activity, for example, a wealth of evidence could be brought to
light to weaken or refine this view. Such evidence might reveal the
political work that planners must do to allow any technical work
itself to proceed.

An empirical planning theory would suggest patterns of practice to study and data to gather. It would be experientially plausible both to practitioners and to observers of planning, who would be led to say not, "That theory is about some other world," but "Yes! That's how it is!"

Like accounts of problems in the physical sciences, an empirically grounded planning theory ought to be evaluated by comparison to rival and previously offered theories. Does the suggested theory explain what its competitors explain? Does it explain or order more? Can it resolve the puzzles and "anomalies" left as open questions by the competing theories? Any new empirical account of planning practice ought to lead to new research questions, new data to collect, new patterns of action to explore—all of which may inform the effectiveness, efficiency, and morality of planning practice. Informing in new ways how planners work, when and how they are listened to, how they may be effective, any new account of planning practice should teach us—and lead us to question in new ways—the art of the possible: design and implementation in a political world.

To be practically appropriate or "interpretive," a theory of planning practice must not only order data, it must also speak to the working interpretations that planners have of the practical situations and problems they face. For example, an empirical theory might be developed strictly in terms of the formal role descriptions (or job titles) of planning agencies and those with whom planners work. Such an empirical theory, though, would most likely be practically next to useless, for it would likely ignore the vast and essential types of informal roles that make any organization so much more than what its organization chart shows. Thus, an analysis of planning might be empirically verifiable but simply irrelevant to the practical demands of planners' work.

An interpretive account of planning, sensitive to the planners' perceptions of events, would suggest strategies of action that were both empirically concrete and practically fitting in the "real world" of planning organizations and politics. A "rigorous technique" that will take two years to use, when the planners need an analysis done in a month, may do no one any good. Without an interpretive account of their work, practitioners will look at existing theories and wonder if the theorists even begin to appreciate what planners face in everyday practice (Vickers 1984; Rabinow and Sullivan 1979; Bolan and Nuttal 1980; Krieger 1981).

Any practically appropriate account of planning, then, should address (though not necessarily accept) the planners' senses of constraints. It should help us also to understand that one of the most significant constraints that planners face is their own perception of the constraints in any given situation (Catron 1977; Krumholz, Cogger, and Linner 1975; Baum 1980). The account should help the reader to anticipate regular, structural problems of noncooperation, vested interest, conflict, and distortions of information, and then, in response, to reformulate notions of planners' influence and efficacy. Able to understand planning "as seen through the planner's eyes," an interpretive theory can inform the strategic, political reading of situations that planners face and so inform practical responses too. Empirically ordering facts about planning practice is not enough; an account of practice must speak to what those facts mean to planners and those with whom they work. This is the meaning of the requirement that an adequate theory of planning practice be interpretive and practically appropriate.

To be ethically illuminating, an account of practice must begin with the recognition that no theory of action can be fundamentally neutral, for any theory reflects an organization of our attention, to the neglect of other possibilities (Forester 1989; Sandercock and Forsyth 1992). Any account of planning practice makes normative claims to its readers: "You ought to consider *these* variables. To understand what planners do, and how they might act better still, you ought to watch out for *those* problems, or *these* opportunities." A problem-solving theory of practice may neglect goal-setting or value-formulating processes, for example; a political theory may neglect questions of economic exchange or class relationships.

Still, saying that any account of practice is inevitably normative and selective does not yet tell us what might make such an account ethically illuminating. To accomplish this, a theory ought not attempt to specify once and for all formal rules to determine action, for the ethical questions of practical judgment will inevitably arise: "How, in *this* situation, should I apply this rule?" Should another rule then be suggested, the question can be asked again—*ad infinitum*; this "application problem" represents a difficulty faced by any formal rule-based system of ethics. Specifying rules in any case can only be as good, practically speaking, as the ability of planners to interpret those rules in actual situations.

Instead, then, an account of planning practice ought to provide explicit guides for action and explicit justifications for those guides. This is hardly a radical claim, for if any theory must have normative dimensions, this claim simply calls for explicitness about those dimensions.

More importantly, an ethically instructive account of planning practice ought to locate that practice in a historical world of influences supporting and threatening the account's notion of good planning. By doing so, the theory can say more than (to a person) "Do good" or (to a movement) "Make the revolution." Pointing out the *threats* to practice which can be *anticipated and counteracted* is one ethically instructive contribution that, we shall argue, a communicative account of planning practice can make.

Such attention to threats and opportunities, though, can only be helpful if the recommended actions—for example, consulting early with some, supporting particular coalitions—are plausibly rooted in the common-sense and ordinary-life practices of society at large. These recommendations must be plausibly related to notions of fairness, equality, social responsibility, minimizing harm, the prevention of tyranny. They should not, for example, ask us to sacrifice the minority for the good of the majority.

Finally, to be ethically illuminating, an account of planning must address the relationships of planning practice to political inquiry and criticism, to the legitimation of public policy, and to the tensions between the reliance upon expertise and the nurturance of democratic politics (Burke 1986). We might not ask of such an account that it "have all the answers," but we should ask that it help us ask ethically insightful questions about the present and possible practices of planning practitioners—and that it help us work together to resolve those questions in practice.

Conventional Views

Before suggesting an alternative account of planning and policy-analysis practice, we should consider several of the conventional notions we find both in our academic literatures and in "the field." We can review four perspectives, briefly: means-ends models of instrumental rationality; problem-solving, rationalistic, "scientific" models; cybernetic, information-processing models; and "satisficing" models of "bounded rationality" (Friedmann 1987). These are not general theories of planning; they are conventional, partial, and important but problematic accounts of planning practice, accounts of how planners do what they do. By the standards of the previous section, each of these accounts may be empirically based. Yet only the latter two seem to address practical issues of interpretation, and none of the four seems to address ethical and normative issues in a systematic manner. Exploring these views in depth along the lines of the last section is beyond the scope of this chapter. Nevertheless, at the risk of some oversimplification, their strengths and weaknesses can instructively be considered here.

Means-Ends Models

Means-ends thinking "works" as long as ends are given and stable; means are unique and self-justifying; and problems are routine and stable (Tribe 1973). But this is usually not the case in planning situations: (1) ends are not only not given, but they may conflict; (2) there are always conflicting means to any end; and (3) problems change, preferences and tastes change, and new values are discovered. Planners need to reformulate problems, strategies, and solution approaches rather than follow standardized procedures (Churchman 1968; March 1978, 1988; Wiggins 1978; Schön 1983; Feldman 1989).

Furthermore, means-ends rationality falsely separates the value-laden character of any means from the ends. Exponents of this view may think that "means" can be neutral while "ends" only are value laden. Yet as long as there is a question of which means are to be chosen (or then of *how* those means are to be applied), then neither the means, nor the one choosing the appropriate means, can be considered neutral.

Means-ends thinking may also push aside, often to an ill-defined "political process," the problem of the sources of the "ends" or program or policy "goals." When we think this way, we act as if we could bury our heads, be neutral, and apply "means" and let someone else worry about "ends." And this is especially a problem, of course, when ends or goals conflict or promise to benefit different groups of people. Such thinking tends to relegate goals to the irrational, while turning the world of action into a set of possible manipulations (Klosterman 1978; Elster 1983, 1986; Sunstein 1991).

Environmental impact reports, for example, are presumably "means" to report (anticipate) the impacts of a project's development. Were we only to look at such a means-ends relationship, we would miss the significant other aspects of EIRs: shaping political participation, making projects visible, providing a design review tool before EIR completion, providing a basis for negotiations with affected publics to shape project design when EIRs may not even be required. Searching for a one-to-one means-ends relationship here might only obscure the actual process from our view.

Problem-Solving Perspectives

Problem-solving views begin with the engineer's special bias, the rationalism of Descartes' *Discourse on Method*: Take the problem, break it down into its component parts, and let's see what we can do about it. This may serve well for relatively routine, conventional, stable problems—but perhaps not for most planning and policy problems (Baum 1980; Churchman 1968; Elster 1986; Peattie 1987; Webber and Rittel 1973).

Problem-solving views often make social and political questions of values, interests, attachments, and meanings apparently "technical" matters. Procedure or method may threaten to drive out substance (Dyckman 1978; Marris 1975; March 1988; Innes 1990). Problem solvers need to reduce; but analysts need to consider. Problem solvers need to get rid of problems; planners and analysts need to create them, to reformulate them, to make them anew so programmatic strategy is possible and desirable and so that their strategy addresses some notions of "what the problem really is" (Meltsner 1975; Seeley 1963; Churchman 1971; Feldman 1989).

Like facts, problems do not speak for themselves: they are not "given," waiting to be broken down and solved. Planning problems are often ambiguous, vague, full of conflicts and competing interpretations (Wildavsky 1979).

Problem-solving thinking appeals to methods appropriate for technically "well-behaved" problems—methods which may not be appropriate to the types of "wicked" problems that planners face (Webber and Rittel 1973). More serious still, the appeal to method may lead us to neglect the sources of criteria, standards, and measures of cost and benefit without which planning and policy analysis cannot make sense. The choice of "method" is an ethical choice having consequences: costs considered and neglected, strategies deemed feasible and sensible or "inappropriate," not right in the case at hand.

In environmental review situations, for example, problems are so various, so different, that while a few standardized forms exist for the initial information gathering, there is no uniform, codified method by which problem solving might work. Planning staffs cannot derive politically strategic solutions like engineers solving equations. Rather, they need to interpret situations and create plausible ideas about just what the problem "ought to be taken as" (Churchman 1971; Krumholz and Forester 1990; Schön 1983; Reich 1988; Majone 1989; Fischer and Forester 1993). Such problem formulating, problem creating, sets the stage for action: phone the developer, send the plans to architectural staff, involve the neighborhood group. All this depends upon what the planners take the problem to be, what they "make of it" in the organizational and political settings within which they work. Less problem solvers, planning analysts might rather be problem makers (constructors)! As Arnold Meltsner describes the related issue of problem selection,

> Indeed, the analyst makes a primary economic and political decision in selecting a problem to work on—economic in that he is a scarce resource whose talents should not be wasted on trivial or unsolvable problems, and political in that problem selection is the first critical step he takes toward insuring his own political success. Choosing the right problem is crucial in building political efficaciousness. (Meltsner 1975, 122; cf. Innes 1990; Reich 1988; but contrast Forester 1993)

Cybernetic Perspectives

The cybernetic imagery is fitting for many physical and natural systems, but it is more problematic for self-constituting, self-transforming social and political ones (Faludi 1976; Vickers 1970). In the cybernetic perspective the definition of "error" and the evaluation of feedback seem no longer to be fundamentally political and ethical matters.

As one student of politics pointedly put it, social systems, the systems in and upon which planners and policy analysts work, may be no more politically self-regulating than the Bastille was self-storming (the image is Langdon Winner's [1977]). Cybernetics may help us significantly to model systems-*behaviors* but not norm setting and social action; it may be less helpful with "normative" matters of planning practice, the formulation of strategy and effective action (Vickers 1973; Adams et al 1987). How, for example, in cybernetic accounts can persons be held responsible? The language of "feedback" can drive out the moral language of agency and responsibility.

By what processes of (legitimate?) communication are goals to be articulated, trade-offs made, compromises come to, and so forth? If feedback must always be evaluated in terms of rules of the game, how, and by whom, have these rules been made? And how rigid or monolithic is the structure of rules? This is a matter of political feasibility: how might the existing rules change? What systemic changes might be possible, can be imagined? The great contribution of cybernetic theories has been their focus upon systemic relations and interactions as they influence system stability and control. Yet normative issues of system control (e.g., governance, legitimate authority, justice) seem to lie beyond the systematic boundaries of present cybernetic accounts (Vickers 1970; Friedmann 1973, 1979).

Again, in environmental review, it is one thing to speak colloquially of getting feedback on a document or an idea, but that is a far cry from modeling the planning process that way. There are too few well-defined production functions or transformations; errors are continuously being defined and redefined; system boundaries are fluid. Cybernetic theories have been most helpful as systems theories; they have been less appropriate as theories of action, whether of the social practices of planning practitioners or of other social actors (Friedmann 1978).

"Satisficing" Perspectives

The "satisficing" account of bounded rational action (and its disjointed incremental cousins) has been particularly provocative and troublesome (Simon 1957; March and Simon 1958; March 1978, 1988; Friedmann 1987). The essential contribution of theories of bounded rationality has been their rejection of the practically irrational rationality of comprehensiveness, collecting all the facts, surveying all possible alternatives, tracing all possible consequences, and so forth. Yet we may not be left with a substantial account of rationality in its place, for satisficing becomes an invitation to "make do."

We may bound rationality by adding constraints of time, resources, and knowledge, but there the questions begin; they do not then end by "settling for less" (Denhardt 1981). Like incrementalism, satisficing threatens to be myopic, perhaps a strategy of "making do" and no more. It separates from practical action the questions of the political and ethical norms that ought to be satisfied in the particular cases at hand. Satisficing accounts may reduce "politics" to "disruption" or to the perpetual, seemingly insoluble war of conflicting interests of all against all. Given reprieve from the utopian demands of Comprehensive Rationality (omniscience), planners are not given a substantive account of practice instead.

Once more, in environmental review, satisficing may cover too many cases of planners doing what they can (independent of quality!): with every project there comes some point at which the planners stop and feel that they've done enough, given the constraints of time, poor information, and so on. Satisficing does help to avoid supercomprehensive EIRs. Yet, since satisficing seems too easily to justify many actions that are practically possible, once utopian comprehensiveness is rejected, Aaron Wildavsky's polemical quip about planning might be adapted: If satisficing is everything, then maybe it's nothing. Satisficing accounts offer too little protection from opportunism, and they indicate little along the lines of understanding the planner's actions as they influence, for better or worse, any political world encompassing the domain populated by formal and informal organizations. Compromises might be reached with local agencies, but if planners were to think predominantly about satisficing, getting along, they would likely then neglect a host of pressing concerns: the contingency of plans and outcomes upon relations of influence and exclusion, levels of neighborhood involvement, access to information and expertise, the openness of review processes, and so on (Simon 1957; Perrow 1972; Denhardt 1981; Forester 1982a).

Planning Practice as Communicative Action

Planning and policy analysis can be understood as forms of social action. But what is social action? Colloquially, we tend to think of our actions as tools. When we act, we say that we're trying to "get something done." Yet our actions are not only often tool-like, but they are practically communicative as well (Vickers 1965; Habermas 1970). Actions as diverse as threatening, promising, and encouraging can illustrate the point; each one may be instrumentally oriented toward some end, but each is fundamentally and practically communicative too. To varying degrees in each specific case, action seeks ends *and* meaningfully communicates: the most instrumental action without meaning would be simply *meaningless*, not even recognizable as an action. In a nutshell, while social action may be instrumental at times, it is more fundamentally and always communicative as well. But this does not mean that action, or planning in particular, is just "talk," merely a matter of "effective communications skills." For communicative action is always interaction between persons, thus political in a very broad sense, reproducing, whether maintaining or altering, social and political relations. To think of communicative action as just talk is to miss the point altogether and to ignore such important actions as challenging, criticizing, announcing, exposing, threatening, predicting, promising, encouraging, explaining, insulting, forgiving, presenting, recommending, and warning, among many others (Austin 1965; Wardhaugh 1985).

As a form of social or communicative action, the planners' actions shape others' expectations, beliefs, hopes, and understandings, even though planners do not strictly control any of these outcomes. The planners' work may be threatening to some but promising to others, for action shapes meaning (Marris 1987; Berger and Luckmann 1966). Planners know this, of course, and they try to anticipate such effects. In community meetings, for example, people often take planners to mean more than they intended, even though the planners may have had only the "best of intentions."

Even a planner's deliberate silence in a meeting may be meaningful and make a practical difference to the flow of events and citizens' participation. Yet if we think of action only as instrumentally "doing things" or "getting things done," such an effective silence becomes difficult to understand. Planning, then, is not instrumental *or* communicative. Always *communicative* action structured by social and political rules and conventions, planning practice may sometimes also be, in addition, more narrowly technical, structured and evaluated by technical conventions and rules too (Pitkin 1972).

To be practical, then, the planner's work has to be meaningful to others; it has to "make sense" to other people, no matter how technically rigorous or correct it may be on its own technical merits. "Being practical" in planning, therefore, should not be confused with "being technical." Mistaking either one for the other may well endanger both. Distinguishing and cultivating both technical and practical planning skills represents a major challenge for planning education or, more precisely, for planning educators to address systematically.

Once we recognize the practical consequences of communicative action, we can develop a powerful account of everyday planning practice. Now we can understand that as instrumental actions "get things done," they also necessarily set up expectations (e.g., no more delays!), affect meanings (they won't cooperate!), influence political relations (trust them?!), and shape understandings (now we can go on...). Once we recognize that the instrumental and communicative aspects of planning practice are inseparable and not mutually exclusive, we may be better able to anticipate the consequences of planners' actions in concrete cases in the future. Our paradigm case of action, then, should shift from the isolated actor's "using a tool" to the interactive case of one actor's "making a promise" (or a threat) to another actor. In both tool using and promise (or threat) making, we may "get something done," but in making a promise or a threat we capture more clearly, paradigmatically, the way that social actions shape meanings and the practical attention of others, as well as shaping any "ends" (Giddens 1976; Bauman 1978; Marris 1975, 1982; Tribe 1973; Vickers 1965; Habermas 1979; Bateson 1975; Forester 1989).

Because communicative action is so much more than "talk," far more than information flows in planners' interactions with others. Responsibility can flow as well. Checking early with a neighborhood association, for example, may involve them in the planning process and also make them partially responsible for the results of that process. Avoiding the charge that "no one from the planning department checked with us about this project," the planner who does such checking does more than gather information: he or she also spreads responsibility. In addition, as planners' actions communicate encouragement or discouragement to others, developers or community organizations, for example, so will the dependency or autonomy of those citizens be influenced as well. As a result of planner's actions, then, the ability of affected persons to respond and act for themselves can be weakened or strengthened.

The common case here involves jargon, of course: the more jargon in planning, the less public understanding, accessibility, and possibility of meaningful action or participation. Yet the cooperative or uncooperative gestures, signals, or timing of planners' actions have a similar, if far more subtle, impact. Planners influence not only what others know, but what they may be able to do as well. By shaping others' perceptions of their own opportunities for effective action, planners shape not only documents but political identities: other people's understandings of themselves, of what they can and cannot feasibly do. Planners may welcome or discourage a community group's involvement: they may suggest strategies for action, or alternatively, imply, "Don't worry; you don't need to get involved." As they work with program or project initiators, developers, community associations, or other agencies, therefore, planners influence who has what information, certainly, but they also and more subtly shift responsibility, and response-ability, or preempt these, simultaneously (Freire 1970; Webber 1963; Meltsner 1976; Forester 1989).

In addition to providing information, then, the planning ana-

lyst calls, directs, and shapes—that is, organizes or disorganizes—
the attention of others (Forester 1989). Just as information is
processed, collected, or spread, so involvements are developed and
participation is shaped, relationships and networks are built and
altered, affected and interested persons are selectively included or
excluded, expectations and hopes are set, raised and lowered differently among different actors, and political engagement is likewise encouraged for some and thwarted for others. The planning
analyst's communicative action, then, is not only to be understood
as information processing, but also as practical social and political
action. By shaping attention, the analyst shapes action and inac-
tion as well. This suggests a particular understanding of the practical role of the planning analyst: the planner is not a processor of
facts, but a *practical organizer* (or disorganizer as the case may be)
of attention (Meltsner 1976; Marris and Rein 1984; Needleman
and Needleman 1974; Teitz 1974; Wildavsky 1972; Benveniste
1977; Forester 1989). For a schematic summary, see table 2.1.

How, though, do planning analysts organize attention in
practice? Analytically, all communicative action makes four inseparable but distinct claims regarding the expressed intentions (1) of
the actors, the supposed truth (2) and conventional comprehensibility (3) of what's said, and the arguably legitimate fit (4) of
what's said with the practical context at hand (Habermas 1979;
Forester 1989). Yet more concretely, as the planner's ongoing practical questioning of options shapes others' responses, so does the
work of planning and policy analysis shape design and even implementation. In the communicative dialogue, conversation, and play
of power that constitute the planning process, the evolution of the
questioning of selective possibilities and the shaping of equally
selective responses, planners' and policy analysts' actions work to
organize (or disorganize) citizens' attention, their engagement,
investment, and participation. Such work is captured far better by
the imagery of "organizing" than by that of "problem solving." In
their everyday, ordinary questioning of possibilities, then, planners and policy analysts open or foreclose possibilities, alert or
ignore others, call forth or disregard particular concerns, and
spread or narrow the bases of design, criticism, participation, and
thus decision making.

Structurally and organizationally, the processes of attention
shaping are those of political and bureaucratic organizing (or again,
of disorganizing, as the case may be). If social action is communicative, then organizations too may be understood as structures of systematically (nonaccidentally and perhaps unnecessarily) distorted

Table 2.1   A Reformulation of Planning Practice: The Shift from Strictly Instrumental to Practical-Communicative Action

INSTRUMENTAL	TO	PRACTICAL-COMMUNICATIVE
processing information	to	shaping attention
problem solving	to	problem reformulating
seeking detachment to further objectivity	to	seeking criticism to check bias and misrepresentation
gathering facts	to	addressing significance: gathering facts that matter and interacting
treating participation as a source of obstruction	to	treating participation as an opportunity to improve analysis
informing decisions	to	organizing attention to formulate and clarify possibilities
supplying a single product, a document with "answers"	to	developing a *process* of questioning possibilities, shaping responses and engagement
reinforcing political dependency of affected persons	to	fostering meaningful political participation and autonomy
passing on "solutions"	to	fostering policy and design criticism, argument, and political discourse
abstracting from social relations	to	reproducing social and political relations

communications. The planner's responsibility to address possibilities of legitimate public policy calls then for work redressing or circumventing unnecessary structural distortions of communications: deliberate exclusion of affected publics, repression of available information concerning policy consequences, ideological justifications of policies, incomprehensible or obscure bureaucratic language, and so on (Dallmayr 1974; Forester 1989; Friedmann 1973; Habermas 1975; Marcuse 1976). When Benveniste speaks of uncertainty management, when Meltsner writes of feasibility testing and preemption, when Rein and Marris write of information-brokering, when the Needlemans write of "public secrets" and "double undergrounds," what we have is an interactive politics of planning analysis: organizing support, checking and co-opting implementers, shaping coalitions, working through networks as well as data bases (Benveniste 1977, 1989; Meltsner 1975; Marris and Rein 1984; Needleman and Needleman 1974). As planners manage attention to possibilities of public action in these and related ways, so is their work politically, and quite obviously, an organizing (or disorganizing) practice.

To assess the traditional political significance of such a communicative, attention-shaping account, we must relate planners' and policy analysts' work to the strengthening or the preemption of democratic political participation and education (Burton and Murphy 1980; Walzer 1980; Barber 1984). Technocratic approaches may neglect or even preempt citizens' autonomous actions: their learning, their abilities to act responsibly, and their knowledge of their own political world (Baum 1980; Meltsner 1976; Friedmann 1987). As an alternative to technocratic styles, planning analysts can try to elaborate roles that seek to employ technical excellence while simultaneously diffusing and spreading design responsibility, promoting critically constructive design and policy criticism, and educating politically—rather than perpetuating exclusion, ignorance, false expectations, deceptive myths of expertise, public distrust, and apathy. Effective planning and policy analysis requires technique, but political and organizational tact too. Planning practice attempting to join critical analysis to implementation requires technical knowledge, practical skills, and political and ethical vision as well.

Treating planning and policy analysis practice as communicative action provides a conceptual (and researchable) bridge from analysis to implementation (via the shaping of attention), from information to organization (via the shaping and reproduction of political identity), from cognition to action (via the claims-making structure of communicative action), and thus from the analysis of abstract meaning to a pragmatic assessment of practical professional activity.[1]

Finally, the analysis of planning and policy analysis practice as communicative action has deep ethical roots in "the ethics of ordinary discourse" we generally presuppose in daily life. As we ordinarily appeal to the *possibility* of communication free from domination when we speak ("What time is it?"), that is, we assume we shouldn't need to coerce others to understand our questions or to accept our claims, so are planners and analysts called to work to clarify, reveal, and communicate to citizens actual possibilities of life-enhancing, emancipatory actions.[2]

Implications for Research and Practice

Finally, if planning and policy analysis practice can be understood as the organizing (or disorganizing) of citizens' attention to possibilities of public action, a host of research questions follow. We can discuss these practical implications at three inseparable but analytically distinguishable levels of analysis: the structural or political-economic level, the organizational and interorganizational level, and the level of action and interaction.

At the structural level, the ability to direct attention takes the form of the ability to invest or control various forms of capital. For as capital is accumulated, controlled, and invested, so is the social capacity to pay attention concentrated, organized, allocated, and invested. Yet attention may be directed in two distinguishable but related ways: *productively* toward some goals and not others, toward the articulated needs of some and not others; and *reproductively*, socially and politically re-creating the form and content of existing, more or less structurally functional social relations, patterns of attention (commitments, loyalty, allegiance, preferences, wants, values, roles, and responsibilities) themselves.

If planners and policy analysts are concerned with occupational health and safety, for example, they must anticipate both of these structural dynamics of attention setting. The abstract planning goals of minimizing risks to workers' health may, for example, conflict with the productive and accumulative goals of those who control the workplaces. Furthermore, planners and analysts can expect that the present structural relations of control not only structure such conflicts (attention paid to safety and health vs. attention paid to profit rates), but also work to encourage employee attitudes of trust and resignation, of acceptance of whatever health risks are present as "necessary evils" or as "all part of the job," thus discouraging employees from actively participating in decisions about the work process.

Providing the context in which planning takes place, these two structural processes of attention-direction can be understood as generally accumulative on the one hand and socializing (legitimating, politically integrating or disintegrating) on the other. While each process may be contested at any point in time, the point here, simply, is that planners and policy analysts can practically anticipate both of these structural processes of the management of citizens' attention. For insofar as these processes are indeed structural, fundamental to the organization of the political economy, they will be regularly expectable: planners and analysts can anticipate and respond to their influences regularly as these structure the conditions in which actual planning and policy development take place (Lukes 1974; Gaventa 1980). Here, of course, the research questions only begin. How do these attention-directing processes work in particular policy domains? How do they frame or stage the practical work of planners and analysts? How do planners and analysts now anticipate and take these influences into account in their practice? How could they? What are the obstacles? How might planners' and analysts' organizing of attention strengthen, or subvert, various forms of the structural processes of attention investment? Such questions need to be addressed through case studies and comparative institutional analyses.

Organizationally, attention is framed by organizational mandates, responsibilities, and precedents and reproduced through the concrete communicative interactions of organization members with one another and with the larger public. Just as action is not only instrumental at times but also and always meaningful, so are the organizations surrounding and facing planners both instrumentally achieving objectives and communicatively shaping expectations. But what sort of expectations are created? As I have indicated above but argued at length elsewhere, communicative action works practically in four dimensions: shaping the listener's sense of truth or *beliefs*, sense of rightness or *consent*, sense of sincerity or *trust*, and sense of understanding or *comprehension* (Forester 1989). While I have argued that the management of these dimensions, deliberately or systematically, can tell us much about concrete relations of power in the planning process, an organizational analysis building on the study of practical communicative action could develop many more insights.

For in each dimension of the practical reproduction of citizens' beliefs, consent, trust, and understanding, interesting research questions arise. Just how, actually, do organizations structure and change the beliefs of their members and those they affect? How are factual claims made and backed up? How is credibility maintained? And similarly, through what processes is consent appealed to, gained, or lost? By what organizational processes is trust strengthened or weakened?

A study of the organizational (re)production of beliefs would involve the assessment of organizational "intelligence," reporting and information systems, research units, the use of studies and scientific analyses, and so on. The study of the reproduction of consent would lead to assessments of formal and informal precedents, mandates, sanctions, threats, bargains and deals, the political, legal, and ideological culture of planning organizations and those organizations with which planners work. The study of processes of gaining trust would lead to assessments of myriad taken-for-granted social rituals whose performance provides planners, and those with whom they work, with the means of evaluating one another's intentions in deed(s). And the study of the organizational management of understanding would lead to a host of questions not only about the use of clear and obscure language, but to far more subtle questions about the abilities of affected citizens to bring up and articulate issues, needs, and concerns in the first place (Wilensky 1967; Gusfield 1981; White 1985; Nelson, Megill, and McCloskey 1987; Todd and Fisher 1988; Throgmorton 1991).

Again, the point of such analyses can be practical, not simply abstract. The planner preparing a presentation to a planning commission, a neighborhood group, or a union meeting, for example, should not go into such a meeting blind. He or she might well wish to know: what preconceptions or beliefs do they have that I must address; what positions do they support or oppose that I should know about; how am I likely to be seen by them—as a trusted staff planner, as a suspicious professional, as an untrustworthy delegate from city hall, as someone with my own hidden agenda; how is what I have to say likely to be understood or misunderstood; and how will I best be able to make clear what I have to say?

These are all practical questions, but they are also distinct questions about organizationally produced and reproduced patterns of belief, consent, trust, and understanding—and the following chapters will explore these further. The planner ignores these issues at his or her own risk. The analysis of communicative action may help planners and researchers practically to ask these questions, but the work of finding answers is the practical research task that remains to be done, both generally across various planning domains and more specifically in particular, concrete cases.

In each case, also, planners may ask the critical normative questions—how might the processes shaping citizens' beliefs, consent, trust, and understanding be systematically skewed, biased, or distorted unnecessarily and how, then, might these distorting influences be counteracted? These research questions promise practical payoffs: the encouragement and realization of increasingly democratic and richly informed deliberative planning and policy processes (Reich 1988; Forester 1993).

Finally, the analysis of planning practice as communicative action provides a research framework for the empirical, interpretive, and critical assessment of the daily interactions of planning practitioners. Empirically and interpretively, we can examine the processes by which, and the conditions under which, planners succeed or fail in shaping others: (1) beliefs (by reporting, stating, informing, asserting, representing or presenting, suggesting, indicating, and so on); (2) consent (by judging, evaluating, recommending, advising, criticizing, correcting, objecting, supporting, affirming, dissuading, persuading, and so on); (3) trust (by disclosing, expressing, avowing, wishing, hoping, dreading, fearing, committing, "waffling," and so on); and (4) framing of issues (by formulating, clarifying, translating, depicting, focusing, selecting, simplifying, teaching, explaining meaning, and so on). As the following chapters will show, such are the ordinary practical actions through which planners and policy analysts direct their own and others' attention in daily practice (Austin 1965; Searle 1969; Wardhaugh 1985; Habermas 1979; Bruner 1990).

If their statements and reports are not believed, for example, planners will feel that they're wasting their time, and they would probably be right. If they cannot gain acceptance of their judgments and evaluations, planners will feel powerless, recognizing that they are not being taken seriously. If their expressions of intentions, feelings, desires, and hopes cannot gain others' trust, supreme frustration rather than cooperation is likely to result. And if planners cannot present information clearly and understandably, they are unlikely to be working as planners for long. Yet *how these four dimensions of practice actually work in practice* has hardly been addressed in any systematic way in the planning literature, in planning theory, or in planning research.

The view of planning practice as communicative action poses these practical questions for analysis; the answers must be given in terms of the varieties of concrete situations in which planners are actually working. Since these questions point to the conditions for the success and failure of planning practice, and to the practical reproduction of citizens' patterns of beliefs, consent, trust, and understanding, assessing these research questions might be both theoretically instructive and practically useful, informing planners' anticipation of practical obstacles faced in their everyday work. Keyed to planners' and citizens' understandings and interpretations, the analysis of communicative action is at once empirical, for it specifies a domain of observable speech acts and nonverbal acts as well, and it is interpretive, tied to the meaning-giving capacity and predispositions of diverse social and political actors.

What, though, is normative or critical about such an account of planning practice? Recall that the analysis of communicative action leads immediately to questions of communicative distortions: necessary and unnecessary (or unavoidable and avoidable) ones, and ad hoc or alternatively systematic ones, as chapter 4 will explore in more detail (Forester 1989). Here again, at structural, organizational, and interactive levels of analysis, research questions arise concerning the actual ability of affected citizens to check factual claims; to participate democratically in establishing claims of right; to distinguish genuine intentions from deception; and to formulate or clarify issues, needs, or problems affecting their lives. The analysis of planning as communicative action leads to normative issues of legitimacy at the political-economic level, to questions of procedural fairness and accountability at the organizational level, and the questions of communicative ethics at the level of ordinary interaction. A critical and communicative account of planning practice, then, seeks to integrate not only questions of action and questions of structure, but also questions of empirical and interpretive research with questions of normative and ethical rightness, that is, critical questions probing the obstacles to assuring the democratic and legitimate character of existing and future planning processes (Giddens 1976; Habermas 1979; Hemmens and Stiftel 1980; Kemp 1985; Healey 1992).

Conclusion

These last remarks point to several interrelated levels of analysis and research whose study might bear practical fruit for planning theory and practice. The analysis of structural conditions can be integrated with analyses of organizational processes and concrete planning interactions. At every level, we find essentially a politics and an economics of citizens' attention, a political economy of attention, whose kernel is not only productive labor, but social interaction. At every level, we find dynamics of power and distortion that jeopardize democratic participation and autonomy, and we can identify, anticipate, and work to counteract such influences.

If such an analysis can clarify the everyday working situations that planners must face and respond to practically, then perhaps the schematic arguments of this chapter can inform concrete applications by planning researchers, educators, and practitioners. This analysis provides, then, no definitive "last word," but instead elementary steps toward a renewal of empirically based, practically sensitive, and ethically illuminating planning theories that can help us better to understand what planners actually do, and what they can and should yet do.

3

The Micropolitics of Planning and Policy Practices: Questioning and Organizing Attention[1]

What good can city planners, public administrators, and planning analysts more generally do?[2] Maybe none, cynics suggest. Yet we should not be too quick to judge. If we set planners up to know everything, to devise, implement, and then coordinate comprehensive social systems and soon change these once again, then surely planners will fail, as Aaron Wildavsky (1973) says. If we lower our expectations and "satisfice," as Herbert Simon suggested, then the task that our planning analysts face may only be that of "making do," and just about anything may come to count as success, under the given constraints, of course (Simon 1957; Mechanic 1976; Perrow 1972). Our idea of "what good" planners and analysts can do, then, depends upon our theories of what planners and analysts do, in fact, do, and so upon what we might expect them to do in the future.

We need, then, an account of planning analysis that explains how planning analysts are effective in shaping design, and how, furthermore, they can be effective in the future. As the last chapter argued, we need an empirical, interpretive, and ethically insightful theory to help us understand what is going on now, to help us evaluate the significance of these activities, and finally to help us recognize possibilities for improving that practice in the future.

In this chapter, we consider examples from administrative and planning situations in a metropolitan city planning department, but the argument is intended to apply to city planners, policy analysts, and program evaluators, as well as to public administrators more generally. For the sake of brevity and to avoid terminological confusion, we will often replace the cumbersome "planner, evaluator, or public administrator" with "planner" or "planning analyst" to refer to the range of professional roles performed by public administrators, program evaluators, policy analysts, and city planners as well. In the same way, "design" will often be used to include "implementation," "project development," or "program development," for just as planners shape built designs, so do administrators develop and implement programs. Accordingly, this chapter addresses basic practical, political, and ethical problems shared in the daily work of public administrators, program evaluators, and planners alike.

Realism: Opportunistic Ideology Or Critical Pragmatism?

The theories of practice we now have reflect not as much realism as an exaggerated Realism (Euben 1970). To be Realistic is to muddle through, if we believe the incrementalists. Thirty-odd years ago Charles Lindblom depicted the incrementalist vision, and we are still taken by it: the "test of 'good' policy...is agreement on policy itself, which remains possible even when agreement on values is not" (Lindblom 1959). Whose agreement, and whether it is voluntary, coerced, legitimate or not, seems not to be at issue. To his credit, Lindblom drew out the implications of such a view: "In an important sense, therefore, it is not irrational for an administrator to defend a policy as good without being able to specify what it is for." Lindblom argued for expediency and the later chance to try (but try what?) again. We still face the question: How can we inform not simply any design, but good design? In the political sense, how is good design, or right action, possible?

The tradition of political Realism and incrementalism has left us with a planning and administrative ethic that amounts to Herbert Simon's satisficing, all too easily (mis)understood as making do. We have come to think of "ethical" actions as impractical actions, whatever their content, and of "democracy," "freedom," "participation," as concepts so general as to be nearly meaningless for purposes of our actual planning and administrative practice.

Students of the field are happy to leave these concepts to the political philosophers—the "real world" calls. Yet thinking this way asks for problems. This leaves planning practitioners all too often as frustrated Machiavellians, technicians, or rule-mongering bureaucrats; what we are missing, and what we in the planning and policy fields anxiously, if not desperately, need, is the illumination of questions of "how to" with a politically and ethically articulate and critical sense of "what for." Without a developing critical theory of our practice, of the possibilities of right action and good design, our pragmatism can only remain myopic. We need, simply, a critical pragmatism, *pragmatics with vision.*

The questions of good design, right action, good planning, are deeply tied to our commitment to a model of rationality (Habermas 1975). As we choose a mode of rational action, so do we choose a framework for the conduct of planning analysis. We can consider three related but distinguishable forms of rationality:

1. purposive-rational, or instrumental, models of rational action;
2. systems-rational, or cybernetic, models; and
3. practical-rational, or critical-reconstructive, models.[3]

If planning is to illuminate and serve social action, the pervasive questions of "what can we do?" then we ought not limit ourselves to either of the first two models or frameworks. Instrumental rationality is appropriate to conventionally technical problems; it cannot address questions of value formation, value change, social growth, or learning. At best, it represents a codified paradigm of practice, embodied as "know-how"; it can serve but not guide our knowing "what for" or our knowing "what should be." Systems rationality threatens to subordinate issues of right action and the responsibilities of persons—moral and political life in a community and polity—to matters of system maintenance; like incrementalism but writ large at the societal scale, it offers us no protection from opportunism and the abuse of power and control.[4]

Critical practical rationality encompasses, but extends beyond, the limited province of these models by posing action (therefore planning) as fundamentally communicative and so interpretive, practical, tied to the possible meanings of specific situations. The practical-rational model allows us to preserve and enhance processes of interpretation and value formation, dialogue and political discourse; thus it promotes critically reconstructive decisions gathering together instrumental know-how and systems knowledge to explore and formulate responses to questions of right action, good design, and good planning in specific cases. As it con-

siders action fundamentally communicative, socially constructivist, so does the practical-rational model extend beyond and overcome the systematic inadequacies of instrumental and systems
rationalities. Only if we understand administrative and planning
practice as practical-communicative may we be able to assess
objectively (openly and intersubjectively) questions of value and
legitimacy apart from only solipsistic or decisionistic perspectives
(Habermas 1975, 1983; Kelly 1990).

The practical-rational view works from the premise that
"facts" are social products, subject to description in particular languages and interpretation in particular historical contexts. The systems and instrumental rationalities, though, work from the
premise that facts are "brute," more or less "simply out there in the
world." The practical-rational view leads us to recognize the representation of "the facts" as historically contingent and socially constructed; thus we are led systematically to ask, "How might we
reconstruct our representation and understanding of the problems
we face? How might we act differently?" Instrumental and systems
views lead us rather to collect *more* facts or look for alternative
explanations of the same facts, without addressing questions of "for
what?" The instrumental and systems rationalities have fundamentally different epistemological premises than the critical practical-rational model. The practical-rational view leads us to a *critical-
pragmatism*; the others may leave us only with a naive Realism.

The narrow view of Realism leads us only to accept and con-
done powers that be and conventional opportunities as they are. It
does not lead us to develop a genuine realism that would actually
help us evaluate existing social and political practices and illuminate
strategies of action directed toward real, if innovative, alternatives.
Thus, Realism obscures actual realism behind the apparent necessi-
ties of existing belief systems and structures of power: so we as planners, administrators, and students of planning and administration
do not see what we might, understand what is possible, suspect
apparent necessity as other than "all there is." Indeed, Realism leads
us to view the promise of "theory" in a tragically limited way (Habermas 1975, 102–10; Rorty 1988; Sandercock and Forsyth 1992).

Our Demand from Theory:
Correspondence or Sensitivity?

As long as we hold the correspondence view of theory, that "theory" describes the world, corresponds to it, through explanatory

propositions, "theory" will always appear to be largely irrelevant to practice. The world is just too complex; situations are too diverse, too specific, "theories" too general. "Fact is richer than diction," Austin wrote (Austin 1961). This understanding of "theory" (and thus of knowing) leads us to systematic failures of policy analysis and explanation. Even where situations are routine enough for apparent correspondence, such "theories" will be at best instrumental or technical. They will not allow us to read situations, to understand experienced meaning, to interpret and address questions of value and significance. They will not open up or explore for us questions about what "should be" done; they will be instrumental but not instructive, tools for manipulation but not for learning, deliberation, and evaluation.

But alternatively, we can understand a theory not to *correspond* to brute data, but to *pattern attention* selectively to meaningful parts of our world. What difference does this make? This view tells us that the power of theory may well not be in its present degree of "operationalism," but rather in its power to sensitize us to the important variables in a situation, to illuminate and disclose significance for us.[5]

Faced with situations of action, we need to ask not only "how do things work here?" but more: "To what ought I pay attention?" The correspondence view can only address instrumental, mechanistic relationships, whether among variables or people. The "critical-pragmatic" view includes attention to mechanistic patterns, but it also leads us to respect and interpret actors' meanings in specific cases and reinterpret them where contexts change. The correspondence view leads us to isolate or control contextual variables, the critical view leads us to understand their contingency and significance. The correspondence view leads us to clarify behavior; the critical view seeks to illuminate action, to *attend to* the meaning and value of any behavior. The critical-pragmatic view asks not only "what?" but "so what?" as well. As long as planning analysts look to discussions of "theory" only to document correlations and mechanical relationships, they will neglect their own perpetual dependence upon working theories (patterns of attention) that provide them with insight, sensitivity, and ideas of possibility and desirability in everyday work.[6] Just because theory is fundamentally a matter of attentiveness and not correspondence, an insightful case study may be far more revealing, instructive, useful, and relevant for a planner or administrator than a "rigorously tested theory" may be.[7]

Theory: Abstraction or Pattern of Attention?
The Planning Analyst as Organizer of Attention

We seem to be captives of two traditions of thought about implementation and design—one Cartesian or rationalistic, including variants of social engineering views, and the other narrowly pragmatic, including incrementalism and related philosophies of "satisficing" by lowering expectations. The former gives us principles without pragmatics (formalism); the second too easily gives us pragmatics without principles (opportunism). Both relegate "theory" to disembodied ideas; neither understands a theory as a claim, theorizing as action to call and shape attention, analysis therefore as inherently a process of communicating, shaping actions, organizing and designing.

Hanna Pitkin's work and Wittgenstein's later writings free us from these misleading and inadequate notions of planning theory and analysis.[8] Wittgenstein tells us that "every particular notation stresses some particular point of view"; we might say, then, that every analysis shapes our attention and concerns in selective ways (Wittgenstein 1972a, 28). The language that we use is not an instrument that is separate from the problems we discuss (as in "language here-problem there"). Rather, by saying what the problem at hand is (in a particular language in a particular way, with specific concepts, perhaps "class," perhaps "marginal utility"), we act to frame the problem and point to possible resolutions, often for example, in highly gendered ways (Todd and Fisher 1988; Davis 1988; Sandercock and Forsyth 1992; Edelman 1978; McCloskey 1985). As Jan Dekema writes, "Language constitutes aspects of an object as well as denotes them."[9]

Our problem formulations are patternings of attention, and more: They are callings of attention, recommendations and requests to consider "the problem" and its uncertainties, threats, and opportunities in the ways we have stated them. This is no less true of the junior planner or bureaucrat on the telephone to the neighbor of a building site than it is of academics writing "planning theory." In each case, the work of analysis functions to develop a point of view and *call and direct attention* as a result. But now theory is no longer some formal scholastic game. As our theories shape our attentiveness, so do they also shape our neglect—even *as* we work within structures of power. A theory is a pattern of attention, and theorizing is the patterning, calling, directing of that attention (if, as always, with criteria of explanatory power, suggestiveness, elegance, and so forth). Theorizing is thus a practical communicative activity. We have here, then, an operational understanding of planners and policy analysts as practicing theorists: posing and explaining problems and plausible solutions, questioning possibilities with others and influencing their responses and actions. Planners and policy analysts are thus brokers and managers, organizers of attention, shaping attention to the desirability and feasibility of actions, alternatives, and possibilities.[10] Before assessing the ethical and political implications of this analysis, we consider first the organizationally pragmatic issues of how the planners', analysts', and administrators' organizing of attention works.

1. Shaping Attention through Questioning: The Planning Analyst as Organizer of Attention

In practice, planning analysts organize attention (and so too involvement, participation, expertise, support) through the concrete everyday activity of questioning possibilities.[11] As the planning analyst's questioning shapes diverse activities of response, so does the administrator's or planner's analysis shape design (Freire 1970; Krumholz and Forester 1990). This is the kernel of the communicative theory of analysis and design proposed here. Once we recognize design as an ongoing historical process of social and political construction, and no longer only Platonically as "the elegant idea," we can then better understand the work of planning analysts as a form of organizing (or disorganizing) rather than as map making or organization-chart "designing" (Lukes 1974; Gaventa 1980; Forester 1989).

The planning analyst selectively asks questions of program or policy possibilities and so calls and directs attention in particular ways—and so, too, shapes the actions of others and thus the ongoing process of design. Once we understand that the analyst's or administrator's work is fundamentally communicative, both literally and metaphorically questioning possibilities—opportunities, threats, consequences, values—and shaping various responses of others, we can see that "analysis" need no longer be separated from "implementation" and action. In the next section, we examine the planning analyst's role as an organizer of attention. We ask, "How actually can planning analysts organize attention? What sources of power or political strategies make any of this possible?"

But before addressing those questions, we must ask, "To what is practical attention called and directed in the first place?"[12]

Attention to What?

Planning analysts shape attention to (1) the stakes, (2) the setting, (3) the approach, (4) the political positions, and (5) the effectiveness of the possible actions they assess. In each case, there are a number of issues to which attention is often addressed.

(1) The Stakes of Design. Problems are not simply given once and for all. Activities of problem formulation, shaping attention to just what the problem ought-to-be-taken-as, are fundamental to problem-solution (Seeley 1963; Churchman 1968, 1971; Innes 1990; Forester 1993; Anderson 1985). Questions soliciting responses defining "what the problem here really is" allow planning analysts to involve others early, check their opinions, watch out for their special perspectives, and take advantage of their particular experience and knowledge. Asking for "inputs" or less mechanically, more truly, "responses" concerning costs and benefits allows the planning analyst to assess not only the stakes of the problem at hand, but also the political environment in which it exists. Such probing of "interests," for example, is central to a great deal of ongoing negotiation practice (Susskind and Cruickshank 1987; Lax and Sebenius 1986; Fisher and Ury 1983). At the same time, the planning analyst's questions here inform others as well, by letting a neighborhood group know of estimates of long-run "need for services," for example. Then, in the routine course of problem assessment or plan making, analysts often call attention to possible *clients*, possible beneficiaries—and those possibly suffering from given actions as well.

(2) The Setting of Design. Just as problems don't speak for themselves, neither do the social and political settings in which they arise. By calling attention to the political and organizational context, planning analysts can shape expectations of support or opposition; by asking questions, formally and informally, of the possible "significant others" who may care about these alternatives, planners can anticipate needed negotiations and prepare for them. By judiciously questioning possibilities of specific alternatives, planning analysts can create images of possible futures: "Yes, we could do that; that might work." Working with developers, questioning possibilities leads to design refinements; working with community organizations, the same type of questioning and

attention shaping by the planner is similar to community organizing. Underlying this work, of course, is a continual payment of
attention to particular social relations; as analysts ask questions
of "who will be affected?" by various alternatives, so may they
shape the awareness, concern, and attentiveness of others to possible actions at hand (Benveniste 1977; Marris 1987).

(3) Design Approaches. The eclecticism of planning and policy
analysis reflects the lack of any dominant paradigmatic approach.
In everyday practice, as analysts raise questions of method, they
shape the perspectives that may be taken to assess the problems
they face. Posing questions of alternative methods can, for example, legitimate attention to alternative interpretations of problem
scope, and thus content, as well.

Since analysis cannot appear arbitrary if it is to be credible,
planners must pay attention to questions of objectivity. Since facts
do not speak of their own accord, analysts can, and even must,
organize the "relevant" and significant facts to be used. Raising (or
planting) questions of objectivity calls attention to the adequacy of
data collection, processing, and presentation; so analysts can
inform or warn others of systematic omissions of data, neglected
alternatives, or otherwise faulty analysis or design.

Then, just as problem scope may be delimited by a method
adopted, so do problem resolutions depend on attention to explanations of the problem at hand. A planner's explanation to a community group that a developer's project should be redesigned because
of technical inadequacies, or alternatively, because of a hostile
political environment, can lead to quite different strategies of
action: the marshalling of expertise or the organization of political
pressure. Shaping strategies of action follows directly from attention to problem explanation (Peattie 1987; March 1988; Innes 1990).

(4) Political Positions in Design. Planning analysts typically
shape attention to the political positions inherent in various alternatives. By raising or spreading questions of justification, formally
and informally, always judiciously, they can develop processes of
argument, consultation, and participation in the design process
(Faludi 1987; Fischer 1980; Fischer and Forester 1993). By questioning in its early stages the range of participation and political
processes influencing a proposed plan, analysts may call attention
to the legitimacy of various alternatives and modify design as a
result (Krumholz and Forester 1990). No matter how implicitly
questions of legitimacy or justification are raised, planning analysts call attention as well to issues of responsibility for design.
Any anticipation of implementation (problems or success) leads to

specifications of organizational and political responsibilities. As planners search for possibilities of design, so do they pose questions of the corresponding responsibilities to be attributed to private developers, affected members of the public, and state agencies as well.

(5) The Effectiveness of Design. Their concern with efficacy leads analysts and administrators to shape attention in still other ways. By questioning constraints, they call attention to issues of feasibility (Meltsner 1972; Benveniste 1977; Reich 1988). To be responsive, adaptive, flexible, and capable of learning and changing, administrative and planning staff must pay attention to ongoing problems of their own listening (Forester 1989). Simultaneously, they can attend to those who they hope will learn from and be able to act upon their analyses. Attending to problems of "listening" can help develop networks of formal and informal contacts and ties. Attending to those acting upon the planning analysts' work can help to prevent analyses from collecting dust on forgotten shelves; here the anticipation of "implementation" can lead to early involvement, but perhaps also to the preemption or co-optation of a broad range of eventual users.

Shaping Attention Is Shaping Action

Planning, policy, and administrative processes have both formal and informal sides, and on both sides there is room for discretion and the analysts' influence (Rohr 1978; Lipsky 1980). Formally, analysts must interpret the spirit and letter of mandating rules or laws, regarding the delays "necessary" or desirable in "moving a project along," regarding the degree of cooperation with another agency or a community organization ("I called right away" or "I really couldn't call sooner; I had other priorities to attend to"). Informally, analysts and administrators may favor certain projects; they may tip off constituents to upcoming meetings or decisions or to "someone you should talk to," or perhaps to key issues to be brought up at any of several occasions. Thus shaping *who* finds out about *what*, to what extent and for what purposes, the planning or administrative staff can indeed shape the attention and so the actions of others who might participate in the planning, policy, or administrative process (Wilensky 1967).

To do all this, the planner or policy analyst uses political and organizational savvy, experience, whatever "methods" are available to organize the attention of others. Of course, such organizing is influenced by existing structures of power and authority, but wide areas of discretion exist nonetheless. So, by shaping attention to issues of (1) problem formulation (the stakes), (2) strategy and context articulation (the setting), (3) fact selection and scope (the approach), (4) processes of management, intervention, and implementation (the political positions), and (5) responsiveness and learning (effectiveness), planners, policy analysts, and public administrators shape practice. In the actions of questioning possibilities, calling of attention, and so too shaping involvement, participation, and response, the planners' theory, or better, the planner's *theorizing*, can shape actual practice.

Planning and Administrative Strategy: The Organization of Attention as the Exercise of Power

Have planning analysts any power to influence action, though? Has their shaping of attention anything to do with their sources of power, their effectiveness?

Actually, the idea of "organizing attention" helps us to explain more elegantly, and to integrate for the first time, six well-established but previously unrelated theses regarding the sources of power in the planning analyst's role. First, Arnold Meltsner's insights regarding client preemption is most clearly a case in which the analyst sets the agenda of attention for the client. Having little formal political power, and indeed working for and subordinate to the client, the analyst nevertheless can exert power by delimiting the scope of attention to be paid, a scope sensitive to the feasible, one arguably desirable and necessary to the tasks at hand (Meltsner 1975).

Second, Guy Benveniste's notion of uncertainty management as a source of influence can be understood as the consideration of apparent threat; thus it is the management of the client's attention to anticipate and prepare for recognized uncertainties (Benveniste 1977, 1989). Benveniste argues that decision makers must listen to analysts precisely because as decision makers they are not capable of attending to all the uncertainties themselves.

Third, Benveniste's thesis that planning analysts' power comes as well from an ability to invent images of the future for others is also a matter of the analysts' organization of attention (Benveniste 1977). Here, rather than having a lone decision maker make a pronouncement, Benveniste argues, an analyst can exert influence by creating a shared and politically supported agenda, upon which the decision maker may then act. In this role, the planner is a bureaucratic and political organizer, shaping the attention (to a plausible, desirable, perhaps bargained-for future) of actors who depend on one another, for example, who must work together continually.

Fourth, Eliot Freidson's notion of the *gatekeeper* role of professionals also falls within an attention-management explanation of the planner's role (Freidson 1970). If both neighborhood residents and developers' consultants alike, for example, *need* to go to the planning staff for support, cooperation, and general advice, then the planners exert power as they regulate, shape, and channel the attention that those residents and developers' staff can pay, and gain from.

Fifth, the more common notion of "information is power" is easily explained by the organization of attention thesis; indeed, the shaping of attention extends far beyond mere information flow (Marris and Rein 1974; Forester 1989; Needleman and Needleman 1974; Lukes 1974; Gaventa 1980). Information is power as long as planners, analysts, and administrators have relatively greater access to information which others need. How and when a planner tells a developer or resident about a coming meeting shapes the value of the information about the meeting time. Here we have not only information flow, but attention management as well.

Sixth, and finally, our thesis explains the classical dynamic of co-optation (Selznick 1966). By bringing in from the political environment a potential source of resistance, the planner or administrator not only shapes the attention they will pay to issues at hand, but also the investments which that attention will bring with it. With attention paid, investments made, subsequent resistance to the planning and administrative process may be co-opted. Once again, the source of the planning analyst's power and influence is rooted in their ability to manage and organize the attention of those with whom they work.

2. Organizing Attention in Practice: The Power of Questioning

Most fundamentally but not exclusively, planners, analysts, and public administrators shape attention through the political and linguistic activity of asking questions—not forbidden questions, but quite ordinary ones (Forester 1977). Asking a question is performing a deceptively simple action. Unlike our making an ordinary statement, when we pose a question, we not only perform the act of requesting (or challenging, or perhaps invading, someone's privacy, for example), but we also shape actions of response (informing, authorizing, telling, answering) as well (Bell 1975; Searle 1969; Austin 1965, 1979; Wardhaugh 1985). Questioning is no simple matter of mere "talk"; it is rather a mode of interaction, a form of action: communicative action. Because it is an activity of everyday ordinary language use, we are often not aware of how much we actually do when we ask questions and shape responses (Bruner 1990; Todd and Fisher 1988; Davis 1988). By revealing the ordinary power of questioning, we can reveal what we can do in everyday planning and policy analysis practice too. As questioning calls forth acts of response, attention is organized; theory, thus embodied in the planner's communicative action as a pattern of attention, then shapes practice.

Consider how much planners and analysts do when they ask questions and how much they take their everyday effectiveness for granted. Planners and analysts often do recognize their power as closely tied to "the politics of information." They have information—or access to it—that others need, and they have some influence in the politics of the planning and policy process as a result. There's even more to it, though. At stake in "the politics of information" are not only "facts" or "tips" or "leads" or "warnings." This becomes clear when we recognize that the planners' or analysts' questioning not only "gets information," but does much more as well. We need to ask, then, how our understanding of analysts as questioners of possibilities can expand or improve upon our more conventional idea of analysts as "brokers of information." How else might planners or analysts be effective? What else, besides channeling information, is involved when we ask questions? When questioning shapes response, much more than information flow has taken place, but what more? How much can we do when we ask a question?[13]

Questioning in Practice and Praxis

Posing questions carefully, we can build relationships. We ask questions of persons and as persons, and often with an eye to our future. We pay attention to the people we ask, perhaps showing them respect as well (for example, "What do you think about the proposal?" "I wanted to be sure to check with you for your feelings.") We can develop working relationships that both of us will be able to trust and count on in the future. We can ask questions outside of formal channels and so develop a wide range of liaisons with people not necessarily connected formally to the planning or administrative process at all; here we see the common nurturance and use of "networks" and "contacts" (Tronto 1987; Conley and O'Barr 1990).

In questioning we can also shape the involvement and participation of the people we ask. The planner who asks neighborhood organizations for "input" on particular proposals is getting much more than information, whether intentionally asking for more or not. The asking of the questions gives [others] a certain amount of time to respond, a certain opportunity to be included or excluded from the local planning process. *How* questions are asked will often be taken to represent planners' and analysts' stances toward others; a seemingly formal question may be taken as the rejection, rather than the encouragement, of citizen participation or agency cooperation. A more open question may encourage further participation, and so questioning may also be a strategy of co-optation; anticipating concern and possible opposition, bringing outsiders "in," the process of questioning reflects and respects the basically political nature of planning analysis.

We can selectively orient others' responses too. The planner's or administrator's questions cannot refer directly to everything about a particular proposal or problem; some aspects will be stressed and others ignored. Just how this selection occurs is a political as well as a technical matter. As Meltsner emphasizes, the policy analyst may "preempt" the client or decision maker by initially formulating "the problem" and the relevant uncertainties and opportunities; what the analyst asks is not all there is to ask (Meltsner 1975). To a community group, a planner's questions orient response to project uncertainties or strategies of bargaining with building developers; to the developers, the planners' questions may orient response to project alternatives that may be less objectionable to community groups than the original plans. Our questions get information, but they shape attention and response—they shape thought, worry, anger, effort, and constructive response—as well. They inquire, but they also design and organize.

Through questioning we can also open up possibilities for action; we can illuminate alternatives, shape the consideration of new ways of acting. Planning staff hardly have the power to be directive; any "Thou shalt" comes only after a long process of asking "What if we took this alternative?" or "What about doing *that*?"

Questions are modes of exploration—but not only for the planning or policy-advising staff, for all those with whom they work as well: other agency staff, community members, builders, and project initiators. In each case, asking about possibilities is often less effective in gathering facts than it is in directing attention to ways of acting, alternative strategies, the "what can be done." Questioning is an action of alternative-generation, by setting others off, provoking, shaping responses and critical disagreements which then become bases for refined alternatives. By so stimulating criticism and insights (grossly, "feedback") regarding possible action, in questioning possibilities planners and administrators alike work to improve the quality of design and implementation (Susskind and Ozawa 1984; Roe 1994).

Our questioning does not call for just any answers, any facts, or any responses. Our questions call for relevant and significant replies, thus calling forth concern and care. When the planner asks a neighborhood organization for comments about a proposal, or "checks with them for their feelings about this project," the question gets not neutral bits of information, but a significant response—interested or apathetic (both count). We find out what others care about, perhaps what they are bored by, perhaps what they are deeply committed to. Questioning can probe care and concern; and we can stimulate concern as well as we call for response.

Furthermore, when we ask questions regarding possibilities of action, we can spread responsibility just as we shape involvement and participation. What flows in questioning is not only information, but responsibility as well. When an advisory board or a community group is asked for comments on a proposed project or building design, for example, the administrator or planner who asks them requests not only information, but their complicity, their sharing of responsibility in the review of the proposal, as well. We see the special case, which we mistake for the general case, when a planner asks a licensed soils engineer to check a sloping site for safety; then what flows is not only information, but the assurance of credentialed expertise. Whether to authorities with credentials or others, though, the planner's and administrator's questioning shifts responsibility for response to those asked. When responsibility spreads in this way, so too can the bases of creativity, insight, and support, the bases of design, spread as well.

We can also trigger action, both in direct response to our question and in further "follow-up."[14] Unlike other communicative acts such as making statements, for example, questioning directly calls forth the action of another person. Questioning not only refers to an issue and opens it up to response, it calls for the other's action. Here the planner or administrator becomes an organizer and not simply an information processor.

With the activity of questioning, then, shaping participation and involvement, spreading responsibility, selectively orienting response, calling forth care and concern, opening up possibilities, and building relationships and the bases for future efforts, planners, analysts, and administrators set the stage for future actions of others and shape their efforts as well. Here questioning is a strategy of design, a strategy of political, perhaps bureaucratic, perhaps community-based organizing too.

Questioning How? Organizational Intelligence, Political Networks, and Informal Communications

But how can the work of questioning take place practically? The strategies are many. Some questions must be asked face to face; others will take advantage of the distance of the telephone. When the administrator or analyst is not trusted or doesn't "have the contacts" to ask the questions necessary, he or she will have to ask "by proxy." Some questions will only be asked of specific persons, as when we need to find out something from an expert; others will be more effectively asked of a group, as when a planner wishes to raise an issue for a number of people to discuss, or when information is missing, but it's not clear who in the world might know the answer. Some questions will be properly asked in formal channels (before I delay this project I have to ask my supervisor); others may only be asked informally, within or outside organizational boundaries (if I take this position in the meeting, would you support me?). Some questions will take advantage of the fact that someone can respond, think, and answer; other questions will be asked of documents that can't talk back. Generally, our informal questioning will be politically more significant than our formal questioning, both within and beyond any given organization's walls. Carolyn and Martin Needleman described this strikingly as the "double underground" of community planners, the first within the planning department among sympathetic supporters, the second extending to other organizations and community contacts (Needleman and Needleman 1974). Possibilities for questioning will always extend far beyond formal channels and role definitions. Even under conditions of extreme secrecy, information may leak, and questions may be spread to others who may be able to do the asking (shaping attention, involvement, concern) without threat of reprisal.[15] The questioning of program, project, or policy responsibilities, then, can be undertaken through formal channels and informal ones, to specific contacts and groups, directly or by proxy, through networks or first contacts, with political protection or (but not necessarily) vulnerability. The planners', policy analysts', or administrators' questioning is an ordinary practice of speaking carefully, a richly practical communicative activity, and its possibilities—our opportunities—are many.

3. Systematically Distorted Communications and Critical Theory in Practice: Questioning and Shaping Attention as Planning Strategy

Planning Analysis: Incremental, Scientistic, Error-Correcting, or Argumentative

What organizational and political form can the planning analyst's questioning and organizing of attention take? The literature of social science, the "policy sciences," and the philosophy of science offer us preliminary, but inadequate, answers.

Three views of planning inquiry, for example, provide us with "instructive mistakes." First, the incremental versus comprehensive planning debate told us that questions asking for "all the facts" ask for frustration instead, while less ambitious questions about the bits and pieces still only make sense in some larger context—we do not want to increment our way to hell (Etzioni 1968, chaps. 11, 12).

Second, Thomas Kuhn's seminal work freed us from the traditionally rationalistic understanding of scientific progress; now we can understand scientific inquiry as a socially constructivist process, scientific inquiry as a mode of action in the world (Kuhn 1972; Lakatos and Musgrave 1972; Feyerabend 1975).[16] We need no longer denigrate planning inquiry for being largely performed outside of the experimental laboratory. (The formal experiment is no more essential to science—although dialogue and criticism *are*—than the automobile is to travel; it may help, but it may hinder as well.)

Third, the literature on "learning organizations" teaches us that in a turbulent environment, organizations must be adaptive, flexible, continually testing, "error-correcting," and innovating

(Schön 1971; Michael 1973; Landau 1973). Still, the "learning theorists" leave unasked the basic political questions: what ends ought these organizations to serve and who ought to learn what? Surely our organizations ought to be "error-correcting," but then we need to ask, "What sorts of judgments will determine error, undesirable activity, and who will have the power, with what accountability, to make these judgments?" If we ignore these questions, we are left with the struggle only for organizational survival and self-perpetuation; we are asked to keep the organizations we now have, whether or not "might makes right," and only then, if at all, are we to ask what we ought to keep them for.

Incrementalism offers us too little protection from opportunism. Scientism mistakenly sends us to the laboratory, where we tend to ignore rather than address interpretive problems of application and implementation. Learning-systems notions threaten to reduce the world to a population of organizations or systems—rather than persons—and threaten to neglect political life altogether.

Nevertheless, planning analysts are *not* "free" either to ask whatever questions they might wish or to involve formally whichever groups of people they might desire; they can expect that work within any historical setting of power, authority, and conflicting interests will mean work within a setting of institutionally, systematically distorted communications (hardly reflecting, needless to say, whatever truly necessary, inevitable distortions there may be in "the Good Society"). Thus, when Habermas draws our attention to these systematic distortions of communication limiting our actions, he can write that "the analytic resolution of distorted communication...is at once theory and therapy."[17] For if we understood *how*, and not just *that*, our open questioning as planning analysts was systematically distorted, we would then be better able to work toward overcoming those distortions, to work toward the organizational possibility of more open questioning, political discourse, and the criticism and improvement of policy and action. Habermas thus provides us with the beginnings of a foundation for a "critical pragmatism" (Habermas 1968, chap. 5; Dewey 1927, 1960; Bernstein 1971, 165–229).

Planners and public administrators themselves have often attempted to address these problems by calling for participatory rather than technocratic decision-making styles. Without questioning the legitimacy of existing processes of participation, Melvin Webber provides a clear example of a contemporary planner and planning theorist attempting to reformulate the direction and calling of planning practice.

The growing involvement of lay groups bodes well for the prospects of a politically responsive mode of planning. It suggests that an effective style of planning does not call for plans that present right answers, rather that it calls for procedures which might help plural publics reach decisions in acceptable ways.... Its special task would then be to help assure that all parties' voices are heard; that available evidence, theory, and arguments are weighed; that potentially useful options are considered and evaluated; that latent consequences and their distributions among the many publics are identified and assessed. (Webber 1978, 158)

Webber is concerned with attention to "the ways decisions get made, rather than to the specific preferred substantive content of those decisions." The planner becomes, then, "a facilitator of debate," rather than a "substantive expert." Webber's planner must work to foster open communications but leave the content of the communication to those concerned with the policy issues at hand. But when lack of wealth, power, status, or other resources prevent those to be affected from participating equally and freely, Webber's "argumentative" style of planning is thwarted by political problems of what Habermas calls "systematically distorted communications." Webber realizes that these problems arise, but the limitations of treating planning as an argumentative cognitive style prevent him from then treating these political interferences in any systematic manner.

Planning Analysis as Communicative Action: Critical Theory Applied

Habermas gives us the beginnings of an analysis of systematic distortions of communication—in terms of power, ideology, organization; he provides us as well with the practical tasks of exposure, challenge, clarification, and illumination of possibilities, work toward communicative action and self-reflection free from *unnecessary* distortion and domination.[18] Webber's procedural model seeks to make democratic discourse—political discourse openly suggesting, testing, and arguing for alternative actions—possible and actual, but it lacks attention to the systematic but unnecessary distortions of participation and communication that threaten to make any such model simply idealistic, "impractical," politically and organizationally wanting. Habermas's "critical communications theory of society" provides the counterpoint and substantive foundation so that participatory models for planning and policy analytic deliberation can be developed that account for (and challenge) those contingent systematic distortions, by poverty, power, and ideology, of the communicative actions of planners and the persons with whom they can work.

In ordinary communication, we anticipate certain uncoerced idealized possibilities of mutual understanding—otherwise we would not presume to be able to argue coherently at all (let us say, e.g., that power *does* or does not matter to the planner's efficacy).[19] But these possibilities are often obstructed in practice by the particular, historically structured political and economic conditions in which we live.

Distorted communications, interactions shaped by existing power and ideology, are commonplace, hardly exceptions. This is precisely why Habermas seeks to clarify what communication free from domination, open communicative interaction, presupposes and requires—so that we may have a normative basis for evaluating the situations in which we *now* find ourselves (Forester 1989). If communication free from unnecessary distortion were not possible, how could anyone suppose that a claim that a program is inadequate, or that a community is underserved, or that a policy is repressive, could ever be communicated well enough to be understood to be true?

Habermas is asking the political question, "How is legitimate public action possible?" What might conditions of authentic political discourse involve? Through argument in dialogues concerned with possibilities of action, speakers could put forth proposals, criticize and be criticized, come collectively to construct courses of action justified with reasons subject to public examination. In the ideal situation, people could do so without the threat of force; disagreement might be rampant, but conflicts would still be structured by an underlying agreement to negotiation, argument, and to taking generalizable, shared interests into account to balance "private wants."[20] Trent Schroyer makes the point as follows:

> The fundamental idealization made in every act of human speech assumes an ideal of reason which does not exist empirically but which every human assertion anticipates in practice. In every communicative situation in which a consensus is established under coercion or under distorted conditions, we are confronting instances of illusory discourse. This is the contemporary form of the critique of ideology. (Schroyer 1973, 162–63)

The practical critique of systematically distorted communications becomes the basis, then, for a vision of legitimate political action, for a vision of democratically deliberative planning and policy analysis practice (Forester 1989, 1991).

Rather than base legitimacy in the "needs of the system," as some modern systems theorists would wish, Habermas argues that political legitimacy must be rooted in the critical meaning giving, interpretation, and "will-formation" of human beings, persons acting and interacting, arguing and agreeing, shaping and reshaping their political institutions. In the face of increasing social and political complexity, and administrative and economic complexity as well, Habermas takes Niklas Luhmann to task, for example, for placing "the rationality of the system" above the inherent value of democratization, developing conditions of more open communication and public deliberation (Habermas 1973; Pateman 1970; Bachrach 1967).

Planning Analysis for Democratization: Toward the Possibility of Political Discourse, Articulation, and Dialogue

Habermas's appeal is not to some ideal communications community, but rather to the continual democratization of political discourse (Forester 1991, 52–56). He calls our attention to interaction and not argument because he wishes to stress that democratization is a matter of action and interaction, not only one of information and traditionally conceived rationality. Setting up a call for action, then, he uses the ideal of pure communicative action, free from the constraints of external power and ideological structures, to provide the counterpoint to any simple acceptance of the communication structures and processes we now have. Thus he calls for a continual exposure of unnecessary distortions in communications, for the continual attention to unequal opportunities for political debate and argument, for continual criticism of prevailing ideological beliefs and rationalizations.

Habermas calls for rationality, to be sure—the rationality of critical argument and citizens' action. Rationality becomes a matter of action, rather than one of "systems performance." His closing lines of *Legitimation Crisis* are to the point here:

> Even if we could not know much more today than my argumentation sketch suggests...this circumstance would not discourage critical attempts to expose the stress limits of advanced capitalism to conspicuous tests; and it would most

certainly not paralyze the determination to take up the struggle against the stabilization of a nature-like social system *over* the heads of its citizens. (Habermas 1975: 143)

This is more than empty rhetoric—for such exposure is quite possible and quite connected to what planning analysts can do in practice by the very nature of their profession (Krumholz and Forester 1990). In the most technocratic terminology, such exposure is "monitoring feedback for possible systems failures." In more ordinary language, such exposure is warning of problems of unmet needs, inadequate services or budgets, unresponsive programs, or threats to democratic processes, participation, or popular control (Forester 1987a). In planning and administrative language, such exposure means stressing the uncertainties of existing policy, examining the false promises of others; it means the continual search for system failure and democratic solution, the continual effort to prevent illegitimate structures of power from developing further—informed by our attention to the basic communicative action of consensus-building processes necessarily lying at the foundations of political legitimacy (Habermas 1975, 130–43). This is not a call for public debate in the midst of a police state; it is a call for continual work toward the possibility of open communications, political discourse, and dialogue, authentic political argument.

This is a call to rework and alter the organizational structures now existing from where we are, rather than to create wholly new organizations in some mysterious, politically fantastic manner (Needleman and Needleman 1974; Marris and Rein 1974). As the existing institutional structure becomes more repressive, as communications between those shaping and those affected by policies become more distorted (or token), Habermas's argument sounds like one calling for subversion. In the context of a technocratic or bureaucratic state, indeed, the call for democratization, for creating the conditions of open political discourse, for rational argument and criticism—this becomes a call for subversion of antidemocratic structures of investment and control.

Questioning and Organizing for Democratization

What, then, can our analysis of questioning and Habermas's call for the democratization of political discourse imply for planning and administrative practice? The proponents of error-correcting systems give us problems of planning and administration as the organization of learning, without politics. Habermas runs the opposite danger—of giving us an analysis of political discourse, planning, and administration as political processes, without organizational form.[21]

But if we consider planning and policy analysis practice as the questioning of possibilities and so the organizing of attention and response, then we can give such practice political *and* organizational meaning. We need neither to build politics into learning organizations nor to give organizational form to some abstract political discourse, for planning analysts shape others' attention by probing policy or project possibilities every day, in both political and organizational settings. We need to direct our attention neither to ideal reorganizations nor to utopian political changes to improve planning and administrative practice.

The planning analyst's questioning and attention shaping is already organizational, but not strictly limited by organizational form. Informal networks of contacts, sources of advice, support, and warning supplement formal institutional channels. If planners and public administrators are to make democratic political debate and argument possible, they will need strategically located allies to avoid being fully thwarted by the characteristic self-protecting behaviors of the planning organizations and bureaucracies within which they work.

Planning analysts who use their questioning activity to democratize the planning process and the larger political process will have to work and build relationships with "friendly outsiders"—or, to be more directly political, "democratic outsiders"—who may be able to support the planning analyst's work or carry it further than apparent organizational constraints facing the analyst allow (Evans and Boyte 1986). Just as Martin Landau called for internal criticism and self-questioning in error-correcting organizations, the democratizing planner or administrator will call for and work to establish strategic external criticism (Landau 1973). For example, community planners use a variety of practical strategies, cultivating and using informal networks, a "double underground," within and extending beyond the boundaries of planing organizations (Needleman and Needleman 1974; Wilensky 1967). Planners and administrators can organize internal and external advocates for institutionally excluded interests and support networks and coalitions connecting planning staff, program staff, beneficiaries and others affected, and community organizations to work to correct systematic distortions of democratic communication, threats to public deliberation (Reich 1988; Forester 1993). Consider the common planning case in which this already happens: the planning staff enable a concerned community organization to raise questions about a project—questions that the planners could not "touch" themselves for "political reasons." In the first and second parts of this chapter, we discussed practical strategies available to planners and administrators, from relationship building to uncertainty management. All of these strategies are modes of action that planning analysts can use as they seek to correct unnecessarily distorted communications, to try to democratize planning and policy processes. To illustrate how this might be so, we can explore the planning analyst's organization of attention to uncertainty at greater length.

For Political Discourse: Selective Attention to Uncertainty

Planning analysts can organize networks to manage, or produce, uncertainty as a political tool when policy decisions are likely to be made with virtually no public deliberation. Uncertainty production is one strategy for setting up outside critics as "checks and balances": as Benveniste emphasizes, much of the planning analyst's power derives from his or her management of uncertainty. Spreading "uncertainty management" to friendly outsiders may be a necessary organizational strategy for the democratizing planners concerned about their own job stability. Such attention to uncertainty in a forthcoming project is likely to be listened to—as Taylor (1977) illustrates from the testimony of an Army Corps of Engineers analyst:

> The worst thing in this business is to be surprised by some serious environmental issue. That throws doubt not only on the district's credibility for candor and neutrality, but also on its technical competence. If they missed this issue, what else have they screwed up on?

Sensitive not only to what others want to do but also to what uncertainties they face, what they need to "watch out for," planners find that information, advice, and counsel about these matters becomes a source of power. If the developer's team does not want to bog down in bureaucratic detail, they will have to listen to the planning staff. As one planner put it, there may be no "inside" to the system, but developers and community persons alike may *need* to work with planners to deal with the practical uncertainties of their own strategies. The planner's power, here, comes not only through withholding strategic information, but through using it as well, often bringing up and clearly posing important uncertainties for the first time. Here the planning analyst's probing of opportunities and dangers creates its own basis of power and self-protection. Similarly, spreading questions of uncertainties to "friendly" outsiders committed to democratizing further the planning process can empower them as well in particular cases. Knowing that a developer is lining up political support for an industrial park proposal, the city planner who spreads to community groups questions of design, costs, and alternatives may act to democratize the planning process where otherwise a project may have been "snuck in through the back door," or "railroaded" past a planning commission before significant community involvement and participation had been made possible.[22] Here, the organizing and educative effects can be as important as a given project's modification.

Since "the powers that be" need to protect themselves from mistakes, poor investments, inopportune policy positions, they must beware of uncertainty; when these powers must pay attention to uncertain internal or external environments, then planning staffers gain power and discretion of their own. By carefully questioning possibilities, planners and analysts exert influence, and so such spreading of questions of uncertainty can be a practical tool for democratizing planning analysts.

The Politics of Planning and Administrative Practice and the Ethics of Questioning

Planners and analysts who seek to democratize planning and policy processes will necessarily at times be in conflict with the everyday routine, precedents, and structure of those planning and policy processes. As we shift away from the informational imagery of the planner who is politically determined to process policy-relevant data in set ways, though, the possibilities of effective, increasingly democratic, practice grow. Information will still be gathered, screened, and channeled along to "decision makers," but the practice of questioning will accomplish much more as well. And these political functions of the planning analyst's questioning can serve to open communications, spread responsibility for action to other actors, inform concerned but excluded groups about upcoming proposals or opportunities for action, and so on—as sketched above in the first and second parts of this chapter.

Thus, the planner's practice of questioning is already organizational and political—as communicative action. Yet because in planning theory we have not understood the power and effectiveness of questioning (and speech acts more generally) and thus analysts' organizing of attention as practical-political communicative activity, we have neglected a wide range of opportunities for action in planning and policy analysis. To understand how our practice is thwarted by systematic distortions of communications, and how we might expose and correct these distortions, we need to understand better the possibilities of the planning analyst's communicative practice, organizing attention and shaping the practical activities of response.[23]

If the traditional "critique of ideology" becomes now the critique of systematically distorted communications, this critique must involve:

1. The articulation of a democratic political vision of open communication ("voice" free from domination) and dialogue, and, simultaneously, for

2. The organizing, the practice and praxis, working concretely day to day to correct and overcome the domination of the unnecessary systematic distortions of communication in the organizational and political settings in which we live.

So we must immediately confront the ethics of planning analysis, planning and administrative practice (Krumholz and Forester 1990; Burke 1986; Wachs 1985).

Will the analyst allow distorted communications, distorted communicative action, to continue as is, or will the analyst or planner work to create more open public deliberations, more open, less needlessly distorted, planning discourse?[24] Will the analyst simply participate in and perpetuate existing forms of interactions and political participation—or work to change them toward increasingly dialogical and democratic forms (Barber 1984; Cohen and Rogers 1983)? Whether or not the planning analyst can formally challenge existing power and authority, will encouragement and support, motivation and information, be given to others who may mobilize politically, foster political argument, and work to correct distortions of discourse and dialogue?

The ethics of planning analysis are the ethics of communicative action, and these are the ethics of everyday speech and discourse.[25] As I ought not manipulate the reader in these pages, and as we ought not ordinarily mislead one another in ordinary talk, the planning analyst ought not perpetuate distorted communications between "client groups," "decision makers," "planning staff," and others. If this means that democratizing the planning process, and the larger political process, will threaten the bureaucratic routines and "business as usual" of existing organizations, this, of course, becomes a problem for planning staff to address in turn. The point is *not* that planning analysts should "always tell the truth, the whole truth, and nothing but the truth," but that they should make truth telling and obfuscation, criticism and false promises, integrity and deceit problematic, a focus of practical attention, insofar as the character of political participation and decision making depends upon them (Forester 1991).

To support existing organizational structures while ignoring distorted communication is to perpetuate and re-create deceit, dishonesty, manipulation; it is to continue to fabricate a society—or a neighborhood development project—which is at best a half-truth, at worst a lie in terms of the human possibilities discoverable and realizable under conditions of more democratic communication. The imposition of ideology in a totalitarian state, the spreading of systems-myths by a technocratic elite—these are "reality constructions" that are not socially rooted in the concerns and practice of the broader populace; their truth must be partial, simple fabrications for the consumption of others.

We can be responsible when we are able to respond to the world about us; thus, talk of formal political responsibility under repressive regimes may be meaningless. An ethics of everyday discourse calls upon us not just to hear, but to listen to those with whom we speak, to try to answer genuinely when we are spoken to, to seek to speak the truth rather than to create a false world. So, too, planners and administrators who speak within conflicting ideologies, within systems of authority and status, always face the question, "How to speak and respond?" Shall we simply nod mechanically to those about us as C. Wright Mills' "cheerful robots" or work to build cooperative relationships, to free ourselves from unnecessary repression, to create a better world, however local, and sometimes necessarily, to the same ends, refuse to be an accomplice in others' repression, as well? These are everyday questions we face with co-workers, friends, family, and "acquaintances" too. Verbal or otherwise, communicative action is the texture of our relations with others—and how we shall respond, how we shall act, is always a question with which we are faced. We perpetually answer and respond to this question as we live; and as moral and political beings we are perpetually responsible for how we respond to this question.[26]

The planning analyst is one of us—a human being with others, speaking and being spoken to, called to consider possibilities for change, to respect traditions as well. Working within structures of power and ideology and knowing better than many others the local opportunities and perversities of those structures, planners and administrators must continue to speak and listen critically; they must continue to communicate, not as machines transferring bits of information, but as caring persons acting with other caring persons. The questions of "How?" will perpetually arise. How shall we handle this case—shall we involve the neighborhood group (much) or not? Shall we simply bargain for design changes with the developer's staff (program staff) instead? Whom ought we to talk to about this case, and what might we do?

The planning analyst faces such questions continually, in a thousand varied forms and circumstances. Of course, *all* the people affected by policy or project proposals may never be consulted. Under certain circumstances planners may deliberately withhold information from others. Yet the basic political and ethical question remains: Shall the planning analyst maintain, or work to change, given conditions of unnecessarily distorted communications—the given conditions of distorted communicative action: inequitable distributions of opportunities and resources for participation in political discourse, illusions of possibilities and impossibilities perpetuated by dominant ideologies, the protection of bureaucratic exclusiveness rather than encouragement of others' political action (Forester 1989; BenHabib and Dallmayr 1990)? The ethics we share in everyday discourse, the morality we anticipate in ordinary language use, obliges and guides us as planning analysts to work toward the democratization of public deliberations.

Conclusion: Analysts' Questions
Organize Attention and Response

By paying attention to the many functions of our questioning, we can find planning and administrative strategies to shape design and work toward more open public deliberation too. Once we free ourselves of the image of the planning analyst as information gatherer, we appreciate instead the analysts' organizational and political relationships and their activities of speaking and listening, opening possibilities for action, searching for and responding to concerns, spreading responsibility, questioning and so organizing participation and involvement in response as well as eliciting information. The planner or administrator does not simply make plans, but rather shapes the network of relations and the attention of those who care about plans. Focusing on the formal product of a plan as a document runs the risk of substituting concern with graphics for that of deliberation and implementation.

We should understand planning analysis, then, as a form of organizing (or, as it fails, one of dis-organizing). The communicative activities of questioning options and shaping responses are political and technical actions; they are not just "talk." The planning analyst directs attention selectively, highlighting certain strategies and downplaying others. As the planning analyst's questions shape responses and still further actions, so are they part of the ongoing processes of design. The questioning of neighborhood groups can encourage and develop participation; the questioning of project developers can open up further refinements in originally proposed designs. What flows in all this is more than words, though argument, negotiation, checking, bargaining, and testing others' positions are all common enough. In the practice of questioning, relationships are built and the extent and timing of political participation is shaped too. Thus planning analysis is far more than formal symbol manipulation; instead, in the critical and pragmatic activities of probing possibilities, the administrator's or planner's analysis is at once theoretical and practical.

A critical-pragmatic theory of the practice of questioning allows us immediately to relate activities of analysis to design; we no longer need to separate radically analytical activity from implementation, "critique" from "emancipation." By using a communicative model of planning analysis as questioning, organizing attention and response, we can free ourselves of the subordination of the politics and ethics of planning to the preoccupation with analytical technique. Questioning is inherently revealing, opening, searching; as action calling for action in response, it is at once analytic and synthetic in intent and practice (Freire 1970).

Through questioning possibilities and shaping attention, then, planning analysis is an activity of organizing. Embodied as questions shaping responses, so does theoretical attention shape practical action—so does theory shape practice. Our attention to the practice of questioning shows us not only the relationship of analysis to design and the problems of political criticism and democratization, it shows us how we can effectively work, shape design and implementation, toward democratization as well. As the dialogue and argument of question-response anticipate and counter the domination of systematically distorted communicative action and provide the bases for action, design and implementation, a critical-questioning style of administrative and planning practice shows us that rather than analysis or formalism alone, thought and action together, politics and vision, lie at the heart of planning and administrative practice.

4

Practical Rationality: From Bounded Rationality to the Critique of Ideology in Practice

Introduction

In planning and policy analysis, rationality is not simply a cognitive problem. If we treat it as a matter of knowing—or, more precisely, following conventional accounts, as a matter of calculation—we are liable to ignore the historical contingencies of practical rationality in action (Faludi 1984; Reade 1984; cf. Forester 1989). Investigating rational mental processes, we may neglect rational conduct and practice. This chapter proposes an account of practical, situated, rational action as an alternative to the common instrumental view of rationality as means-ends calculation.

After offering a Weberian critique of instrumental rationality and an account of practical communicative action, this chapter: (1) reformulates the "boundedness" or constrained character of such action; (2) assesses the practical significance of that reformulation; and (3) considers the ethical, critical, and political implications of this account of rationality in planmaking.

Herbert Simon and Jurgen Habermas, leading exponents of the Carnegie-Mellon school of decision making and the contemporary "Frankfurt School" of social theory, respectively, point to similar problems and new directions: the analysis of situated practical

action. Simon rejects the notion of rational decision making as constrained optimization, and he calls instead for a program of economic behavioralism, the investigation of the procedures actually
used by decision makers in real-choice situations. Simon (1979, 85)
writes:

> Economics is now focusing on new research questions whose
> answers require explicit attention to procedural rationality.
> As economics becomes more and more involved in the study of
> uncertainty, more and more concerned with the complex actu-
> ality of business decision-making, the shift in programme will
> become inevitable. Wider and wider areas of economics will
> replace the over-simplified assumptions of the situationally
> constrained omniscient decision maker with a realistic (and
> psychological) characterization of the limits on Man's rational-
> ity, and the consequences of those limits for his economic
> behaviour.

And Habermas, as we shall see, has sought to develop a model of
practical communicative action, action understood not as the
result of a formal means-ends calculation, but as a pragmatic
socially meaningful performance.

The Critique of Instrumental Rationality— and Practical Communicative Action

In *Toward a Rational Society* and the more recent *Theory of Communicative Action*, Habermas works to reformulate Weber's theory
of social rationalization (Habermas 1970, 1983). Seeking to articulate a model of social action through which rationalization
processes take place, Habermas distinguishes two candidates: purposive-rational or instrumental action and symbolic interaction.
The purposive rational actor is the functionally rational calculator;
the symbolic interactor is the practically rational member engaged
in a conversation.[1] For the calculator, rationality produces control;
for the engaged conversationalist, rationality produces understanding and consensual decisions. This distinction, Habermas
and Robert Bellah more recently remind us, derives in various
forms from Aristotle's distinction between techne and praxis (Bellah 1982; Habermas 1973).

In the first model of action, questions of value and significance seem to be given, already provided, without incompleteness, ambiguity, or bias. Questions of political legitimacy (calculation for whom, solving which and whose problems?) are ruled out of court. Rationality here pretends to political neutrality or, better, to indifference and disregard for encompassing (and more subtly constituting) political influences. Thus a murderous regime may be served in rational ways; murder might be performed not just efficiently but rationally—if this account of rational action is accepted. This is an awkward if not outrageous position, as C. West Churchman (1962, 73) points out:

> It is simply a mistake to think that game theory, or much of so-called decision theory, is an analysis of rational behavior. The work in these fields is undoubtedly very important, but it has very little to do with our learning about rationality. This is because the problem of rationality is not to define rules of behavior, given the goals, but rather to define rational goals. To relegate rationality to the study of means only is to trivialize it. It is to lose the whole traditional spirit of the concept of rational behavior to say that a man may "rationally" murder his friends in cold blood, as long as he structures his choices according to "rational" rules.

The strictly means-ends calculating approach to rational action, then, may lead to embarrassing (not to say repugnant) results. If instrumental rationality cannot address the issue of desirable goals and norms—if it must rather assume those as standards with respect to which to calculate streams of benefits and costs, pleasures and pains—then the purposes for which rationality is used are nonrational, perhaps irrational (and it is not clear how we would draw this distinction). Worse still, technical or instrumental rationality then involves us in a process of calculation in which we are to believe that we are sophisticatedly and rationally pursuing the nonrational or irrational. This deeply violates our most basic common sense. Peculiarly, then, in an important sense, we do not know what it is that we are supposedly rationally doing when we act instrumentally. This result should give us substantial pause and reason to doubt the adequacy of such an instrumental, calculating view of rationality (Elster 1986; Mansbridge 1988).

This embarrassing result echoes the pathos of Weber's lifework. Eric Reade (1984) has suggested that Weber took instrumental rationality to include the assessment of ends in themselves. This is ambiguous at best, if not incorrect. Chosen ends might lead us to differing clusters of consequences, and, to this limited extent, Weber thought, ends might indeed be assessed. Yet Weber despaired of ever being able to compare and evaluate ends with respect to one another—and he pointed to the problem by distinguishing purposive rational (zweckrational) and value-rational (wertrational) action. Had Weber thought that ends themselves could be compared rationally, he would not have found it necessary, in his famous "Politics as a Vocation," to distinguish the "ethic of ultimate ends" from the "ethic of responsibility"; the former would simply have been reducible to the latter—a conclusion Weber obviously and strenuously rejected (Weber 1958a, chap. 4). Respecting the doubt that a rational evaluation comparing ends was possible, Weber repeatedly warned of the consequences of rationalization—overvaluing the calculating, instrumentally rational competences of human beings to the neglect of other virtues (and other conceptions of rationality as well). Two quotes suggest Weber's own critique of the problematic character and adequacy of understanding rationality to be essentially instrumental in nature. The first passage is often quoted; the second, though far more striking, is less well known.

At the close of *The Protestant Ethic and the Spirit of Capitalism,* Weber points to the significance and implications of a society organized increasingly upon the lines of purposive rational, calculating action. He referred to the spread of such rationality as rationalization, and he wrote of its secular and ascetic capitalist manifestations as an "iron cage":

> No one knows who will live in this cage in the future, or whether at the end of this tremendous development entirely new prophets will arise, or there will be a great rebirth of old ideas and ideals, or, if neither, mechanized petrification, embellished with a sort of convulsive self-importance. For of the last stage of this cultural development, it might well be truly said: "Specialists without spirit, sensualists without heart; this nullity imagines that it has attained a level of civilization never before achieved." (Weber 1958b, 182)

In another essay, "Religious Rejections of the World and Their Directions," an essay aiming "at contributing to the typology and sociology of rationalism," Weber notes that "[T]he cosmos of natural causality and the postulated cosmos of ethical, compensatory causality have stood in irreconcilable opposition" (Weber

1958a, 324, 355). Yet Weber did not celebrate the scientific realm of increasing instrumental rationality at the expense of the religious and ethical life; he was far too astute a moral observer. Weber thought—as Popper was later to think as well—that the scientific or critical attitude itself could not be systematically justified on its own standards. The foundation of the scientific community was nonrational, then: moral decision or commitments. This ironic, if not self-contradictory, result led to disturbing ethical conclusions, as Weber forcefully and poignantly pointed out. He wrote a profound indictment whose deep charge of senselessness must be addressed by all those advocating any reduction of rationality to instrumental rationality:

> Science has created this cosmos of natural causality and has seemed unable to answer with certainty the question of its own ultimate presuppositions. Nevertheless science, in the name of 'intellectual integrity', has come forward with the claim of representing the only possible form of a reasoned view of the world. The intellect, like all culture values, has created an aristocracy based on the possession of rational culture and independent of all personal ethical qualities of man. The aristocracy of intellect is hence an unbrotherly aristocracy. Worldly man has regarded this possession of culture as the highest good. In addition to the burden of ethical guilt, however, something has adhered to this cultural value which was bound to depreciate it with still greater finality, namely, senselessness—if this cultural value is to be judged in terms of its own standards. (Weber 1958a, 355)

As Weber knew, then, the first model of rational action, instrumental rationality, leads to embarrassing and morally troubling results. Actors seem to pursue the nonrational rationally; as calculators they seem to mistake in the Golden Rule the gold for the spirit of the rule. They seem to emulate the latest and most efficient model in evolving generations of computer systems— rather than emulating the most profound models of civic virtue, brotherhood, or Aristotelean ethical maturity (Bellah 1982).

The second model of rational action suggests that conduct be understood not as the use of a tool but as the making of a promise. As social beings, actors shape each other's attention to the world and expectations of it. Such communicative action ordinarily makes both *content* and *context* claims; we promise or agree to or threaten or ask something, and we do so in particular social or institutional contexts. Habermas argues at length that such action is never guaranteed to succeed. Communicative action is a contingent, skilled, practical performance, and when it breaks down, two options arise. Either actors give up the attempt at mutual understanding and cooperative interaction (perhaps to resort to coercion), or they may momentarily step aside from the stream of action to participate in "discourse": a forum in which they may attempt, respecting only the force of the better argument, to resurrect and sustain the conversation—to test a factual claim against the evidence or to justify a normative claim with reasons, so that noncoercive communicative interaction may proceed. In this way, Habermas suggests, situated communicative action involves practical claims made (testably, subject to criticism via discourse) between social actors; thus social action is contingently rational action (Forester 1989). This model of action makes possible a powerful empirical analysis of practice—an analysis both structurally informed and phenomenologically sensitive. For our purposes here, though, we can concentrate not on the anatomy of communicative action but upon its situated character and its notion of criticism and discourse.

The practical communicative model of action suggests a rich notion of rationality, for here questions of norms and values are not presumed to be undiscussable but yet necessarily influential and constitutive of the very sense of action itself. Here we need, then, to address the conditions under which action, criticism, and justification take place—and allow ourselves to grant that justification of normative positions might be as rational, infinitely more context-sensitive but less precise, as any utilitarian calculation (Fischer 1980; Klosterman 1978). Here we need a theory, not of risk and rankings, but of conditions of action and discourse, debate and argument, and, in an overall sense, democratic voice (Habermas 1975; Barber 1984; Forester 1989; Fischer and Forester 1993).

Situated Rational Action

If we explore the problem of rationality as one of practical communicative action, we must ask: "Who acts? In what contexts? In what situations of choice? Constituted by what norms? Limited by what sorts of bounds and constraints?" The situated rational actor inherits an historical starting point in which information and misinformation, help and hindrance, support and opposition, are likely to be contingent, variable, always ambiguously forthcoming.

At the worst, if the nature of the constraints and obstacles to action varied across all situations—for example, health policy, land-use planning, environmental policy, and so on—then the resulting account of rationality would be, it seems, unacceptably relativistic. But, if we can typify expectable constraints across various planning and policy situations, we can see how the theory of rational action depends in part upon a theory of historical context or, sociologically, a theory of the institutional and structural contexts of action. Here the major social and political theories offer partially complementary and partially contradictory accounts of the real contexts of action.

As facts do not speak for themselves, neither do contexts; their interpretation is just as theoretically informed as that of any "fact." The Marxist, Weberian, and Durkheimian anticipate differing structural constraints and obstacles to practical action. But just how their paradigms call attention selectively and practically to differing aspects of a given situation is neither well understood nor yet clearly articulated.

If we can assess the situated character of our rational actor (a policy analyst or planner, for example)—not to leave him or her in the abstract, out in the cold—we can ask the following social questions: How do the institutional structures and social processes of the society at large reproduce and re-create the decision context of the planner, of the actor? How is the decision situation, the problem-solving or the advice-giving situation, socially and politically constructed? What pressures, incentives, temptations, confusions, threats, seductive techniques, or professional expectations are pressed upon the planner or policy analyst? These influences extend far beyond any cognitive sense of bias or ideology—and Habermas's reformulation of the problem of ideology as that of "systematically distorted (pragmatic) communications" opens up a rich set of practical influences to investigate.

So to understand a planner's action as more or less rational, we may well need to understand how the planning organization itself reflects, in Schattschneider's brilliant phrase, "the mobilization of bias" (Schattschneider 1960, 71). Some citizens or interest groups, for example, may systematically have access to local government or federal agencies, whereas other citizens do not, and knowing that may be important in gauging what is to count as rational action by a planner or policy analyst mandated to serve both groups of citizens. Notice that if analysts treat all similarly, under the banner of equal formal opportunity (that is, the door being open to all who can knock), the analysts help to ensure that the given inequality of access will be perpetuated. Significantly, though, analysts' efforts to improve access to those without it may be seen as wasteful and even inequitable if the organizational biases that constitute the actual work setting are *not* taken into account.

The Rebounding Of Rationality: Practical Anticipation And Response

Simon, of course, broached this line of analysis long ago. If Simon had not used, however, the passive voice of "bounded rationality", but had referred to "the bounding of rationality" instead, his readers would have been drawn much more quickly by the grammar of the phrase to ask: What bounds rational action? How does such bounding take place? Can some of the boundedness of action be prevented, whereas some cannot? How might social structure influence the boundedness of action?

Two crucial distinctions need to be drawn if we are to clarify the actual boundedness of rational action. The distinctions have force when we note that Simon's paradigmatic notion of boundedness, namely the cognitive limits of decision makers' brainpower, is one that is apparently both (1) inevitable and (2) not socially systematic (it is nonstructural). Simon's own emphasis seems to beg two questions, therefore. First, might not some practical bounds, instead of being inevitable, be artificial and unnecessary, mere artifacts of personality or power relations or custom—any of which might be changed, thus rebounding the action situation at hand? Second, if bounds can be socially constructed by virtue of organizational design or political structure, might not some bounds be socially systematic, derived from existing patterns of social structure rather than from wholly random or ad hoc sources? Posing these questions allows us to reformulate the boundedness of rational action (Forester 1989; Kemp 1980, 1982). Bounds or constraints upon rational action not only vary along two dimensions, nonsystematic or systematic, and necessary or unnecessary, as suggested by table 4.1, but correspondingly practical responses to such varying "bounds" will vary as well.

The practical implications of these distinctions are substantial. The person who always anticipates systematic distortions or constraints when random and usually nonsystematic ones exist, we are likely to call paranoid; the person who treats inevitable constraints as if they were transient artifacts of the situation, we

Table 4.1   Bounded rationality: a critical theoretic reformulation to distinguish *types of misinformation* or communicative distortion (bounds on the rationality of action) (adapted from Forester 1989).

	Autonomy of the Source of Distortion	
	socially ad hoc	socially systematic-structural
inevitable distortions	idiosyncratic personal traits affecting communication random noise	information inequalities resulting from legitimated division of labor transmission-content losses across organizational boundaries
Contingency of Distortion	**1 Cognitive limits [Simon]**	**2 Differentiation [Weber]**
socially unnecessary distortions	willful unresponsiveness interpersonal deception interpersonal bargaining behavior; for example, bluffing	monopolistic distortions of exchange monopolistic creation of needs ideological rationalization of class or power structure
	3 Pluralist Bargaining [Lindblom]	**4 Structural legitimation [Marx]**

are likely to call impractical at best and a fool at worst (the geniuses who transform the inevitable into the artificial notwithstanding). More interestingly, though, we can anticipate structural and systematic constraints, whereas nonsystematic ones will be more uncertain; we may devise a strategy to get information that another organization is expected to withhold, but, in the face of random staffing problems, we may be forced to hedge our bets by allowing some additional increment of time to do what we are trying to do.

Distinguishing these bounds upon rational action also has political implications. Liberal political theorists, for example, focus attention far more to nonsystematic conflicts of pluralist interest groups, while Marxist theorists focus attention instead upon structural constraints on social action. Technically minded analysts attend to inevitably "given" problems, while political and entrepreneurial analysts make an art out of assessing the political "givenness," the artificial social construction of the problems they face (Meltsner 1976; Baum 1987, 1990; Benveniste 1989; Clavel 1986; Healey 1992; Hoch and Cibulskis 1987).

If this analysis of the variable boundedness of rational action is half-right, then the empirical study of planning and policy analysis practice might produce insightful accounts of the practical repertoires of strategies that analysts actually use in the face of these various sorts of practical constraints. By informing the practitioner's anticipation of different types of constraints upon his or her action, such a planning theory of the variable boundedness of rational action might also directly inform practical planning strategies. For example, responses to ad hoc but necessary constraints (quadrant 1, table 4.1) include strategies of risk analysis, the hedging of bets, allowing redundancy; responses to necessary systematic constraints (quadrant 2) include boundary spanning, specialization of function, and socialization of risk (when, for example, knowledge or commitment is systematically diffuse). Responses to ad hoc but unnecessary constraints upon action (quadrant 3) include strategies of bargaining, sanctioning others' behavior, checking and monitoring, and using legal remedies. Finally, responses to systematic and unnecessary constraints (quadrant 4) may include strategies of community, class, or political organization, the use of coalitions, and the exposure and critique of ideological claims.

These responses, organized into table 4.2, provide only the barest glimpse at the wealth of the practical repertoires of strategies that are likely to be found in practice—in response to these distinctive types of constraints upon action. Just as table 4.1 suggests how various major political theories might focus attention upon differing practical constraints upon action, so does table 4.2 suggest how and why these major theories find such different practical strategies of action to be rational!

A further, more challenging problem remains. Judgments of value and significance must be made in situations of action, even if they might now be partially protected from the mystifications and biases reflected in unnecessary constraints upon action. The work of judgment, what Sir Geoffrey Vickers described so lucidly as the appreciation of fact and value, remains as a practical problem demanding a theory of ethics and evaluation, understood within a broader a theory of society as well.[2]

Table 4.2   Examples of responses to particular types of bounds or constraints upon rational action.

| | Autonomy of Distortion | |
	socially ad hoc	socially systematic-structural
inevitable distortions	risk analysis	boundary spanning
	hedging	specialization of function
	allowing redundancy	socialization of risk
Contingency of Distortion	1	2
socially unnecessary distortions	bargaining	political or community or class organizing
	sanctioning behavior, checking and monitoring	exposure and critique of ideology
	legal remedy	coalition utilization
	3	4

Bounded Rationality and Ethical Responsibility

"Bounded rationality" in its standard political and administrative form had perversely *socialized* rationality by presuming existing relations of power to be fully legitimate (or, in what amounts practically, if not theoretically, to the same thing, by presuming them to be above challenge in any specific case). If policy analysts and planners, as satisficing rational actors, are ever to assess potentially illegitimate or unjustified coercive influences constraining their satisficing solutions, they must consider the political legitimacy of the relations of power at hand.[3]

Simon's satisficer, no less and no more than Lindblom's incrementalist, is a political animal, though a potentially rational one—but as along as questions of illegitimacy and the abuse of power are neglected, that satisficer and incrementalist will be only a deferential and quiescent—and thus an ethically dangerous and hardly professional—political actor. So the question arises: Should not the ethically responsible rational actor in real constrained situations of choice and action distinguish, anticipate, evaluate, and act correspondingly differently toward political constraints that have strong claims to legitimacy and those that do not (Krumholz and Forester 1990, chap. 15; Burke 1986)?

Rationality and Criticism

How does our Habermasian account suggest anything helpful in the face of such problems? The Habermasian rational actor is a practical communicative agent who makes claims in a community of affected persons, claims for which he or she would be willing to offer justifications and arguments in discourses where (in principle) only the force of the better argument may prevail. Thus the counterfactual willingness to engage in processes of criticism, to subject one's views to the force of the better argument, is as central to Habermas as it is, in another variant, to Popper (Faludi 1984; McCarthy 1978; Smith 1981). For Popper and Habermas both, an appeal is made to a counterfactual (existing in principle, if only imperfectly realized in fact) community of inquirers and affected persons having the freedom to offer and challenge arguments, to put forth evidence and justifications, to seek the better argument. The detailed epistemological differences between Habermas and Popper notwithstanding, the Habermasian model of discourse underlying the practical claims made in communicative action is no more—and no less—counterfactual than the Popperian notion of the critical attitude and the critical scientific community of inquirers (McCarthy 1978, 44–52).

Yet, although Popper suggests that the critical attitude itself cannot be systematically justified, Habermas argues, extending the arguments of Karl Otto Apel, that the *counterfactual* ideal of an ideal speech situation in both theoretical and practical discourses is inherent in our ordinary use of language with one another, in our ordinary communicative competence (Habermas 1975, part 3; 1979 chap. 1; cf. Forester 1991, 52–55). Habermas suggests that while factual claims anticipate the court of theoretical discourses for their in-principle establishment, normative claims anticipate instead the court of practical discourses for their hypothetical justification.

Habermas argues, then, that our notion of rationality is systematically connected to the consideration of the conditions of criticism that may exist. Instrumental action may be criticized as correct or not, as more or less effective or efficient; communicative action more broadly may also be criticized as justifiable within the affected community (Habermas 1970, 1979). As a result, the crux of the problem of the possibility of rational action will not be the weighting of consequences and, as Simon says, the mathematically straightforward optimization of a payoff; it will be, instead, the anticipation of threats to conditions of free discourse and unhampered argumentation. Thus the problem of communicative rationality is intimately linked to questions of freedom and justice (the essential conditions constituting the community of inquirers and all those affected). To the extent that an action might in principle be ratified by all those investigating it or affected by it in a discourse based upon the strength of the offered arguments alone, to that extent might the action be called "rational".

The imagination called for, here, by the potentially rational actor is that searching for action which would meet generalizable agreement by all those affected. Rationality thus—whether of the most technical instrumental actions or the most ethically charged communicative action more generally—becomes a function of in-principle consent, roughly as the Popperian notion of scientific results appeals to the in-principle provisional acceptance by the community of scientific inquirers.

Conclusion

If we treat rationality as a problem purely of epistemology, cognition, and instrumental calculation, then, we run several risks. First, we may ignore the real lived situations of people needing to make practical judgments, needing to act, and so our notion of rationality will be far too abstract and impractical. Second, we may ignore the historical constitution of any potentially rational actor's entangled situation, and so we will fail to appreciate the institutional complexities (the biases, prejudices, partial formulations) of "the problem" at hand.

Third, we are likely to ignore the pressures upon potentially rational actors to act in particular political ways. Subscribers to the cognitive calculating view of rationality, we are likely then to be less able to *anticipate and counteract* those practical social and political influences that render planners' and analysts' conduct contingent and vulnerable to distortion (for example, the play of arbitrary or organized, but illegitimate, power).

Fourth, if we fail to distinguish unnecessary from necessary, ad hoc from structural bounds constraining rational action, our calculating view is likely to suppress questions of justice and legitimacy altogether. Yet, in fact, advocating such a narrow view would imply that existing constraints must be accepted—as if any play of power bounding action (limiting information, for instance) were in fact legitimate. A more effective self-imposed discouragement of normative criticism can hardly be imagined. What appears to be an apolitical "satisficing" account of rationality in the abstract, then, may be in the actual concrete case the most quiescent, blindly deferential political action possible. The relations of power that shape the bounds of action, and thus the satisficing action or decision, would be accepted in principle (!), however illegitimate they may be.

Fifth, if we ignore the social and institutional context of action, our instrumental or calculating view is likely to ignore the practical problem of ideology: the ways in which issues of problem formulation, scope, time horizons, weightings of consequences, and so on may be practically constituted, prejudged (pre-judiced), and influenced by elements of the social environment that hardly reflect the interests of those to be affected by the action or decision at hand.

Sixth, thus, our calculating view would reduce rationality and questions of rational action to apparently technical problems when they are quite obviously (also) political and ethical (normative) through and through. Because the consequentiality—the value and significance—of consequences cannot be given before questions of rational action arise, attempts to formulate a powerful notion of rationality must recognize the potentially rational actor to be a participant in a community of potentially affected persons—whose free consent and assent (in principle) to the actor's decision might be taken to establish the very rationality of the decision.[4] This discursive or argumentative model of rationality in planning depends upon a notion of the planner as a potentially rational participant in a political and social world—a notion excluded and obscured by a purely instrumental, calculating view of rationality.

By taking the problem of rationality to be a problem of situated action, more than one of epistemology and cognition, a practical account of planners' behavior in choice situations can be given. The problem of rational action in planning can then be recognized as socially situated, politically contingent, facing bounds potentially ad hoc or systematic, necessary or unnecessary, in a political world, and affecting others who might in principle criticize and accept or reject particular planning actions. Hardly solving questions of choice for once and for all, such an account of situated and bounded rational action—an account of practical rationality—might at least enable policy analysts and planners better to anticipate a range of distorting and biasing "bounding" influences that they are likely to face in practice (Forester 1989, chap. 4). Such anticipation may help planners and analysts to counteract those forces and thus to protect the quality of a planning and policy-analytic practice in which rational action is intimately connected to the possibilities of its criticism and consensual acceptance.

5

The Geography of Practice and
the Terrain of Resistance

As a profession, planning has been too timid. This criticism is pointed less toward the rank-and-file staff of most agencies than at their directors. They are the individuals confronted with the challenge and opportunity to create an activist role for their organizations, and they have the freedom to do so because there is much 'slack' in local government and because planning practice is not uniform by law or tradition. Beyond the narrow powers and responsibilities mandated to planners by their city charters, the scope and context of the planning function in most cities waits to be defined by the planners themselves, by their planning commissions, and by their mayors. However, mayors and planning commissioners will rarely provide leadership, especially toward equity objectives. This means that the planners themselves must seize the initiative and define their own roles relative to the real needs of the city and its people. This course of action involves some political risks, but as our experience...indicates, the risks are manageable. I believe that planners can do much more than they are now doing.

(Krumholz 1982, 173)

Introduction[1]

City planners have always been concerned with issues of space, geography, and territory. Zoning has its own lurid history, and industrial location remains central to planning for urban and regional economic development. Ironically, though, these conceptions of space seem to have left little room for the planners themselves. Property owners, developers, builders, and industries bid to make moves on the territorial game board, and planners from afar seemingly seek to maintain order, to provide incentives for desirable industrial location, to protect residential neighborhoods, to promote and channel growth, to protect the environment. Action in this world is either a competition between property owners and investors (seen pluralistically from a neoclassical perspective) or a struggle between capital and labor (seen dualistically from a neo-Marxist perspective). In either view, strangely, the institutional world of the planners themselves may be altogether missing, despite the recent attention paid to the neo-Marxist theory of the state.[2] In what territory and space, then, institutionally, culturally, and politically, do planners act to affect the ongoing productive and reproductive processes of our society? This chapter attempts to answer this question and thus to elaborate a practical geography of planning practice, so providing an account of the geography of planners' actual day-to-day professional conduct.

Why is a "geography of practice" an issue at all? Consider four reasons. First, planners bewail the irrelevance of much theory to their real-world work. These same planners do not doubt that the academic theories are often about important problems, rather they suggest that these theories do not "tell them what to do" in the situations in which they find themselves (Baum 1983). This reaction is less anti-intellectualism than the cry of the drowning man who is thrown not a rope but a book on water quality.

Second, a growing number of planning academics are now calling for a planning theory grounded in the practical organizational and political realities of planning practice (Baum 1983; Bolan 1980; DeNeufville 1983; Forester 1982a; Roweis 1983; Schön 1983). These writers share a dissatisfaction with planning practice understood as technical problem solving, and thus they have been forced to characterize planning as some sort of interactive process—as socially constructing meaning, as shaping public attention and conversation, as influencing social learning, and so on. In each case the questions arise, "interacting with whom and in what institutional contexts?"

Third, planning practitioners and academics alike stand to benefit from the growing appreciation in several disciplines that questions of individual action and social structure cannot be addressed separately (Bryson 1982; Gaventa 1980; Giddens 1979; Habermas 1979; Lukes 1974; Thrift 1983). Accounts of action alone risk treating planners as if they worked in a vacuum. Accounts of political and economic structure alone risk treating planners as if they were wholly determined, their function and accomplishments foregone conclusions, the practical matters of their judgments and choices simply dead and illusory issues. Between practical actions to be attempted and political-economic structures that provide the settings for those actions lie the situations in which planners find themselves. If these situations could be mapped at all, we might then illuminate the practical terrain of planners' work, the spatiotemporal, normative, and institutional geography of their practice.

Fourth, several influential accounts consider planning practice as a form of mediation linked to processes of social reproduction and learning (Bolan 1980; Burton and Murphy 1980; Forester 1989; Marris 1987; Roweis 1983; Schön 1983). Not only technical but political and ethical questions as well are at stake here. Calculating the tax advantages to be offered as locational incentives is one thing; recommending alternative development schemes that shun tax abatements is another. If planners are to treat social learning as more than an intriguing metaphor, then we must explore the ways planners can actually further or hinder "social learning" in practice (Argyris and Schön 1978; Baum 1987; Schön 1983). If planners are to shape social learning in deed, we must map the terrain of learning processes and planners' possible interventions too.

Each of these reasons to elaborate a geography of planning practice raises particular problems, to be addressed in turn in this chapter:

1. To address the situated character of planners' work, we must abandon the image of practice as context-free technical problem solving and replace it with an image of an attentive, practical, context-dependent response to particular situational demands (Forester 1993).

2. To clarify the social and interactive nature of practice, we must set out an account of planners' work as communicative action to show how much more than information is at stake in day-to-day interaction.

3. To link action and structure in a reading of planning practice, we must then assess how planners' actions can influence the ongoing processes of social reproduction that regularly routinize diverse actions into more stable patterns of social structure; and

4. Finally, we must distinguish specific types of social-learning processes and assess their implications for the practical work of planning analysts. In particular, here, we need to recognize the differences between acting in the face of uncertainty and acting in the face of ambiguity.

If we can address these four problems, we might understand planning realistically as a practical communicative activity, structurally staged, situationally contingent, and encouraging or discouraging, organizing or disorganizing, ongoing social processes of social learning and reproduction. Put more simply, we could analyze planning practice as iffy and political, shaping others' attention selectively and so helping or hindering their learning about their own world. If this is so, then the geography of practice will tell prospective planners just what they are getting into—and it might suggest to practicing planners certain regions of swamp, forest, quicksand, bramble, bush, and meadow, regions opportune, fertile, or dangerous, that lie ahead. Furthermore, as the epigram from Norman Krumholz suggests, the geography of practice would then be at once political *and* communicative, historically and structurally framed, situationally uncertain and ambiguous, mapping both opportunities for and obstacles to public-serving planning practice.

Planning Practice Is Situated—Precariously

What does it mean that planning is a practical situated activity? Were history a predictable process, planning problems well defined and stable, social values clear, consistent, and constant, the situation-bound character of planning might be less important than it is. Yet the opposite attributes of planning seem to be the case: history is turbulent and minimally predictable; planning problems are notoriously ill defined; social values are plural, conflicting, and fluid (tastes and preferences change); and, as a result, planners often have little opportunity to apply comprehensively rational problem-solving techniques routinely in their daily work. This much borders on banal incrementalist cliché, yet the implications for planning theory, theory useful for and grounded in planning practice, are striking.

What is at stake here is not only what sociologists call a model of social action, but also the fundamental distinction that must be drawn between context-free technical problem solving and context-responsive practical action. If we understood planning practice as the former, akin to technical calculation or instrumental action, we would expect improvements in practice to come in the form of technological innovations. But if we understand planning practice as the latter, akin to making practical judgments or participating in social interaction, we would expect improvements in practice to take more explicitly moral and political forms: enabling, for example, participation, voice, mediation, argumentative and learning processes, grievance procedures, and so on.

Indeed, attention to the limits of rational-comprehensive planning and elaboration of models of "bounded rationality" and "disjointed incrementalism" have clarified these problems in much gory detail (March 1988). Yet these satisficing and incrementalist accounts of practice too often go to another extreme; rejecting a fully specified style of planning in the name of cognitive, political, and organizational realism, these remedies can be as troublesome as the disease they seek to cure. They may be so vague that they only tell us as planners to take whatever we can get. Here, as we have seen, planning may be reduced to opportunism. Bounded rationality aside, though, two further problems arise: the political structure of the planning environment and the presence of uncertainty and ambiguity in analytical practice.

Environmental Structure

First, while prudence recommends incremental steps in a turbulent political and organizational environment, we need still to explore the structure of that environment. Are there groups or classes likely to make demands upon the planning department? Are there sources of initiative and power, public or private, seeking further power or profit, that can be expected to be more or less cooperative with the planning staff? Are other public agencies a source of support or competition for the planners, or both? Are demands and requests made by independent citizens likely to receive the same consideration by the planning department director as those of corporate representatives?

These questions are theoretical and practical at once. They are theoretical because they ask whether a given planning situation is to be understood as set within a class-based or a pluralist theory of politics, within a liberal or structuralist theory of the state, or within some eclectic but systematic combination of these (Alford and Friedland 1985; Saunders 1979). A planner's hypothesis or bets about the salient aspects of his or her situation reflect in practice his or her working political theory. Little work has been done, though, that suggests just how alternative social and political theories might inform practicing planners' readings of their organizational environment's composition of conflict, cooperation, opportunity, and resistance.

These questions are practical, too, because they call attention selectively to potential sources of support and opposition, to those who may help and those who may hinder the analyst's work. Suggesting bets about who may be more or less friendly, trustworthy, informed, influential, and so on, these questions suggest strategies of action in the face of scarce time, poor information, and complex political constellations of power and influence.

Analysts on both sides of the political spectrum might agree, for instance, that the state in capitalist society has at least two conflicting functions: to pursue both efficiency and equity in the liberal formulation and to further accumulation and legitimation in the neo-Marxist account. Planners could well expect, then, to face a similar dual imperative, even if how best to do so may never be spelled out by a written theory.

Uncertainty and Ambiguity

Second, the major analytical response to the demands of situation-dependent action has been the elaboration of models of decision-making in the face of *uncertainty*. Adapting the earlier work of Thompson and Tuden, Karen Christensen, for example, has argued that planners face potential uncertainties of two types, those of the technologies of problem solving and those of the goals to be addressed (Christensen 1982). This analysis is useful because it begins to match appropriate planning actions with the character of the specific situation at hand. Yet this formulation perpetuates an important shortcoming as well: the reduction of questions of normative ambiguity to questions of cognitive certainty or uncertainty. Whether we use the language of economy and society or productive forces and productive relations, efficiency and equity or accumulation and legitimation, it seems safe to argue that the environment of planning *structurally* presents planners with problems of distinctly differing levels of technical uncertainty and normative ambiguity. Faced with uncertainty we wonder if a particular strategy will work; faced with ambiguity we wonder what we should take as the standard of what works in the first place.

The point here is no quibble about semantics, as if semantics did not matter, distinguishing uncertainty from ambiguity. The point is threefold.

First, as a problem confronted in ordinary life, ambiguity is irreducible to and indeed fundamentally different from uncertainty. *That* an event will take place may be uncertain but not ambiguous; a pun is ambiguous but not uncertain. Questions of purpose and intent, or ethical and political choice, of obligation and responsibility, of the proper interpretation of meaning—these are issues of ambiguity; we look not for certainty but for justification (March and Olsen 1976; March 1988). Questions of scientific and technical results, of systems performance or the prediction of consequences—these are primarily issues of certainty and uncertainty; we look for evidence, not for interpretations of precedent.

Second, as suggested above, the social structure encompassing planning in an advanced capitalist society can be expected systematically to present planners with distinct challenges of facing uncertainty and ambiguity. Pressures for growth and accumulation will press questions of technological innovation and systems performance; here decision making under uncertainty may appropriately be one paradigmatic strategy to be considered. Yet pressures of legal responsibility, equity, and legitimation will press different questions, questions of rights and entitlements and justice; here one paradigmatic strategy to be considered will be one of practical political action in the face of ambiguity, in the face of conflicting claims, interests, and ideological interpretations, and here models of decision making under uncertainty may be more distracting than helpful.

Third, if these distinct problems of ambiguity and uncertainty continue to be confused, if the two are not properly distinguished, then political, normative, and "value" problems will likely be reduced to matters of supposed scientific certainty and uncertainty. Practical normative problems will be rendered technical and apolitical. Planners' and the broader public's attention will continue to be distracted, both from the historical and political bases of conflicting and shifting goals and interests, and from the reconstructive moral, legal, and political processes that may yet address such issues of conflicting or ambiguous wants, needs, desires, interests, precedents, and obligations. Wondering about uncertainty, we look for evidence. Wondering about the ambiguous, we look for precedent; tradition; a source of legitimacy; a consensually based interpretation; an appropriate, fitting response. Overly attentive to "scientific" questions about certainty, planners may fail to work skillfully in a variety of politically and socially interactive processes (consultation, bargaining, consensus building, structured argument, and so on) that might actually foster an effectively democratic, not technocratic, planning process.

The Anatomy of Planning Practice: Communicative Action[3]

How a planner talks to colleagues, public officials, building developers, neighborhood residents, and others is neither merely a matter of talk nor of information alone, nor even of personality. For how that planner talks is an important part of how that planner acts toward these others—effusively or reticently, encouragingly or discouragingly, blindly or creatively, naively or astutely, sensitively or callously, tactfully or ineptly. Insulting, promising, agreeing, and refusing to agree are actions, usually taken in speech but sometimes in gesture, actions for which the agent is responsible. As planners talk, write, or avoid these at times, so do they shape other actors' expectations, their perceptions of problems and opportunities at hand, and their abilities to act as well. Neoconservatives suggest that planners confuse issues better left to the market; left-liberals suggest that planners often legitimate decisions already made, that their practical communicative actions do not so much confuse issues but rather placate potentially rebellious and disaffected citizens (Wildavsky 1979; Piven and Cloward 1975). In either case, here, the planners' actions can be understood as significantly communicative, practically shaping—organizing or disorganizing—the attention of others to problems at hand.

How does such practical communication work? Communication theorists seem to agree on one simple but fundamental point: that all communication consists of two deeply related aspects, content and context. *What* a planner talks *about* is the *content* of what is said; *when and in what situation and with whom* the planner talks begins to define the *context* of what is said.

To communicate content, planners and their audience need to

share a language—of word or gesture—with which first to call attention to particular things in the world and second to say something coherent about these things. A building site presents an infinity of detail; speaking about it, a planner must not only refer selectively to it, referring to soil conditions, economic values, and so on, but then the planner must say something about what he or she refers to: the soil is not stable; the cost figures are inflated; no low-income housing units are to be provided; and so on. So the content side of practical communicative action has two components:

1. attention is called selectively to something (call this simply a *claim upon attention*); and

2. a statement is made about that something (call this a *factual claim*).

Now the context of what a planner says is defined by the historical, political, and social relations that provide the stage upon which the planner has anything to say to anyone in the first place. The planner speaks first of all as a planner, as an actor on a professional-political stage rather than on the stage of a Broadway theater (practitioners' sarcastic allusions to the "theater of the absurd" notwithstanding). Presentation of a report at a meeting of the planning commission—or at a meeting of a neighborhood association—may be taken for granted as being "in context," yet presentation of that same report in the same manner in the middle of the intersection outside would likely get the planner taken away to an asylum. Context counts; content alone is meaningless.

The context of what is said depends upon more than the structural legal-political relations making up the institutional and historical settings in which planners and others talk. Consider how in ordinary speech we understand joking, exaggeration, whining, parody, satire, anger, or hopelessness in another's words. Understanding here depends upon a reading of the other's intentions, their expressions of self, their personal stance providing an essential orienting element of the context at hand. So we may think of others, as we listen to what they say, "they're angry" or "they're kidding" or "they've got an axe to grind," and our evaluations of their intentions help to put what they say in context. At a planning commission meeting, the professional intentions of the staff presenting a report may be simultaneously taken for granted by the commissioners, yet suspiciously distrusted by building developers and neighborhood residents alike. Institutional rules and roles may be clear, providing one aspect of the context at hand, but developers may nevertheless wonder, "Are the staff favoring the neighborhood?" And neighborhood residents may wonder, "Are the staff really in bed with the developers?" What is said and done, then, is evaluated and understood in the context of institutional structure and of speakers' intentions.

So the contextual or relational side of practical communicative action also has two components (in addition to the content side):

1. speakers invoke the political-legal norms of the institutional relations at hand to give meaning to what they say (call this a *claim to legitimacy*, to be speaking legitimately-in-context); and

2. speakers color what they say with their own intentions and stances—to rein in or express emotion, to be overtly or covertly partisan (call this an *expressive claim* disclosing the speaker's self).

These four aspects of practical communicative action are only analytically separable. They are elements of the anatomy of action, but none take place in a vacuum, separated from social actors supporting, challenging, fighting, agreeing, caring for one another. This anatomy of action can be quite useful, not simply for purposes of further discussion (ordinary language philosophers will do that), but to inform the investigation of the health, vulnerability, and contingencies of actual planning practice.

The Systematic Place of Ambiguity and Uncertainty in Action

Notice that when questions of content are raised, issues of uncertainty (at least) appear. When questions of context or actors' institutional relationships are raised, issues of ambiguity arise (Bolan 1980). Precisely because practical action is never guaranteed, but rather always an historically and situationally contingent performance of fallible human actors offering both content *and* context claims in practice, those same actors (as speakers and listeners both) may always experience both uncertainty and ambiguity in practical life. *Uncertainty and ambiguity are systematically related, then, to the anatomy and structure of practical social (communicative) action.*

Yet how can issues of ambiguity and uncertainty be resolved? In part, resolution takes place through conflict and social learning (March and Olsen 1976; Marris 1975).

Conflict and Social Learning

How can the characterization of planning practice as communicative action account for conflict? What if any of the claims made (of either content or context-relationship aspects of practice) are contested? What if a developer claims that "minimal environmental impact" is likely to result from a proposed project, and local environmentalists argue precisely the opposite? What if a local hospital claims that an expensive equipment purchase is "needed," but a local health-care consumer organization claims just the contrary?

In such common cases, a continuum between two polar extremes presents itself. At one extreme the contested claim is settled by raw power—one side simply prevails, independent of the merits of the opposing claim. At the other extreme, both sides work to establish their case, making the merits of related arguments a matter of public scrutiny and legitimate political debate. In the first case, power displaces both democratic politics, a functioning public sphere in which legitimate authority may be constituted and renewed, and science, a functioning arena of criticism and conjecture in which competing explanations may be advanced, tested, and refined. In the second case, processes and institutions of debate, criticism, and discourse make possible (if always contingently) social learning in two dimensions: the practical-normative and the technical-instrumental (Habermas 1979).

In practice, actual conflicts will often fall on the continuum between these two extremes. One interesting implication of the notion of planning as communicative action, then, is the practical question: to what extent in actual practice can contested claims be debated or tested in anything like a social-learning process? Are contested claims decided purely on the basis of relations of power? How might planners anticipate and counteract obstructions to social learning? To address these questions practically, we need to map out a geography of practice, a geography of contingent and ever-vulnerable social learning.

The Environment of Planning Practice: Power and Organization

This anatomy of practical communicative action can inform the analyses of power and organization in planning. The exercise of power, for example, is likely to be more pervasively influential as the communication of the threat of sanctions than as the raw exercise of force. Indeed, power may be exercised in any or all of the four dimensions of social action, as (a) the mobilization of bias and selective attention; (b) the control of technical and factual information; (c) the invocation of myth, symbolism, precedent, tradition, and ideology legitimating social relations; and (d) the manipulation of trust and dependency. The analysis of these dimensions of power leads us directly to distinguish possible practical responses and forms of resistance in each dimension as well.

Because analysis of communicative action can inform the anticipation of power and possible resistance to it, we can then ask the further question, "Does this anatomy of practical action suggest a geography of power and a terrain of resistance? Can a terrain of resistance (Giroux 1983) be charted so that illegitimate authority, the illegitimate use of power, and the perpetuation of massive social and political-economic inequalities can be counteracted?" These questions are taken up below.

This anatomy of action also suggests a distinctive reading of organizational behavior. If organizations are evolving patterns of social action, then they might be expected—imperfectly, to be sure—to reproduce the types of claims made in ordinary communicative action. Consider the effects of the four claims when they are accepted by listeners. Factual claims (1) shape beliefs and knowledge when accepted; and claims upon attention naturally (2) direct listeners' attention selectively. Accepted legitimacy claims (3) shape deference and consent; expressive claims (4) shape social trust and recognition. As structures of practical communicative action, then, organizations are social forms that variably reproduce social relations of knowledge, consent, trust, and attention. If this is plausible, then the particular organizational and interorganizational processes of such social reproduction should represent key institutional elements, definitive regions, of a practical geography of planning practice. If planners are to influence the social and political processes by which public knowledge, consent, trust, and attention are reproduced, they must learn where and how best to intervene in these regions of the ongoing organizational play of power, domination, and resistance. But how is this possible?

Linking Action and Structure: The Practical Geography of Planners' Work

Certainly planning practice is more than face-to-face communication. Even if planners—as communicative actors—influence variable relations of belief, consent, trust, and attention as they act, how do these relations become established as stable patterns of interaction, as elements of social structure? How, that is, can a planner's practical claims-making actions ever make a difference in the context of already established and routinized social relations?[4] We can explore four dimensions of the geography of practice as an initial answer to these questions.

How might a neighborhood resident's claims about the facts of a case ("this will lower property values"), for example, become incorporated into the existing social stock of knowledge? To assert or challenge "facts" effectively, planners need to learn (1) a cognitive geography—not only a mapping of who knows what, but also one of the processes (including methods and procedures) by which claims to knowledge are established.

How might a developer's prescriptive claims ("this regulation should be abolished") become incorporated into the normative structure of social relations (law, custom, morality)? To establish or challenge norms, planners need to learn (2) a political-legal geography—to recognize the formal and informal processes of discussion, consensus, review, legislation, mediation, judicial hearings, suits, appeals, and grievance processes through which normative claims are set forth, rejected, or established.

How might an agency staff member's "expressive claims" of intention, desire, wish, and interest ("I'd like to stay away from politics") become patterned into others' stable expectations of that person, into stable senses of social identity? To gain the trust of others, or to recognize and be recognized in stable ways, planners need to learn (3) a ritual geography of practices by which practical social identities are constituted, re-created, and publicly recognized.

Finally, how might a citizen's attention-directing claims ("check out the revenue projections") become patterned into a socially structured division of the investment of attention (and so labor as well)? Here planners must learn (4) an economic resource geography of budgets, social capital, and the specialization of function and labor.

The geography of practice consists of four overlays, then: cognitive, legal-political, ritual-structured, and economic. To illustrate each briefly, in turn, we can consider an example of a local health-planning problem.

Take the case of a health planner who staffs a formal planning review committee to consider a hospital's proposal to purchase a new piece of equipment, a CAT-scanner (computerized axial tomography scanner) costing $500,000. By law the hospital is required, let us suppose, to bring this proposal to the regional health-planning agency for review. Such legislation was passed in an attempt at cost control, in the hope that some unnecessary and inflationary equipment purchases and facilities expansions might be restrained.

The "review committees" of such agencies are advised and served by professional health planners. Each review committee is mandated to ask questions such as: "Is the desired new equipment really needed? Will the cost of local medical care be inflated if the purchase is made? Do more cost-effective alternatives exist? Might the purchase be delayed—allowing other providers to meet existing needs or taking advantage of technological innovations producing less costly and more effective equipment?"

The questions that the review committee and the planner face are hardly amenable to straightforward technical solution. Often neither the data nor the proper economic and organizational simulation models exist to make the necessary calculations possible in the time required. So such planning review committees face not only uncertainty but ambiguity as well.[5] Future events—the rate of radiological innovation, for example—are uncertain, and their value or significance is ambiguous, issues of judgment not certainty. Given a high rate of innovation, that is, should this hospital lease now and buy later, or let someone else (a doctors' group practice or another hospital, for instance) provide the service?

Like matters of fact, these issues of uncertainty and ambiguity do not speak for themselves in the planning committee. How uncertainties and ambiguities are addressed and resolved in practice will depend upon actual organizational relations of expertise, power, participation, and resources. The review committee discussion is a politically structured conversation. Different participants will call attention to different issues and questions; some people will stress financing, others will ask about need, and still others will point to the hospital's public-service record. In this world of many-layered questions and conflicts, the planner must act.

Confronted by a situation loaded with uncertainty and ambiguity, structured by and potentially reproducing existing relations of power, how can the planner respond? How can the planner *anticipate* the play of power here, acting to protect the relatively powerless and defend the always precarious integrity of a public-serving planning process as well? A fully developed geography of practice could begin to answer these questions, for it would map out those overlapping regions in which the reproduction of the relations of everyday life—and thus of knowledge, power, status, and hope—takes place. Consider briefly, then, the basic dimensions of such a geography of practice and terrain of resistance.[6]

The Cognitive Geography of Knowledge Production

To anticipate how beliefs about the forthcoming hospital proposal might be shaped, the planner must in effect be a practical sociologist of knowledge. Faced with conflicting claims about the facts of the case, what can a planner do? What must the planner know?

Certainly, the planner can expect that large organizations, public and private, are likely to present information that favor and legitimate their own purposes rather than slight them (Edelman 1977; Krumholz and Forester 1990). Hospital staff may use technical languages that are clear to a few people, mysterious to others. Data and records will be accessible and comprehensible to some, not available or meaningful to others. In the smallest meetings, planners can expect a carefully and skillfully conducted 'presentation of self' by all participants. Thus the institutional landscape of the planning process can be defined, in part, through an analysis not only of "who knows what" but also of "who collects, checks, reports, and regulates access to information" and who thus shapes public knowledge and belief.

Knowing that the hospital may selectively present information favoring its case, the planner is likely to look, of course, to other sources of data as a check. So the experience of other hospitals in the same or similar regions becomes important. A local health-services researcher doing utilization studies may be consulted. Health-care providers who compete with the hospital may be asked for an assessment of local needs.

Information in the review process is not only a scarce good, but it is a political and institutional good as well. Access to information may be an organizational issue, and the planner who is blind to such an informational geography will likely fail and suffer, being first surprised and then embarrassed by others with information that he or she might not even have known to exist.[7] Here the planner is faced with problems of interorganizational learning, work with networks, the cultivation of contacts, and the development of strategies of information checking and testing (Schön 1971).

Furthermore, knowing who is ignorant and who on the review committee believes any of a number of health-care myths may be as important to the planner as knowing who has any more "solid" information. Reading the landscape of knowledge production is no less important than knowing who might have particular information.

The Political-Legal Geography of Relations of Power and Consent

The planner who knows that information may be monopolized or used as a source of power also knows that the review committee meetings are inevitably and deeply political. Rational discussion takes a political cast here: not all questions can be asked, not all consequences can be assessed, not all value positions can be considered impartially.

Seeking to serve ideals of the public interest, a democratic polity, or even the public health, the planner must explore issues of representation, access, participation, accountability, and more. Does the review committee, for example, represent particular organizations, groups, or classes of the population, or more general "interests"? What political ideologies are held by committee members? Do some believe that medical care should be allocated by the market while others support decentralized community control? Will particular coalitions of committee members who represent special interest groups control the agenda of the review session or lobby for votes?

At stake here is a practical reading of the politics of the review committee—both of the committee itself and of its organizational and structural setting. Only if the planning staff can anticipate that certain interests or concerns are likely to be neglected or minimized can they begin to counteract such influences. Only if the planning staff can anticipate that the committee discussion itself may be somehow less than just, providing, for example, a falsely legitimating consensus about social needs, can they then begin to counteract such possible abuse of power. Norman Krumholz, Cleveland's planning director for ten years under three radically different mayors, illustrated this cogently. Speaking of his equity-planning work in Cleveland, Krumholz (1982, 165) described his staff's attention to the local political geography of influence in this way:

> Influence, like wealth, was unevenly distributed in the population. When goals conflicted, groups with wealth and influence were likely to win every time, although it was hard to see how such winning contributed either to democracy or to

the public good. The result was that public facilities rotted without attention in low income neighborhoods while public and philanthropic resources were lavished on public spaces and old buildings downtown. Within the context of this contending but unequal power and influence, placing priority attention on the needs of the poor would tend to provide them with countervailing power and, like universal suffrage and majority rule, would help strengthen democracy.

Democratic discourse is an institutional attempt to achieve political rationality—a social and political learning process characterized by always vulnerable relations of uncoerced participation and justice. The political geography of planning practice, then, is a mapping of the terrain of power, participation, and authority that might enable practitioners in each particular case to identify those influences (managing decisions, agendas, or needs) that threaten to make a subtle mockery of the supposedly democratic planning process at hand.

The Ritual Geography of Social Identity Formation (Knowing Who's Who)

However knowledge and information is distributed and reproduced, and however the political-economic staging of the review committee is structured, the planner must address somewhat more personal and interpersonal questions as well. Who are these people who come before and who sit on the review committee? They have names, faces, jobs perhaps—but who are they? How can the planner work with them? Who will be defensive, who open, who suspicious, who antagonistic, who cooperative? Who will take all information gratefully but then act in the committee meeting as if they had just arrived on the scene like an utter novice? Who will promise to work or report back on an important issue and then fail to do it? Who will "talk tough" outside of the committee sessions and then be mysteriously deferential in the meetings? Who will take risks and who will not?

How can the planner learn even some of the answers to these questions about her or his practical social and interpersonal environment? By considering others' reputations? How does a planner know that someone's reputation is more than mere hearsay? What can the planner do to form reliable judgments about others and check any reputation they have too? The answer here is quite ordinary, but surprising as well. Of course the planner needs to learn from experience—but the experience of what?

Only in the evaluation of others' ordinary and mundane ritual performances do planners really begin to find out who is to be trusted and who not, who is conscientious and who not, who stays tough in the face of opposition and who wilts. For in our performances of the little rituals of conversation, argument, turn taking in ordinary talk, letting someone speak their piece, defending someone interrupted in a meeting, and so on, do we disclose ourselves to one another in ways that our self-descriptions can never do (Kertzer 1988; Myerhoff 1982; Lukes 1975).

Each and every meeting and the contacts outside of those meetings provide a varied field of socially defined and normatively structured ritual performances through which actors manifest their commitments and stances to one another. For example, the significance of one committee member's continual interruptions of others' ordinary conversations can extend far beyond the immediate occasions at hand. For those interruptions disclose an attitude and practical orientation toward others; breaking the rituals of organized talk may signal here egotism, disrespect for others, arrogance, or simply an incompetence for cooperative working relations—"He's impossible to work with!"

Knowing how someone has acted under unique circumstances will be less useful than knowing how he or she acts on the day-to-day conventions of social life, for out of those day-to-day elements are the planner's (and everyone else's) working relationships constructed. Sensitive to these ordinary ritual performances of others—committee members, other planning staff, 'providers', 'consumers', and still others—the planner becomes a practical historian and anthropologist. At stake are continuing and trusted working relationships and the possibilities of new ones, without which all the data analysis and political analysis in the world will amount to just that, analysis, without any forthcoming action yet informed or guided by it.

Distinct from a cognitive terrain of knowledge production and a political terrain of relations of power and authority, the ritual-structured geography of practice is a mapping of social identities, of a practical "who's who" for planners: who is committed to defending (or stopping) the hospital no matter what; who is more or less even-handed; who is organizationally astute and who not; who handles conflict well and who avoids it altogether—and so on.[8] This aspect of planning practice is at once mundane and mysterious, ordinary and extraordinarily complex in practice as well—as any one personality, not to say the hundreds with whom any one planner might work, can be.

The Economic-Resource Geography of Attention

Finally, planners can recognize immediately that attention is a scarce and unequally distributed resource. Information is poor, and often little more can be collected in the time available. Various criteria might be used to evaluate a project, but full analyses of need, cost, and equity considerations are likely to be impossible to carry out. Review committee members have limited time to spend either on the seemingly incessant meetings or on the careful reading of the stacks of project documentation materials that they receive. The applicant who proposes a project, of course, may have a staff of experts whose attention has been focused on little else than this project for months.

As political scientists are fond of quoting, every organization reflects a particular "mobilization of bias" (Schattschneider 1960; Lukes 1974; Gaventa 1980). Formal organizations and social organization more generally reflect particular patterns of attentiveness and neglect. Budgets are only the most common accounting device of the distribution of deliberately organized attention, but the division of labor reflects a more subtle and pervasive patterning of attentiveness and neglect as well. How does this matter for our health planner preparing for the review committee meeting?

If attention is unevenly distributed, the planner wishing to foster a public-serving review process must seek to assure that important public-disserving aspects of the proposed project are able to be considered, not pushed aside, scheduled so late that they cannot be discussed, or raised in only a token manner (Krumholz and Forester 1990). The applicant and the review committee members alike bring a type of social capital with them. Depending upon their skills, interests, and political dispositions, they will press attention to certain issues rather than others. Whenever a practitioner wonders, "How might this committee pay attention to the issues?" a question of practical economic geography is being asked. In this review process, attention will be invested selectively, but how? What skills do the committee members have; to what and in what ways are they able to pay attention; and what might they neglect?

More generally, of course, the planner must read the environment of the planning process in the same way. Who will bring pressure to bear on which issues? What can be publicized and what not? What role might the media play in bringing attention to the project at hand? What about local community organizations, or local government? Does the structure of the health-planning process itself ensure that some issues receive attention while others never do?

Here the planner is a practical political-economist, asking in what ways the existing institutional structure patterns the investments of attention and resources, and to what public or private purposes and results. It is simple enough for the planner to anticipate that Mr. Murphy will once again ask his question about Big Brother and the role of government. Yet it is something else altogether for the planner to recognize practically that public-serving review processes have politically vulnerable and produced agendas—agendas that distract or otherwise focus, disorganize or otherwise organize, public attention to issues of significant public concern.

The Significance of the Four Geographies

These four geographies—cognitive, political-legal, ritual-structured, and economic—are overlays of course, overlapping and complementary mappings of the world of planning practice. If planners ignore the cognitive geography of practice, they will risk producing documents that few people will read, fewer will believe, and fewer still will be able to use. If they ignore the political geography of practice, they will find politics not supporting planning but only thwarting it—and miss legitimate practical opportunities as a result. Blind to patterns of conflict, bureaucratic self-protection, class and group interests, planners may—against much experience—fail to cultivate support and find that their plans go unimplemented and unappreciated.[9]

If planners ignore the ritual geography of practice, they are unlikely to develop trusted (if cautious) working relationships with a wide range of citizens—officials, developers, professional staff, organized and unorganized neighborhood residents, and more. Failing to pay attention to the ordinary ritual performances of those citizens, planners may assume reliability where it is not to be found, may trust where they will instead find betrayal, and may miss opportunities for substantial cooperation where these present themselves.

And if planners fail to attend to the economic geography of their practices and practical settings, they will be far less efficient and effective than they might be. Presenting information and counsel without regard to the social organization of attention to the issues at hand, planners will find their advice heeded at one moment, overwhelmed more often. If this practical geography of attention is itself neglected, planners working in a setting of severe inequalities of resources may work to provide equal opportunity for all to speak, and find again and again that the less powerful, the less resourceful, will be the systematic losers.

These four aspects of the geography of practice suggest regions for empirical, practical, and theoretical investigation. Each of these four regions requires an extensive analysis of its own. With that done, these geographies might then inform actual planning practice by showing how the reproduction of belief, consent, trust, and attention constitutes the practical environment of planners' work.

Conclusion: Implications for Social Learning

We have seen that planning practice is a contingent, situated communicative activity that regularly confronts issues of uncertainty and ambiguity. Since such communicative action always involves questions of content and context, we saw, too, that uncertainty and ambiguity were systematically tied to the structure of social action and thus planning practice as well. We then set out a preliminary sketch of the geography of practical communicative action as we mapped the domains in which the pragmatic claims of action are established or contested. Now we can argue that if planners are to be sensitive to the continual reproduction of relations of knowledge, power, trust, and attention, they must assess practically this institutional geography of four dimensions—cognitive, political-legal, ritual-structured, and economic. We can assess, finally, the implications of this analysis for the problems—and prospects—of social learning.

Commentators from diverse backgrounds agree that social learning occurs—when it takes place—in two dimensions, broadly characterized as technical and practical. Even if a consensus upon goals and norms were to exist in a given organization, strictly technical questions might yet be unanswered. Given a consensus, let us say, about the desirability of protecting patients' health, what medical technologies or public-health preventive strategies will be most effective at particular levels of expenditure?

Alternatively, not technical, but practical moral questions and issues may be contested: how most legitimately or justly to distribute the social product, to protect the health of workers, to resolve the problems of multiple and conflicting goals when personal preferences can neither be compared nor perhaps even reliably measured? Democrats regard these questions as those of continual debate; others regard them as issues of class struggle; liberal conservatives regard the unfettered market as the appropriate learning mechanism to deal with these problems. Despite these differences, the question for planning practice becomes: How can planners improve rather than obstruct social learning in these two dimensions?

Our analysis suggests answers to this question. First, it warns that questions of ambiguity, questions of conflicting norms, ought not to be reduced to technical questions of uncertainty. For if practical planning will systematically confront problems both of uncertainty and of ambiguity, then reducing ambiguity to a technical issue will lead to the practical failure to anticipate and respond to the regular sources of such ambiguity: the shifting constellations of group and class interests, changing legislative mandates, multiple and conflicting goals and obligations, and so on.

Action in the face of technical uncertainty calls for experimentation and the hedging of one's bets. Action in the face of ambiguity calls for uncoerced moral and political discourse, argument, debate, or appeal, for a new interpretation of precedent or obligation or a new consensus upon a course of action. But if planners treat issues of ambiguity as ones of uncertainty, they will systematically ignore opportunities for moral and political learning—opportunities for possible consensus building, legitimate compromise, mediation and fair bargaining, political discussion and democratic debate (Susskind and Cruikshank 1987; Forester 1992b). Issues of political and moral discourse will be depoliticized and rendered technical, the province of experts perhaps but not political participation and representation. If planners render the ambiguous as simply the uncertain, they will fail to learn about the normative and contextual dimensions of their work—and their practice is likely to suffer. Such planners would be sensitive perhaps to the cognitive geography of their work, the informational and even the ideological environment, but they would most likely be blind to—and pay the price of neglecting—the political, ritual-structured, and economic geographies of their own professional practice.

Second, our analysis suggests that actual social learning of either a technical or practical sort is likely to be a multilayered, precarious process of practical communicative interaction. This seems true enough for project-review processes, legislative arenas at all levels of government, citizen participation processes, neighborhood organizing efforts, or attempts at environmental mediation and conflict resolution.[10] If this is so, then planners who hope to foster democratic learning processes will have to work to anticipate and counteract those particular forces and exercises of power that threaten present attempts to institutionalize widespread democratic participation and discourse. This is a problem not only of democratic theory but of professional, organizational, and political practice as well.

In each of the dimensions of practice discussed above, planners can play organizing or disorganizing roles: (1) keeping information restricted from those affected, or seeking to provide access to such information; (2) enabling or undercutting popular political participation and autonomous political organization; (3) building cooperative coalitions and networks that seek to overcome social inequities and inequalities, or accepting "given" social roles and contacts as immutable; and (4) working to call attention to the needs of the relatively disenfranchised and unorganized, or assuming that the present structure of control of investment and attention optimally addresses social needs. Planners do not solve the world's problems in their day-to-day work; yet they do serve practically and professionally to shape others' perceptions, expectations, senses of problems and opportunities. Thus, in part, planners help to organize or disorganize social efforts seeking social justice—and they do this on the cognitive, political-legal, ritual-structured, and economic terrains of their daily work.

Just as defining democratic processes is a significant analytical problem, counteracting the institutional and structural forces subverting such processes is an equally significant analytical and practical problem. Interested planners might begin to anticipate and formulate responses to these antidemocratic influences by surveying and probing a powerfully articulated geography of practice: concretely assessing in each case the plays of information, power, ordinary performance, and selective attention through which domination in several forms may be reestablished—or resisted.

6

Challenges of Organization and Mobilization: Examples from Community-Labor Coalitions

This chapter explores the empirical dimensions of critical social theory, as articulated most systematically in Jurgen Habermas's *Theory of Communicative Action* (1984). The argument develops as follows.

Part 1 briefly describes three cases of political conflict. The first involves the efforts of a citizens action movement—the New York Citizens Action Network (NYCAN)—linked to a national campaign to fight toxic chemical threats to workers and community residents. The second case concerns the Philadelphia organizing effort of the Delaware Valley Toxics Coalition, a community-labor coalition that won communitywide right-to-know legislation (Chess 1983). The third account briefly describes a successful labor-community effort to resist the privatization of health services in Sheboygan, Wisconsin (Montouri 1984).

Part 2 shows how Habermas's critical theory helps us to account for the complexities of these political conflicts and the strategies and tactics used by all participants. While the cases lend concreteness and specificity to Habermas's conceptual framework, Habermas's formulation provides insight into the political and practical dynamics of these cases as well (Misgeld 1984; Thompson 1983; Giddens 1982; Wellmer 1983). If this much can be accomplished, we would be on the way to specifying an empirical research program along Habermasian lines—something that has hardly been done (Forester 1985; Alvesson and Wilmott 1992).

Part 3 briefly sketches the continuities of Habermas's present critical theory, as elaborated selectively here, with the traditional Marxist project and the broader aims of a critical social theory (Thompson and Held 1982; McCarthy 1978; Giddens 1982; Wellmer 1983).

Part 4 concludes by outlining an empirically oriented, critical-theoretic research program that could assess ongoing issues of power and domination, policy choice and political action.

Three Cases of Political Conflict

The New York Citizen Action Network (NYCAN) and the National Campaign against Toxic Hazards

Toxic wastes threaten communities across the nation. In recent years citizens have increasingly organized to protect themselves—so much so that Environmental Protection Agency administrators have complained that citizen-initiated suits threatened to obstruct the EPA's efforts to clean up hazardous waste sites. In New York State, this citizens' struggle was illustrated by a short primer distributed by NYCAN (1983) and entitled, *The toxics crisis: a citizen's response.*

The primer begins with eight newsflashes, the typical first of which reads:

> *Hazardous waste exceeds estimates*—The Environmental Protection Agency (EPA) finds that the amount of hazardous waste being generated in the United States is nearly four times higher than previously estimated. (*New York Times,* 31 August 1983)

Noting the multiple threats to our land, drinking water, and air, in workplaces, schools and homes, the primer sets out the following programmatic direction:

> To meet this crisis hundreds of neighborhood, citizen, environmental, worker, senior citizen, and minority organizations across the nation who have been fighting toxic contamination in their communities have joined together to form a new movement. The new movement is the National Campaign Against

Toxic Hazards.... (T)he Campaign will work to: 1) increase the public's awareness of the full dimensions of the toxics problem and its solutions; 2) strengthen existing laws dealing with toxic substances; 3) win passage of a comprehensive legislative program to detect, correct, and prevent toxic problems; 4) make the toxics crisis a critical issue in the upcoming presidential and congressional elections.

The organizing primer continues in two parts. The first, *The Toxic Crisis*, sets out the dimensions of the problem: 1,000 new chemicals are introduced each year in the United States yet inadequate information exists regarding their health effects; the number of poorly controlled hazardous waste sites (at the time, 17,000) is growing; food and drinking water supplies are threatened; and so on: for example, "25 million American workers are exposed to potentially toxic chemicals and an estimated 17,000 die each year from cancer caused by the exposure; when other occupationally-related diseases are added, the estimated toll climbs to 100,000."

In addition, this first part of the primer sets out estimated economic costs of toxics to complement the discussion of health effects. Thus, for example, "the cost of occupational disease is estimated to be $11.4 billion per year in lost income alone. This cost has been paid by the public in the form of programs such as social security (instead of industry-funded worker compensation)." This is an initial portrayal of the facts of the matter.

Finally, the characterization of the problem closes with a section criticizing the existing national response as inadequate. Federal legislation is weak and fragmented. Enforcement has been poor. The Reagan administration had cut back EPA staff and numerous pollution and toxic control programs. Poor information is thus hardly the sole problem: legislative and regulatory measures have not been pressed strongly.

The second part of the primer, entitled *The Toxics Solution*, provides directions for action. The following paragraphs characterize NYCAN's and the campaigns' proposed solutions.

Across the nation hundreds of newly formed community groups are reacting to local problems by demanding cleanup and opposing the use of landfills and other hazardous waste facilities. National environmental, labor and consumer organizations are forging linkages with and between these groups to solidify the base for a country safe from the harmful affects of exposure to toxic hazards.

The National Campaign Against Toxic Hazards has linked the technical, research, political, and lobby components of the national organization and the toxic coalitions in nearly 30 states. The state organizations have a combined constituency of millions—built largely through neighborhood canvasses that will visit 15 million houses.... Through the use of the canvass and organizing staff, the campaign can conduct work in more than 200 congressional districts.

Many of the local and statewide organizations participating in this effort have already achieved victories in the toxics area. In New Jersey, Citizen Action and Clean Water helped lead a network of 100 groups in a campaign that produced this country's strongest state Right-to-Know law. Similar coalitions have been successful in California where tough restrictions on landfilling of hazardous waste and underground storage were enacted. In Massachusetts and Connecticut, state toxic networks succeeded in specific dumpsite cleanups.

Given this organizing thrust, the primer concludes first by noting that Congress was soon to consider reauthorization of many of the laws dealing with toxic substances, and second by setting out in some detail a "Statement of Rights" to be defended. That Statement is worth considering briefly. The statement begins:

The basic principle of the National Campaign Against Toxic Hazards is that citizens have a basic right to a healthy environment. Today we have no guarantee to this right: industry and government too often view public health as an expendable item to be bartered in the name of economics.... The Campaign believes that every citizen has certain rights...:
Right to be safe from harmful exposure...
Right to Know...
Right to Cleanup...
Right to Participate...
Right to Compensation...
Right to Prevention...
Right to Protection and Enforcement...

Finally, the primer sets out a "Legislative agenda." That agenda discusses each of the "rights" listed above in some detail, specifying particular problems (e.g., inadequate prevention) and legislative provisions that respond to those problems (e.g., encouraging "source reduction").

The NYCAN organizing primer thus described the toxics issue, problems of legislation and enforcement, and a set of citizen responses and principles. Little is said about specific actions of industry; more is said about the inadequacies of state intervention—inadequacies at least from the perspective of community health protection, if not from that of industry's prerogatives. Let us return to these issues after reviewing two more cases of political organizing and conflict.

Consider next a case of local labor-community organizing for right-to-know legislation in the city of Philadelphia.

The Delaware Valley Toxics Coalition (DVTC) and Winning the Community-Labor Right-to-Know in Philadelphia

In January 1981 a broad-based popular coalition won legislation in the Philadelphia City Council that both: (1) gave workers and community residents access to information about toxic substances used in workplaces or emitted into the air, water, or land; and (2) gave the city the authority to regulate storage and emission of toxics as well (Chess 1983). How did this happen? How was this possible? As Caron Chess, a DVTC organizer, tells it, the story began many years before 1981. The following summary draws heavily from Chess's account.

In 1976 the Philadelphia Area Project on Occupational Health and Safety (PHILAPOSH) worked with local union members on health and safety problems and began to push the Occupational Safety and Health Administration (OSHA) for a federal right-to-know provision. Residents in local communities had also been organizing around pollution problems. Staff at the Public Interest Law Center had been marshalling statistics documenting cancer mortality rates. The staff, Chess writes, "were researching the ties between industrial pollution and cancer while assisting community groups to organize around toxics issues."

In 1979, Chess continues, "PHILAPOSH and the Law Center organized a 'chemical killers' conference to explore the links between toxics in workplaces and neighborhoods.... Conference participants, including more than 300 representatives of community, environmental, and labor groups...called for the development of a coalition to maximize the power of the diverse groups working on toxics issues." The Delaware Valley Toxics Coalition was born. Its first goal would be a Philadelphia law granting the right-to-know to workers and residents.

In June 1980, DVTC introduced Right-to-Know legislation into city council. They "spent the summer building support for the legislation, doing research, and planning our strategy."

By September, Chess writes, "industry was churning out one argument after another to point out that Right-to-Know would be hazardous to the economic health of the corporate community." DVTC responded with a "highly visible campaign" marshalling the support of "more than 40 organizations as diverse as the United Auto Workers, the League of Women Voters, the Friends of the Earth, the Philadelphia Council of Neighborhood Organizations, and the Americans for Democratic Action." Unity among these groups made it difficult for their opposition to dismiss right-to-know as a narrow labor issue or as simply one more demand from the neighborhoods.

By the day of the October public hearing, coalition members had appeared on almost every talk show in town, petitioned on street corners, met with city administration officials, and made a pitch to just about every organization whose members were touched in any way by toxics issues.... The committee hearing drew more than 200 supporters, who donned surgical masks to dramatize their concern about toxics, making front page headlines. Despite the testimony (of diverse supporters), the legislation stalled in committee after the city administration proposed a watered down version of (the) bill. While the Administration attempted to quietly confuse council members with its complex counter-proposal, industry mounted a vigorous lobbying campaign.

Pointing to DVTC's strategy and tactics, Chess (1983) continues,

Right-to-know became a political football. We stayed in the game by mounting demonstrations, organizing mass political lobbying and letter writing, and keeping close tabs on council members' positions on the legislation. Although the Coalition had a flair for making headlines, substance did not get lost.... The Law Center assisted with analyses of the Administration's lengthy proposals, leading to...position papers which showed the flaws of the Administration's 'Know-Nothing' version.

Pressure from DVTC led city council members to send industry, the city administration, and DVTC to the negotiating table. As noted above, the resulting legislation provided both for public access to toxics information and for the city to regulate toxics storage and emissions. Then, of course, the political work continued: to get regulations that put teeth in the legislation, to ensure implementation, to educate residents and workers to use the law, and to ensure enforcement.

Turn now to the case of a struggle involving a public sector employees union, a county government, and the threat of contracting out several local health services.

Public or Private Control of Health Services: Fighting Contracting Out in Sheboygan, Wisconsin

Consider the following labor-community struggle over the control of local health services. Joe Montouri is worth quoting at length:

> The Reagan administration and private industry both advocate more "contracting out" of public services to private firms. They have hitched their scheme to the public's demand for tax relief.
>
> The situation leaves public sector employees on the defensive, and at apparent odds with the interests of the taxpaying public. But are they?
>
> Experience with contracting out shows the opposite. Not only is the efficient use of taxpayers' money compatible with quality public services and decent public sector jobs, they are, in fact, complementary.
>
> How have unions been fighting the "contracting-out" fever?
>
> In the Fall of 1982, AFSCME Local 2427 organized against a plan to contract out the services of three Sheboygan County, Wisconsin institutions. Over 450 members joined with other employees, patients, and citizens to save quality patient care and jobs.
>
> The County Board of Supervisors set up a committee to study whether Sheboygan County should continue to own and operate three institutions that provide care for drug and alcohol abusers, mentally ill patients, and the elderly and physically disabled. AFSCME rank and filers formed a Fightback Committee, mapping out a strategy that provides a useful model for public employee/community alliance.
>
> A 20-member Watchdog Committee made sure that all open meetings of the county board, its study committee, and

each institution were attended by eight to ten AFSCME members.

A Public Relations Committee disseminated information to community organizations such as the Central Labor Council, the Association for Retarded Citizens, and the Mental Health Association, as well as the patients' families, community leaders, and volunteers. It became clear to all that the county board was interested only in saving money.

AFSCME members and community residents made patient care the issue. For six months the daily paper printed an AFSCME-coordinated barrage of letters to the editor. Twelve thousand signatures were gathered in a three-month period, urging the county to continue operation and ownership of all three institutions.

What clinched the victory, however, was the visible and vocal support demonstrated at each of the three public hearings.

"We knew we would win after that first meeting," says steward Sandy Nytes. "We saw that the public felt strongly enough on this issue to show up. The [county] committee was afraid of all these people at the hearing." The county board decided to keep all three institutions funded. (Montouri 1984)

Montouri continues to discuss other efforts of public employee unions to resist efforts to privatize public services, yet even this brief description of organizing in Sheboygan is instructive.

Each of these three cases illustrates challenges to private economic power, abetted or weakly regulated by the administrative or legislative state. Each of the organizing efforts makes demands upon a nominally democratic state, if hardly suggesting that the passage of legislation will truly or even sufficiently solve any problem. Each of these cases raises issues of corporate "responsibility" and accountability—or lack of such, too.

Interesting practical issues arise as well. Where in the labor-based strategy of organizing does letter writing to the press come in? Why monitor council or committee meetings with more than one or two people? How should we understand the focused attention on legislative arenas? What lessons can we infer from these brief cases to refine our thinking about future conflicts, to inform our possible practice? In the next part we consider whether Habermas's critical theory has anything interesting to say about these cases—and others.

Critical Theory and the Analysis of Concrete Conflicts

The Habermasian Center:
Three Dimensions of Social Reproduction

At the center of Habermas's social theory lie three processes of social reproduction. He refers to these as processes of: (1) cultural reproduction, in which worldviews are elaborated and shaped; (2) social integration, in which norms, rules, and obligations are shaped and adopted; and (3) socialization, in which social identities and expressions of self are altered and developed.

"If, as a first step," Habermas writes,

> we conceptualized society as the life-world, and see this as centered on communicative action, then three components of the life-world, culture, society and personality, can be correlated with the components of action oriented to reaching understanding. As (table 6.1) shows, the maintenance of the symbolic structures of the life-world can be analysed in these dimensions...
>
> The individual reproduction processes can be evaluated according to standards of the rationality of knowledge, the solidarity of members, and the responsibility of the adult personality. (Thompson and Held 1982: 278)

Table 6.1

	STRUCTURAL COMPONENTS		
Reproduction processes	Culture	Society	Personality
Cultural reproduction	Interpretative schemata susceptible to consensus ('valid knowledge')	Legitimations influential in self-formation, educational goals	Behavioral patterns
Social	Obligations	Legitimately ordered interrelations	Social memberships
Socialization	Interpretive accomplishments	Motivation for norm conformative actions	Capability for interaction ('personal identity')

Source: Habermas, in Thompson and Held 1982, 279.

These reproduction processes occur in, and contribute contingently to, a structural, institutional environment. "I am supposing, furthermore," Habermas summarizes,

> that in modern societies two sub-systems have been differentiated out through the media of money and power, namely the capitalist economic system and a rationalized (in Weber's sense) state administration. Each forms a complementary environment for the other...
> Naturally the economic and administrative systems of action have to be anchored in the life-world by way of institutionalization of the money and power media. This means that the symbolically structured life-world is connected with the functional imperatives of the economy and administration through private households and the legal system; it is thereby subject to the limitations of material production within the framework of existing productive relations. On the other hand, the economy and the administrative system of domination, are dependent on accomplishments of the symbolic reproduction of the life-world, namely on individual skills and motivations, as well as on mass loyalty. (Thompson and Held 1982, 279–80)

This sketch raises the following sorts of problems. How do the reproduction processes work? What do they reproduce? If we can show how these processes reproduce the lifeworld, how are they vulnerable to "system" pressures from the economy and state administration? For empirical research, how are we to identify specific actions that contribute to one process or another, or which represent system pressures upon them? Through what institutional channels, in what institutional infrastructure, do these reproductive processes work, perhaps becoming more or less rationalized? How, specifically, are political conflicts about policy issues, and the political organizing that constitutes such conflicts, to be assessed in this framework? These are problems to which we now turn.

As table 6.2 indicates, these processes of social reproduction have pragmatic and phenomenological bases in the structure of everyday speech, in the claims we ordinarily make in any conversation. The factual claims we make regarding the truth of statements about the world may shape beliefs and be organized in social worldviews. The normative claims we make (threats, challenges, requests, offers) in a variety of moral-legal-political contexts may gain consent and integrate our specific actions into

Table 6.2   Performative Bases of Reproduction Processes

Reproduction process	Pragmatic Claims	Output
Cultural reproduction	factual truth	social belief
Social integration	legitimacy	consent
Socialization	expressiveness/sincerity	identity

larger streams of organized social action. The expressive claims we make present our own identities and may be routinized in socialization processes in which we develop—for ourselves and for others—attributions of character, or reputations. "...[F]orms of argumentation," McCarthy writes,

> take shape which may be transmitted and developed within a cultural tradition and even embodied in specific cultural institutions. Thus, for instance, the scientific enterprise, the legal system, and the institutions for producing, disseminating, and criticizing art represent enduring possibilities of hypothetically examining the truth of statements, the rightness of actions and norms, or the authenticity of expressions, and of productively assimilating our negative experiences in these dimensions. *Through the connection with cultural traditions and social institutions the concept of communicative action becomes serviceable for social theory.* (Habermas 1983, xi, Translator's Introduction, italics added)

Now what do these reproductive processes have to do with these cases and with political struggles more generally? If, as Habermas suggests, these reproductive processes are rooted in the structure of social interaction itself, in the possibility of social beings acting in concert, then these reproductive processes will form dimensions in which social and political conflicts are concretely fought out. Again, McCarthy summarizes:

> ...to the different structural components of the lifeworld (culture, society, personality) there correspond reproduction processes (cultural reproduction, social integration, socialization) based on the different aspects of communicative action (understanding, coordination, socialization) which are rooted in the structural components of speech acts (propositional,

illocutionary, expressive). These structural correspondences permit communicative action to perform its different functions and to serve as a suitable medium for the symbolic reproduction of the lifeworld. When these functions are interfered with, there arise disturbances, in the reproduction process and corresponding crisis manifestations: loss of meaning, withdrawal of legitimation, confusion of orientations, anomie, destabilization of collective identities, alienation, psychopathologies, breakdowns in tradition, withdrawal of motivation. (Habermas 1983, xxv)

Thus we might infer, to begin, that effort in each of these dimensions will be required in democratizing struggles. Indeed, in the three cases above we see evidence of conflict in all three domains:

1. With respect to the reproduction of beliefs, NYCAN, DVTC, and AFSCME all mounted "educational" campaigns to alert their members and others to the dangers of toxics, to the inadequacies of present legislation, or to the costs and benefits of various policy proposals (like that to "contract out" services).

2. With respect to the reproduction of consent, the processes of social integration, NYCAN, AFSCME and DVTC organized pressure in legislative arenas, drawing up and assessing legislative proposals, appealing to basic "rights" and marshalling support from citizens.

3. With respect to the reproduction of identity, NYCAN, DVTC and AFSCME each created coalitions of supporters, thus creating new political forces; they gathered signatures, expressing the appeal of the signatories for their positions, they were careful to consider their image, their presentation of self, their organizational identity, how they would be identified (as not narrowly labor-based, for example) (Goffman 1967).

The point here is not simply to find empirical examples for these three central reproductive processes. Instead, the practical point may be put as follows: if democratizing efforts neglect any of these dimensions, they stand to undercut their own power and ability to mobilize support. First, ignoring the reproduction of belief—political and technical education—would allow opponents' statements of costs, assurances of safety, predictions of consequences to go unchallenged; it would provide potential supporters with no evidence to counter what may be opponents' (mis)information. Second, ignoring integrative processes—by which norms or rights or entitlements are established—would undercut the traditional moral, customary, ethical, procedural or legal bases supporting efforts for citizen power. NYCAN can appeal to a "Statement of Rights" because our liberal democratic culture lends such appeals to rights a colloquial legitimacy. Third, ignoring socialization processes would mean neglecting issues of public image, credibility, stature, and popular reputation—to say nothing of internal solidarity—a sure recipe for being discredited, marginalized, identified (n.b.) as anything but a serious political force. We can elaborate in some detail below, now, how organizing efforts can—theoretically and practically—pay serious attention to each of these three dimensions of social reproduction.

Recognizing the Institutional Infrastructures of the Three Reproduction Processes

Habermas suggests that systemic forces toward accumulation and the consolidation of power may penetrate, invade, colonize, or come to control people's ordinary lives by threatening each of the three reproductive dimensions indicated above. This means that each mode of reproduction is *vulnerable*, that each may be commodified, bureaucratized, or be the site of political conflict. Furthermore, each of these reproductive processes takes place concretely through a variety of specific institutions, through (more abstractly) a communicative infrastructure of social action and interaction that shapes and patterns evolving social relations of belief, political consent, and social identity. Consider, then, the institutional forms and organizational processes through which NYCAN, DVTC, and AFSCME (and their opponents) worked.

First, NYCAN sought to shape public belief by appealing to press reports and the findings of specialized agencies like the EPA. DVTC shaped public knowledge by drawing upon the organized expertise of the Public Interest Law Center, the PHILAPOSH staff, and labor and environmental groups. They also worked through the press, publicizing positions papers and expert responses to the city administration's counterproposals. AFSCME monitored the official county Study Committee to keep abreast of any of its findings; the local union also created a Public Relations Committee specifically to educate the public and major constituent organizations and to keep letters coming to the press to keep the contracting-out issue in the public eye.

In each case, though, of course, the claims of NYCAN, DVTC and AFSCME were contestable. As statements of fact, of hazards, costs, scope of the problem, and so on, these statements are political acts. They happen in institutional places, in concrete settings: the Law Center Office, the foyer of the council chambers, a newspaper office, the street outside a chemical plant. The effectiveness of these statements as political acts will in part depend upon the institutional means by which they are made and in which they are channeled: with two supporters present or 200, on a soapbox, or in the mass media (talk shows and all), from an interested party or a disinterested, independently credible research organization...?

Second, consider the institutions that provide the settings in which socially integrative claims—the shaping of public norms, rights, rules, regulations, entitlements—can be articulated, contested, or established. The NYCAN primer points to legislative arenas at all levels of government and to the political traditions legitimating basic universal rights of the citizenry. DVTC fought for right-to-know provisions by invoking the public will, through petitions to legislators, by working through the city council mechanisms and formal procedures, by invoking the expertise of outsiders to legitimate their demands. AFSCME similarly appealed to public opinion channeled through petitions and letters oriented toward the forum of the county legislature. These organizing efforts worked to develop their own legitimacy by appealing to the recognized expertise of particular organizations, to particular political precedents, to the legitimacy of already established organizations (thus in part coalition building), all in addition to making arguments about the merits of the issues at hand.

In each case, too, these claims to legitimacy were contested—in the press and legislative areas, in the judgments of experts, in appeals to the traditions of unfettered (and thus "free") enterprises. In Philadelphia industry representatives held that right-to-know would both duplicate existing federal law and damage the economic health of the region, and thus be unjustifiable. So federal law and business regulatory practices were broad institutional settings in which DVTC fought.

Consider a more local setting. While the local Chamber of Commerce, as the voice of industry, could hardly be taken as a credible source of cancer statistics, still it would be seen as a legitimate representative of local industry. Thus it only helped DVTC gain legitimacy for its right-to-know proposal when the *Philadelphia Inquirer* quoted the president of the Chamber of Commerce conceding..., "this is a very difficult thing to oppose. I mean, it sounds like you are standing up for cancer." Here DVTC's opposition helped to de-legitimate itself. This was possible precisely because reproduction processes are not only sites of argumentation and contestation, but they are also concretely contingent. Actors can go wrong, make mistakes; strategies and tactics are multiple, ambiguous, and conflicting.

Third, NYCAN, DVTC, and AFSCME each paid a good deal of attention to questions of image and identity. They formed new organizations and coalitions, adopting names, purposes, statements of principle, becoming newsworthy. Having created these new identities—coalitions, "Fight Back Committees," and so on—they encouraged public expressions of solidarity through petitions, call-ins to talk shows, letters to newspaper editors and legislators. They wore surgical masks to committee meetings to dramatize—to express, present, act out—their concerns. They developed their own presence carefully and insistently, appearing *en masse* at committee hearings, organizing demonstrations or public displays of support at other times.

Chess provides a striking example of DVTC's careful negotiation of the institutional terrain on which social and political identities are established. "Use care before asking for the support of large entrenched organizations," she writes,

> First try to get assessments from insiders of your chances of receiving an endorsement. A rebuff from an organization such as a local medical society may undermine your credibility. DVTC chose not to approach certain organizations rather than risk rejection that might harm us later.

Besides public education and legislative pressure, DVTC recognized, the coalition itself had to be built and protected.

So to work or organize in these three reproductive dimensions, citizens need to be able to identify the specific institutions and organizational and cultural forms through which belief, consent, and identity are elaborated, patterned, routinized. With respect (1) to the shaping of belief, this calls for attention to government agencies issuing reports and findings; to brokers of knowledge (corporate, labor-based, scientific, and so on) of all sorts; to the institutions of science, learning, and research; even to political action committees, claiming expert knowledge in an area. With respect (2) to the garnering of consent, this calls for attention to political traditions; to the political processes of campaigning down to the ritual objects of picket signs and buttons; to moral, legal, and religious precedent and legitimation. With respect (3) to identity and image formation, this means attention to style; to associations with groups already identified as legitimate by the broader public; to the channels of expression (the media, the press, talk shows, street theatre) that allow social and political position and identity to be expressed; to the dramatic and ritual processes of meetings, demonstrations, and testimony at hearings that routinize and publicize collective expressions of self and identity, that establish reputation (Forester 1992a).

Anticipating and Responding to Hegemonic Power

As the next chapter will also argue, democratizing efforts need to anticipate and resist privatizing or hegemonic efforts to control the "turf" of these infrastructural domains (Giroux 1983). The institutions that make possible the reproduction of belief and worldview, consent, obligation and allegiance, trust, reputation and identity will be contested—for as they are controlled, so will the political definition of issues be controlled; so will political pressure be mobilized and brought to bear; and so will the expression of popular interests and sentiment be molded, channeled, guided, or misguided. This has very specific implications for the politics surrounding policy choices and "social problems."

DVTC could anticipate corporate responses to the coalitions' right-to-know proposal; industry claimed that the policy would be too expensive, that it would drive away jobs, that the legislation was redundant—and they marshalled experts to prove it. So, of course, did DVTC use experts, official studies, university reports, studies and reports done by consulting firms, supporting its own positions.

In such cases in particular, Habermas suggests, we can expect two system pressures to shape the reproduction processes of the ordinary lifeworld: pressures resulting from the imperatives of accumulation and pressures resulting from the protection or expansion of hierarchic-bureaucratic power. In one quick line, Chess pointed to both when she described the DVTC experience: "while the administration attempted to quietly confuse council members with its complex counterproposal, industry mounted a vigorous lobbying campaign" (Chess 1983). The city administration sought to maintain its power and limit the potentially democratic voice articulated in the city's formal legislative processes—and industry, for its part, sought to maintain its prerogatives to accu-

mulate by lobbying to control that same legislative (socially integrative) process.[1]

DVTC fought back, anticipating and responding to these systemic and hegemonic pressures. "DVTC developed," Chess writes,

> a list of points on which we felt vulnerable and developed rea-
> sonable responses. We were rarely caught offguard. Before
> the public hearings, we wrote the most potent industry argu-
> ments and our responses in simple question and answer fact-
> sheets for supporters, council members, and the media.
> (Chess 1983)

Notice that those fact sheets went to three places: to supporters (to
maintain the strength and internal solidarity, the identity, of
DVTC; to council members (to press arguments and justifications
for the regulations in question); and to the media (to keep information flowing to shape public belief). So DVTC's work here was at
once, of course, communicative, pragmatic, and political. Anticipating supposedly expert arguments and industry claims that right-
to-know legislation would cause industries to leave Philadelphia,
DVTC countered with the claims and arguments of a Wharton
School study showing that environmental regulations were "low on
the list of reasons why businesses leave town."

DVTC, NYCAN, and AFSCME focused close attention upon
legislative processes. They monitored hearings, kept track carefully of individual legislator's positions, assessed past conflicts and
alliances in legislative bodies, and built supporters and allies carefully. That industry had such (or greater) access was presumed,
but not taken as cause for resignation. In these cases, the state
functioned as—provided—an arena for conflict, an arena in which
power, rules, decisions, and implementation were contingent, contestable, and winnable.

Further, as noted above, DVTC and AFSCME were concerned
about the importance of political image and internal solidarity, the
creation and reproduction of their social and political identity.
DVTC sought many avenues to express their positions as those of
a broad-based coalition. Anticipating industry's efforts to use the
media to discredit them, DVTC members spoke on talk shows,
worked with the press, organized letter-writing campaigns,
reached out to the League of Women Voters as well as the United
Auto Workers (UAW). Again, the practical political point is that
the social means of identity formation, reputation, and image
building are diffuse and variously accessible rather than monolith-

ically controlled by corporate or bureaucratic interests. Yet too little applied political analysis seems to have been done to examine this infrastructure of identity formation. How do rituals, traditions, styles of language and dress constitute public identity (Kertzer 1988; Moore and Myerhoff 1977)? Research here could provide lessons, to be appropriated differently in different situations, for democratizing citizen movements (but perhaps, too, in twisted ways, for their opposition as well: consider only the propaganda of union-busting firms that exploit this dimension of social reproduction).

Anticipating Issue (Re)Definition

These three cases have a lesson to incorporate into Habermas's critical social theory as well. DVTC, NYCAN, and AFSCME were all concerned to focus attention on the issue at hand in particular ways. Montouri notes this explicitly when he writes that it became clear that the Sheboygan County Council saw the contracting-out issue as an economic one, while AFSCME worked hard to make the issue one of patient care instead. Here not only facts and people's beliefs are at issue, for the very framing of the question, the very framing of the political issue, is at stake. Thomas Pynchon is said to have written in *Gravity's Rainbow*, "If I can get them asking the wrong questions, I won't have to worry what the answers are...." DVTC and NYCAN worked to keep community health protection, rather than narrow economic-efficiency criteria, the issue most centrally in the public eye. Here the social means of communication, the various means to pose, identify, and frame issues, are processes that must be politically identified, worked with, fought for—for the language in which issues are posed is a crucial matter, as any organizer knows.

Habermas's three reproductive processes deal poorly with this matter of problem definition or issue formulation, yet his earlier work did point to a systematic or theoretical solution to the problem (Forester 1989). In that earlier work, Habermas argued that a fourth pragmatic "validity claim" was raised in every speech act: a claim to comprehensibility, a claim to be recognizably using a shared language in significant ways. Notice that when this claim by a speaker fails, the listener ordinarily asks, "What does that mean?" In situations of doctor-patient or more generally expert-client interactions, of course, the professional may speak in professional jargon intelligible to other experts but meaningless (or intimidating) to the lay public. In such cases, experts and strategic advocates mystify issues and cloak them in technical jargon, and if such claims are not challenged, the advocates or experts may well succeed, as they often have, in framing the issue at hand (e.g., the patient's condition) in their own terms, terms they control. Habermas does not seem to recognize such processes as reproductive, though certainly they seem to reproduce patterns of attention, patterns of popular orientations to what is taken to be the problem at hand. We need, accordingly, to explore a fourth contingent and politically influential reproductive process, that of framing or defining the issues at hand.

Requisite Skills

These issues of contestation and resistance in four dimensions of social reproduction involve very much more practically than a 'correct' or rigorous political analysis, anyone's having a 'correct line' on a problem. For the problems of conflict in these dimensions are generally not cognitive problems, though in part of course they are. The practical problems here involve marshalling not only "the facts" but justifications, not only arguments justifying political positions but ways of building commitments, nurturing identifications, maintaining image, and not only that, but framing issues selectively as well. So democratizing organizing requires diverse skills, abilities to act in these arenas of social and political reproduction.

Here we run quickly into the limits of any theory "with practical intent." Critical social and political theory can give us powerful questions to ask, insightful dimensions to explore, but one theoretical account cannot do more than schematically indicate specific organizing or resistance strategies, tactics, skills (Giroux 1983). The theory can generate and call our attention to the structural space in which such strategies and skills come into play, but the choice of a given strategy and the appropriate place of any skill can only be determined in specific settings. Insightful theory helps us to learn from experience, to appreciate what others have or have not yet done, to anticipate what we must do in the situations we face. Combined with the study of real cases, critical theory points us toward repertoires of political practices of several kinds, but taken by itself that theory—or any theory—cannot generate specific strategies, tactics, skills to be used independently of specific contexts (i.e., for all times and places).

Indeed, even different personality types could be sought for particular roles essential to work in these reproductive dimensions—for those most comfortable at data manipulation may be quite ill at ease, if not mal-adept, at building networks, contacts with the press, and links to diverse organizations, and so forth. Some people must be able to translate technical findings into ordinary language, into fact sheets, press releases, newsletter columns, leaflets, justifications in position papers. Some people must be adept at relating to diverse groups of people, at spanning many organizational boundaries and bringing together people with different interests, loyalties, political persuasions. Some people must present the organization to the press or present the organization's positions in council chambers, whether in the front or back rooms. For example, DVTC organized people who could appear on talk shows, draft responses to city proposals, create the surgical mask tactic, lobby legislators, present arguments in crowded council chambers, and so on. If Habermas assesses the differentiation of modern society into distinctly institutionalized reproductive processes, our analysis suggests that successful democratizing movements today will require a differentiated (at least tactical) thrust of their own: recognizing and nurturing differences in staff, functional roles, even coalition members.

Reproduction and the Play of Power: The Empirical Questions

So we can explain the outcomes of policy struggles, the degree of corporate power versus democratized decision making, by considering the degree of control by affected persons over (1) information, (2) rule-making processes (3) social status and expressions of self, and (4) issue definition.

Habermas points to three of these processes of reproduction, and he links them to the structure of social action, to the structure of pragmatic claims making that constitutes communicative action. He does little, though, sociologically, to assess *how* these processes work, how worldviews, allegiances, identities are elaborated, routinized, established, or altered. But *that* is the central issue to be addressed in any concrete analysis of political struggle, policy debate, political conflict, or social movement—and this explains part of the difficulty, to this date, of applying Habermas's work directly and concretely to political conflicts. Only if these reproductive processes become the focus of concrete research will Habermas's critical social theory develop a grounded, and indeed a politically practical, empirical dimension.

This means we must study how systemic imperatives to accumulate surplus or to consolidate bureaucratic power can dominate these processes. Consider a simple example from the *New York Times* related to the Congressional reauthorizaton of "Superfund," the multibillion-dollar, federally administered program to clean up toxic waste sites.

> William Ruckelshaus, administrator of the Environmental Protection Agency, said that giving citizens the right to sue the Agency for failing to meet deadlines for toxic waste site cleanups would only hinder the cleanup process.
> "We're...certain we can't meet those deadlines because some of the site cleanups are too complicated," Mr. Ruckelshaus said. "Having the courts come in and manage the projects is a very profound social question. It would slow the process considerably."
> Legislation that would give people the right to sue, sponsored by Representative James J. Florio, Democrat of New Jersey [later Governor], was approved by the House last week and is being considered by the Senate. (*New York Times*, 17 August 1984)

Here Ruckelshaus plainly seeks to maintain his agency's power—at the cost of limiting citizens' abilities to press their claims of rights and wrongs in court. In Ruckelshaus's lobbying, bureaucratic power seeks to replace relatively more direct democratic power. In Habermas's terms, the system imperatives of maintaining the EPA's strength and prerogatives threaten to colonize lifeworld processes of citizen voice.

We have already seen how in Philadelphia the bureaucratic power of the city administration and the accumulation imperatives of industry sought to influence the legislative processes of the city council. Consider, then, one last example of systemic pressures potentially colonizing citizens' ordinary experience.

The NYCAN primer (1983, 9) points to the threatened transformation of the public's health into an economic commodity:

> Industry and government often view public health as an expendable item to be bartered in the name of economics....
> The Campaign believes that every citizen has certain rights...

NYCAN itself, then, represents an attempt by citizens to defend themselves *as citizens* against the economizing or accumulating forces that would turn their health into commodities, their identities as "citizens" into "consumers." Here system forces threaten to replace democratic processes of political voice with the integrative processes of a capitalist economy, processes in which the controllers of capital do the integrating while the remaining citizens are integrated (though some not at all) according to the "laws of the economy." The same systemic forces are apparent when local industries seek to sway local legislative processes with the threats of leaving the region, threats of taking sorely needed jobs with them (Cohen and Rogers 1983).

Habermas poses the problem as follows:

> The rationalization of society [no longer means] a diffusion of purposive rational action and a transformation of domains of communicative action into subsystems of purposive-rational action. The point of reference becomes instead the potential for rationality found in the validity basis of speech. This potential is never completely stilled, but it can be activated at different levels, depending on the degree of rationalization of the knowledge incorporated into worldviews. Inasmuch as social actions are coordinated through reaching understanding, the formal conditions of rationally motivated agreement specify how participants' relations to one another can be rationalized. As a general principle, they count as rational to the extent that the yes/no decisions that carry a given consensus issue from the interpretative processes of the participants themselves. Correspondingly, a lifeworld can be regarded as rationalized to the extent that it permits interactions that are not guided by normatively ascribed agreement but—directly or indirectly—by communicatively achieved understanding. (Habermas 1983, 340)

In each reproductive dimension we can ask: on what does the balance between normatively ascribed and communicatively achieved outcomes depend? On what does substantive—rather than purely formal—democratization in these dimensions depend? Research to explore these questions must be empirical and historical, describing various issues, relations, conflicts; it must be theoretical, too, as it attempts to account in an orderly, simple, even elegant way for the otherwise apparently random list of contingencies upon which these reproductive processes depend. Such research shifts away from Habermas's primarily metatheoretical focus; it remains within the parameters of the *Theory of Commu-*

nicative Action, and indeed for the most part of *Legitimation Crisis* as well, but it extends the power, scope, concreteness, and specificity of that work (e.g., Forester 1992a). Without such research, Habermas's critical theory will be increasingly about too much in general, and too little in particular.

Continuities with Marx: The Politics of Staged Contra-Dictions

How does this analysis, growing out of Habermas's critical social theory, relate to a broader Marxian project? Discussion of class seems muted if not absent here, though in the three cases discussed the role of labor is central to the resistance of private power, private usurpation of public well-being. Habermas has continued to reformulate the Marxian project by now integrating it with a critique of Weber's reduction of social rationalization to increasing instrumental control.

Habermas reformulates the basic contradictions that Marx illuminated, the contradictions between popular labor and private accumulation, between the abundant capacity of capitalist means of production and exploitative capitalist relations of production. We can now identify these contradictions concretely and practically by recognizing them as *actual daily contra-dictions, systematically conflicting claims* in each of the four dimensions of reproductive processes.[2]

Industry claims that household kitchens are more dangerous than their workplaces; NYCAN and DVTC and a spreading right-to-know movement point to toxic exposures, not soapsuds. Not only can surplus be appropriated, not only can control be exercised or resisted, but so too can worldviews, patterns of belief, "facts" about the world be managed or contested too (Giroux 1983; Scott 1985, 1990). Industry also appeals to its prerogatives as private entrepreneurs, owners of private property, protectors of "trade secrets" vital to their competitive position; DVTC and NYCAN call attention to natural "rights" to be safe, protected; to have access to information about imminent health threats; to have legislation passed, implemented, and enforced, to realize, however haltingly, economic democracy. The contradictions at the site of production can be articulated in just these ways: practical, contingently articulated contra-dictions about who should control or regulate the workplace.

Similarly, industry seeks to commodify labor, to make labor a product and workers essentially agents of exchange, consumers, buyers, and sellers; DVTC, NYCAN, and AFSCME argue that neither workers nor community members are free agents trading on the market; they are instead citizens in a nominally democratic polity, citizens to whom government must be accountable, citizens who will organize to make that government accountable. Thus the contradiction between existing capitalist relations of production and the germ of any free association of producers is expressed actually and concretely in the contra-dictions evoking social roles and identities, in specific tensions between "If our employees don't like it here, they can go somewhere else" and "We produce what this company makes; we have every right to be protected at the workplace."

Habermas has not ignored the fundamental antagonism at the heart of capitalist relations of production. He has instead reformulated these contradictions so they can be identified in several dimensions—cognitive, normative, and expressive—at a phenomenological or experiential level. When Habermas speaks of "system colonizing lifeworld," he uses a shorthand for "Philadelphia industry attempting to control what workers and residents know, what regulations may protect them, what social and political roles (wage-workers, co-producer, client, consumer, citizen) they may play."

Notice too that the Marxian notion of interest is muted here. Habermas implicitly takes the notion of a basic interest in the control over the fruits of one's labor and reformulates control as effective voice. This political and communicative rendering of the problem does not dismiss issues of interest but rather gives them a multidimensional cast—so that we can examine how systemic rationalizing or commodifying forces obliterate or dominate popular voice, so that we can examine particularly the ways that citizens are (or are not) able to speak and act politically, to question facts, rules, or stereotypical identities. Dominated markets, bureaucracies and democratic politics are alternative organizations of voice, alternative organizations of the satisfaction of basic material interests (Thompson and Held 1982, 278–81).

By extending Marx's project beyond the world of capitalist work, though perhaps not beyond labor understood generically as social action, Habermas helps us to assess domination concretely—not simply and undifferentiatedly as functionally serving capital. Habermas points us toward the tensions between system rationalization—through commodification and bureaucratized power, and lifeworld rationalization—or what he more simply characterizes as the tension between normatively ascribed agreement and communicatively achieved agreement (Thompson and Held 1982, 250–63). To the extent that we do not have the latter, we face domination.

Abstractly, this seems simply to be saying that domination is indicated by the absence of democratic discourse or "communication free from coercion"—which may be tautologous and empty. Yet if the tension between the normatively ascribed and the achieved is explored concretely in the dimensions of the reproduction of belief, consent, and identity, then obstacles and impediments to "communicatively achieved agreement" can be revealed in new ways. Notice that the feminist movement, for example, calls attention particularly to such obstacles represented by the patriarchic reproduction of sexual and gender identity; feminism has been less about the philosophy of equality than about what it is to be gendered as a woman, to have a gendered identity, subject to worldviews, norms, and roles elaborated by men.

Habermas does not try to provide a formal rule to distinguish instances of domination from instances of freedom—for there are good reasons to suspect the adequacy of any such rule: no rule is self-applying, and all disputes about how to apply the rule (does it fit here, or not?) would essentially be disputes about the meaning of domination and freedom in any case. Yet Habermas *does* allow us to explore the question of voice and its subversion in a more phenomenological way than we often have done. Again we can ask: what makes possible or impedes a worker's finding out information at the workplace, challenging rules or norms, or expressing needs, feelings, his or her identity, way of being? This sounds deceptively simple, but it is not. The problem here is to link control structures, including (or perhaps made up by) an ensemble of policy measures, to daily experience, voice, and action. Habermas's three reproductive processes are pitched at the level linking these two realms of social and political life.

Notice finally that progressive social movements often need to beware of their own internal dynamics, to guard against the ugly head of domination reared within their own ranks. Our analysis suggests several dangers here, for some members of such movements may seek to monopolize truth and the politically correct line (left technocracy); or they may simply manipulate one another as objects rather than as joint members (however disciplined) of a collective (left instrumentalism); or they may come to identify themselves within the logic and roles of hegemonic forces, co-opting themselves and others (e.g., left electoralism); or they may so narrowly pose issues, goals, the environment, or human nature that they cannot but distract attention from the particular complexities of concrete problems (left reductionism).

Conclusion: Critical Theory and a Tentative Research Program

This chapter began by posing the problem of "the missing middle" in critical theory: the empirically descriptive analysis of political conflict that might learn from historical cases and illuminate concrete struggles as well.[3] Our subsequent analysis can be recapitulated in terms of the following research strategy:

1. Distinguish the central reproduction processes shaping worldview and belief, consent and allegiance, self and identity, and issue formulation and definition;

2. Identify the institutional and organizational infrastructure that makes possible, actual, concrete, and routine those reproduction processes: e.g., schools, the church, rituals of daily life and popular culture, the media.

3. Identify the range and repertoire of pragmatic speech acts that may work particularly in each dimension (so that we might "code" from transcribed interviews, for example, cognitive reports, normative challenges, personal expressions, and definitions or characterizations of issues).

4. Map the variety of claims that such acts make in these dimensions: How are the claims to truth, rightness, identity, and issue definition made? Is a truth claim a claim to accuracy, to precision, to completeness, to objectivity? Is a claim to legitimacy a claim to propriety, to the customary, to precedent, to utilitarian calculation? What is the range of possible forms a claim in any one dimension might take?

5. Specify the "system" forces that foster capital accumulation and consolidate bureaucratic power: what organizations, which actors, what relations?

6. Assess the "lifeworld" background capacities that give meaning to questions, claims, or challenges regarding facts, rules, identity, or issue definition. Consider here formal and informal,

institutionalized and less routinized traditions, cultural values, defining historical experiences, territorial characteristics.

7. Examine the strategies used to rationalize accumulation or bureaucratic power. What choices exist? On what do those choices depend?

8. Assess the strategies available to agents acting to resist such accumulation/exploitation and power, so acting to democratize political relations (in Habermas's terms: to rationalize the lifeworld, or in more ordinary terms, to have a say in directing one's life). Upon what do these strategies depend?

9. Given the analysis of the contingencies of hegemonic (7) and counterhegemonic (8) strategies, locate the possibilities of action in the next round: What is now to be done? How do policy proposals promise (or threaten) to realign relations of interaction, power, strategy? What are the prospects and tasks of the democratizing forces—if only the most elemental popular interest in voice—that exist?

If these nine steps can be carried through empirically, the prospects for developing a historically grounded, politically sensitive critical theory of public life that spoke directly to issues of practice would be far closer to being realized than has been the case to date.

7

Toward a Critical Sociology of Public Policy: Probing Policy-shaped Contra-Dictions in the Communicative Infrastructure of Society

Introduction

This chapter will argue that Habermas's critical theory suggests a powerful structural and phenomenological framework for policy research, analysis, and practical criticism. The theory provides a basis for the empirical and normative assessment of "policy implications," for the analysis and formulation of "what is to be done."[1] Public policy, we shall argue, alters the communicative infrastructure of society that interweaves social structure and social action. The argument proceeds in five steps.

First, we introduce the basic conceptual framework of Habermas's social theory, by focusing structurally upon his reconstruction of historical materialism and phenomenologically upon his theory of communicative action.[2] Second, by noting the complementarity of Habermas's structural and action theories, we begin to specify the important notion of the "communicative infrastructure" of social action and of societal reproduction (production and reproduction) more generally. Third, we consider the historical construction of policy "problems" as selectively established claims in the structural dimensions of social action: claims regarding facts, normative legitimacy, actors' interests and intentions, and languages of attention. Fourth, and most practically, we argue that policy development and implementation can be understood systematically as processes that modify the communicative infrastructure of society. Thus, these are processes altering the institutional elements that mediate between and shape structural developments of societal learning and social interactions shaping immediate personal experience. Here we will consider Reagan-era federal cutbacks of the Environmental Protection Agency to illustrate the argument. Fifth, then, the analysis of blockages and restrictions to social learning and citizens' "recourse to discourse" suggests empirical and normative issues of the assessment of legitimacy and domination so central to a critical theory of public policy.[3]

Historical-Structural and Action Theories: Habermas's Structural Phenomenology

Two of Habermas's central arguments provide the foundations for a critical theory of public policy analysis: his reconstruction of historical materialism as an evolutionary process of social learning and his reconstruction of speech act theory and intersubjective understanding as a theory of claims-making communicative action.

Habermas argues that Marx the historical analyst always distinguished more carefully than Marx the metatheoretician between the work of production oriented to the transformation of material reality and the social interactions of men and women oriented to the constitution and reproduction of their social relations. Habermas attempts to clarify the distinction here between work and interaction, or as he also puts it, between instrumental or purposive-rational action and communicative action or symbolic interaction. Albrecht Wellmer (1976, 245–46) summarizes as follows,

Habermas's reformulation of the basic assumptions of historical materialism...introduces a categorical distinction into the theory of historical materialism which Marx, in his material analysis, had always implicitly presupposed. Marx distinguishes between two different dimensions in which the self-formation of the human species takes place: that of a cumulative process of technological development (forces of production, labor-processes), and of an emancipatory process of critique and class struggle (relations of production). What Habermas shows is that this categorical distinction can be developed consistently and with all its epistemological implications only if it is reformulated on a higher level of abstraction as that between "instrumental" or "purposive-rational" action on the one hand, and "communicative" action on the other.... Only if we make this distinction, is it possible, according to Habermas, to reconstruct the interdependent historical processes of technological and institutional development in a way which would not blur the differences between technical progress and political emancipation as well as those between science and critique.

"The categorical distinction," Habermas (1979, 120) writes,

> between purposive-rational and communicative action thus permits us to separate the aspects under which action can be rationalized. As learning processes that take place not only in the dimension of objectivating thought but also in the dimension of moral-practical insight, the rationalization of action is deposited not only in forces of production, but also—mediated through the dynamics of social movements—in forms of social integration.

In Habermas's reconstruction of historical materialism societal development and social learning take place in two dialectically autonomous but interdependent dimensions, then: the productive forces of society develop with the advancement of science and technology within a given form of social organization; productive relations develop at a given level of scientific-technological capacity reflecting (if not increasing) substantive democratization. More advanced technology, however, hardly guarantees progress toward greater political freedom. Habermas thus reformulates a dialectic of production and reproduction, of forces and relations of production, by clarifying the types of action characteristic of each moment of this dialectic and assessing the corresponding development or rationalization of each type of action.

The distinction between purposive-rational and communicative action can clarify the relationship of social action, practice and praxis, to the development of the forces and relations of production and their corresponding reinterpretation in social learning processes. Habermas attempts to justify the analysis of these two historical-structural dimensions through his analysis of the structure of communicative action itself, particularly in his essay, "What is Universal Pragmatics" (Habermas 1979).

The Policy Setting:
The Communicative Infrastructure of Society

A critical theory of policy analysis must locate concrete policy initiatives, policy development, and implementation in the framework of social learning and social action that we have sketched above. We might expect each policy to alter in its own way the structural processes of social learning, on the one hand, and the character of social action and interaction, on the other. Yet where in Habermas's account of structure and action are we to locate and assess the organizational and institutional forms of policies manifest as reductions in federal spending, alterations in social policy entitlements, subsidies for housing, price supports, and so on?

Habermas's work conspicuously lacks an account of those institutional and organizational forms that mediate between the analytic levels of social system and social action: for example, factories, hospitals, schools, unions, churches, firms and companies, cultural and ethnic associations, and the like. But such an analysis of intermediate social organization can be developed straightforwardly from Habermas's structural and action theories (Forester 1985). Methodologically, this account becomes a structural phenomenology: it is structural because it maps the political-economic, systematic staging and framing of social action; it is a phenomenology because it explores the concrete social interactions (promises, threats, agreements, deals, conflicts) that are so staged.

To assess concrete policies, we need an account of the mediating institutions, the elements of the institutional *communicative or social infrastructure*, that connect actions to structures and vice versa, and *that a given policy may alter,* thus altering both (macro) systemic relations and (micro) social interactions. Working between Habermas's account of historical materialism (societal production and reproduction, learning in two dimensions) and social action as a derivative of claims-making communicative action, then, we must work to fill in the center of table 7.1.[7]

By considering the mediating organizations that support, frame, or generate each type of action (see table 7.1) and so rationalize those actions for systemic ends and the functions of production and reproduction, we can suggest several rough and tentative answers as sketched in table 7.2. Consider briefly each action type in turn.

In the activity of work itself, the knowledge and control of means-ends strategies is distinctive (but of course not sufficient),

Table 7.1 Habermas's Structural and Action Theory, Macro and Micro, Framework

	DEVELOPING STRUCTURAL RELATIONS	MEDIATING INSTITUTIONS	SOCIAL ACTION TYPES (CLAIM STRESSED)
A)	*Habermas's "System" or Marx's Forces of Production:* Instrumental rationalization and technological-scientific learning		A) *Work:* Purposive rational action
i)	Development of technical-strategic and administrative knowledge	?	i) Means-ends and strategic truth claims (reproducing knowledge and belief
ii)	Capacity to attend to nature and material reality	?	ii) Attention-focusing comprehensibility claims (reproducing attention and investment)[8]
B)	*Habermas's "Lifeworld" or Marx's Relations of Production:* Practical communicative rationalization and legal-moral institutional learning		B) *Interaction:* Communicative interaction
iii)	Establishment of institutional normative relations free from domination	?	iii) Rightness or Legitimacy claims; (reproducing consent and deference)
iv)	Capacity for social cooperation, respect, and solidarity	?	iv) Truthfulness or Expressive claims (reproducing trust and reliability)

Table 7.2 Elements of the Communicative Infrastructure

A. PRODUCTION VIA:

Administrative, technological, and scientific organizations; training programs, information services, technical control departments, (representing strategies, means, and findings)	1) work techniques
Financial-economic organizations: corporations, banks, firms, factories, workplaces; (formulating capital accumulation and investment)	2) capacity to invest attention

B. REPRODUCTION VIA:

Legal regulatory agencies; courts; legislatures, regulatory agencies (establishing norms and regulations)	1) norms of (inter)action
Social-moral organizations: cultural and ethnic associations, churches, service programs, family structures, special interest organizations, unions (identifying intentions via organizational performances)[10]	2) actor's intentions [expressions of self]

whether in a chemical manufacturing process or on an integrated assembly line. Organizational forms such as laboratories, research firms, engineering departments, strategic administrative and management units, and certain information-based services provide the setting for individuals' actions that generate factual knowledge or formulate means-ends strategies and thus contribute to advances in the general forces of production. Consider here, for example, corporate-university joint research ventures through which various corporations have acted to firm up the infrastructure for their own efforts to advance productive know-how and technologies of production (Nobel 1982).

In parallel fashion, the social capacity to pay attention to needs finds organizational form largely in the political economy.[9] Financial and economic institutions—banks and Wall Street brokerages, the Office of Management and Budget and the Federal Reserve Bank, corporations, firms, factories, and workplaces, provide the organizational settings in which decisions about the direction and formulation of particular investments are made and selective needs are consequently addressed. Thus capital flight (from Northeast to Southwest or abroad), or concessions made to forestall such flight, mediates between and immediately threatens both regional and personal budgets, the basic abilities of regions and individuals to attend to their needs.

The organization of social relations depends upon both the institutionalization of norms and the social capacity for mutual recognition and cooperation. The formal institutionalization of norms occurs typically through mediating organizational forms such as courts, legislatures, boards of supervisors and councils (at town, city, county, state, and national levels), and agencies of the state (from federal agencies such as the Internal Revenue Service and the Food and Drug Administration to local welfare and unemployment offices, and the police). Here are the organizational settings in which rules and norms, standards and obligations, rights and entitlements, may be proposed, at times contested, established, enforced, and later reformulated. Thus, Reagan-Bush social policy legislation was attacked not only for its budgetary implications and its neglect of social needs, but also because it subverted a normative framework of rights, entitlements, and legal protections thought by many to be already too weak and business-oriented, questions of bureaucratic size, efficiency, and debt notwithstanding (Piven and Cloward 1982).

Finally, then, the social basis for the mutual recognition of intentions exists in the routinized patterns of social interaction and ritual performances that we call "organizations," "programs," and "associations." For as we are able to evaluate one another's participation as a responsible (or lax, or playful, or serious, or scheming) member of a given organization (a church congregation, a rotary club, a political party, a union, a cultural association, and so on), so are we able to judge the (in)consistency of what the other person says and what they subsequently do. In this way, we are able—via the evaluation of mutual participation in routinized, ritual-structured social organization—to gauge one another's truthful intentions and honest expressions of self. In this way, social systems reproduce their social identities; consider simply the socializing functions, for participants and for observers, of the various cultural, ethnic, and national rituals of dress, speech, cuisine, humor, music, and habit, whether rooted in dance, clan, or text (Kertzer 1988).

Table 7.2, accordingly, presents four families of institutions and organizational forms that mediate between specific practical action claims and structural processes of societal development and learning.

These mediating or infrastructural institutions produce conventional results, of course: (1) techniques, work strategies, and propositional, factual, knowledge (beliefs); (2) selective attention and investment (patterns of attention); (3) patterns of consent and deference (political allegiance); and (4) patterns of trust and mutual recognition (patterns of solidarity). When they establish truth claims, these institutions generate factual beliefs and technical knowledge. When they establish comprehensibility or attention-focusing claims—through well-formed verbal linguistic utterances or through conventional, nonverbal economic tokens (value in the form of capital)—then these institutions devote citizens' attention (and possibly labor) to particular concerns and needs. When they establish legitimacy claims, these normative institutions shape citizens' consent and allegiance. And as social organizations pattern and establish expressive and truthfulness claims through any of the various social rituals structuring routinized organizational performances, so do they shape social recognition and contingent patterns of trust.

Yet these mediating institutions develop unevenly, in contested, contingent, and contradictory ways.[11] Systemic pressures push the functional requirements of production and reproduction: so corporations buy university research and laboratories, train their requisite labor force, and so on. Yet popular and oppositional pressure may push in other directions: populist and trade union groups organize for their own particularistic causes; class-conscious union organizations attempt to build a powerful labor movement; cultural and ethnic groups of all types reaffirm their identities and perhaps occasionally distract their members from the conventional status rewards of the larger political economy. Because their relative autonomy varies historically, these mediating institutions may be contested, challenged, or alternatively accepted as proper integrating mechanisms for the larger society.

Policy implementation alters these mediating or infrastructural institutions not "from the outside" as it were, but rather by taking concrete shape, form and substance, *within* them: creating or destroying specialized budgets (attention), jobs and programs (organization), regulations and enforcement agencies (legal-regulatory presence), and information and innovation sources (scientific results, technological capacity, and administrative strategies).[12]

Each particular policy proposal promises to influence these institutions either to enable or disable, empower or disempower, specific possibilities of popular political debate and mobilization, of popular challenge or traditional class struggle. Labor policies can influence unions to raise or to suppress claims upon corporate power (suppressing them through the current Workers Compensation system, for example) (Berman 1978). Court decisions or legislation can influence state agencies to grant or restrict entitlements, services, and information (for example, to implement or subvert occupational health and safety "right to know" legislation). Policy changes can directly affect research, field inspections, and documentation that can promote public awareness and access to information (the National Institute For Occupational Safety and Health, for example) or, alternatively, work as an impediment to public learning.

As these mediating institutions enable or stymie public discourse, politicization, and processes of learning, so do they provide or deprive legitimate public authority of its true possible mandates. As specific mediating institutions block citizens' recourse to discourse, so do they reproduce relations of power but not authority. And so do they then reproduce domination and only a pale legitimating semblance of democratic political institutions and democratic political life. *In sum, by examining specifically the policy influences upon the infrastructure mediating social relations of belief, consent, trust, and attention, and by then assessing the precarious existence of the legitimating conditions of political discourse, a critical theory of policy analysis illuminates the concrete organizational processes that perpetuate, or oppose, illegitimate power and political domination.*[13]

If the families of social institutions and organizations suggested by table 7.2 mediate between structural developments and social interactions, a critical theory of public policy would then lead policy analysts to ask the following research questions: How does the passage and implementation of a particular policy immediately alter, reproduce, replace, or create anew elements of these mediating institutions and organizations? How does the policy being assessed alter the "communicative infrastructure" of societal production and reproduction, as sketched in table 7.2 (mediating the contents mapped in table 7.1)?

We turn to these questions in the following section. Before that, however, we turn to the problem of the context dependency, the historical constitution, of policy "problems" themselves.

If the dialectic between forces and relations of production can be understood as the interdependence of two historical learning

processes, one technological-scientific-strategic and one institu-
tional-legal-moral, any concrete policy problem can be located in
that context. A policy "problem" would thus reflect and be situated
not only in a certain stage of technological, organizational, and
industrial development, but also in a particular stage of relations
of control, authorization, legitimacy, and cooperation. So the
"given" state of "the problem" can be understood through an analysis of historical development in these dimensions: through indus-
trial-organizational innovation, testing, and implementation no
less than through institutional (legal and moral) developments
mediated by political and social movements. At any given time,
though, policy development will depend not only upon a given
social movement, but also upon the particular "background consensuses" that support or obstruct efforts to alter the status quo in
either dimension of social learning, that of "system" (productive
forces) or "lifeworld" (productive relations).[14]

Background Consensuses:
The Problem "Context" Facing Social Movements

We have argued that public *policies* alter the "communicative
infrastructure" of institutions that mediate between structural
processes of social learning and the practical, situated claims-making processes of social interaction. We can now explore the constitution and social context of policy "problems" themselves. A "policy
problem" is not a brute datum, but an historical product of a vast
variety of claims-making activities.

A "problem" is minimally a claim that something is not right.
Indeed, "policy problems" are claims about facts that matter, about
"facts" and "values": claims both about the objective historical and
physical world and claims about social norms, about right and
wrong, just and unjust, legitimate and illegitimate.

More precisely, to understand a "policy problem," we must
assess the four communicative claims that will constitute its presentation: (1) the "truth claims" representing objective states of
affairs ("these chemicals really do contain kepone"); (2) the "legitimacy claims" prescribing legal-moral norms appropriate to the
case ("these substances should be banned from industrial use!");
(3) the "expressive claims" indicating the intentions and perceived
interests of affected parties ("the manufacturer assures us that the
chemicals are safe, 'not to worry'"); and (4) the comprehensibility-

attention-directing claims that formulate the framework in which "the problem" is to be understood in the first place ("the issue should be seen as one of 'rights' not 'dollars'").

Yet as we pursue such an investigation beyond the most simple preliminary problem statement, we come to realize that problem statements abound and, indeed, that they conflict with one another. We soon discover that any concrete policy "problem" is in fact many problems, and "the problem" can be seen as an historically constituted set of claims, some contradicting one another, in the four dimensions of communicative interaction which make social understanding possible. To understand a particular policy "problem," then, we need to assess historically the following four domains of policy-relevant claims:

1. claims established or presented in the cognitive domain of facts through studies, reports, analyses, tests, findings, investigations, testimony, research, historical studies, and objective (vs. arbitrary, biased, whimsical—not vs. subjective) scientific studies and inquiries;

2. claims established or presented in the interactive domain of normative authority and power relations through legislation, regulations, legal decisions, precedents, cultural and social norms, corporate policy decisions, taboos, formal and informal sanctions, and other relations of perceived authority;

3. claims established or presented in the moral domain of actors' expressions of interests and intentions through expressed desires and needs, conflict and cooperation, wishes and preferences, demands and challenges, actions of solidarity and opposition; and

4. claims established and presented in the communicative-linguistic domain of shared meaning-systems, verbal (via words) or nonverbal (via meaningful tokens of behavior, e.g., gestures or money), and communicative competence, through the ability to call attention to the issues at hand through language use, symbolic presentations (art and music), or investment of resources (economic capital as conventional, congealed attention).

As we can identify the particular claims that have actually been established (among different classes, groups, organizational members, or others) in these dimensions, so can we identify the actual historical background consensuses existing that provide the various social and ideological contexts immediately relevant to the issue at hand. Recognizing that conflicting epidemiological studies have been publicized regarding the effects of certain workplace chemicals, for example, we might expect popular understanding of the alleged occupational health and safety "problem" to be less unified (hegemonic) than if all of the publicized epidemiological reports were in agreement with one another. Recognizing that low income communities and neighborhoods have long been threatened by so-called "urban renewal" efforts identified with local planning and redevelopment agencies, we might well expect residents of those communities to view current proposals of planners and city officials with substantial suspicion, distrust, and skepticism, if not outright hostility. Such sentiments simply represent a significant element of the practical background consensus likely to be present in many neighborhoods whose residents have rightly wondered if "urban renewal" did not often mean "urban removal." Any planners, politicians, or community organizers who do not anticipate the existence of such background consensuses are hardly likely to be trusted or seen as any ally of these neighborhoods.

Two points are important here. First, taken historically, particular background consensuses provide the practical social context for the ongoing struggles of diverse social movements pressing demands or programs for policy changes—whether for the development of a local health clinic or national health service, the protection of social security or social service benefits, reductions in defense expenditures, or the end to nuclear power plant construction. Second, and as a consequence, the reproduction of these background consensuses is likely to be essential to the maintenance of established relations of power and to the de-politicization, the discouragement of political discourse, necessary for such maintenance. Consider each of these points in turn.

Social Movements, Background Consensuses, and Contra-Dictions

The practical work of maintaining, organizing, and advancing social movements—here including labor, environmental, ethnic, and feminist organizing, for example—is politically oriented social action. As social action, such practical work addresses others: seeking to build a membership, to educate a base of supporters, to articulate a sense of possibility of a better life, to reveal relations of control that function systematically to repress, exploit, or deprive vast numbers of people of what might otherwise be theirs—the fruits of their labor, a clean and healthy environment, relations of political-economic and gendered equality, and so forth.

The daily work of social movements, accordingly, characteristically takes the form not just of strategic and instrumental action, but of communicative action and interaction as well. Serious claims need to be made about how the world factually is and could be, about rights and injustice, fairness and exploitation, about interests and intentions, feelings and perceptions. And finally all those claims are made in a variety of linguistic modes running from the most informal and colloquial to the most formal legal and contract language.

Background consensuses do not usually reflect conditions of equality of skill, interest, status, power, information or knowledge. At any given time, instead, these background consensuses are constituted by established political, social, and cultural institutions and the conflicting relations of power and influence that these institutions manifest. These established relations of power—the organization of precedent, symbolic resources, capital, legitimacy and status—can of course be invoked in many ways, and challengers as a result can then be made to seem to be naysayers, complainers, troublemakers, opportunists, heretics, traitors, agitators, crazies, "wierdos," the simply "unreasonable," and so on.

In such cases, power is reproduced not simply through "talk" and simple claims about how things are. Instead, both factual *and* normative claims may be established, shaping belief *and* political consent, through the manipulation of the background consensuses that make any shared public understanding of a "problem" possible in the first place.

Yet all of these practical claims made by members of social movements depend upon a context of already established claims, a partial "background consensus," "ready" for their acceptance. This is why public rhetoric and legitimating arguments are so essential to the maintenance of power: they work not only to establish factual claims ("these chemicals are harmless!"), but also, legitimacy claims ("it's only right that each job should have some risks attached to it; if a worker doesn't like it, he or she's 'free' (sic) to go somewhere else..."), and claims of trustworthiness (thus corporations seek to assure the public of their concern with safety by claiming that there are more hazards in an ordinary kitchen than in their workplaces!). The claims of social movements exist in a context of conflicting claims.[15] And these conflicting claims exist not only in political-economic structures and actions of challenge and opposition, but in the very background consensuses of popular beliefs, senses of legitimacy and rightness, perceived interests, and conscious needs. The contradictions between the privatized control of production and the social needs of reproduction are reproduced, manifest, and established as conflicting practical claims: literally as contra-dictions (Habermas 1975, 26–27).

Background Consensus and the Maintenance of Power

How are these contra-dictions established and "stabilized"? The reproduction of power works not only through practical claims having content, but through claims that establish and reproduce contexts of trust and authority. The appeal to understand a health problem in a particular framework (of cost-benefit analysis or, alternatively, of a natural "right" to health) is an action attempting to invoke a legitimate context of understanding and consideration, a background consensus in which many further corollary propositions can then be considered as well. Notice, however, that if the listener equivocates or begins to doubt (is this job safe? is this, what you, the state health official, are telling me about this dump site, really true?), the speaker may act to reinforce the shaky background consensus by invoking previously implicit but potentially binding norms: for example, (1) "If you want to keep this job, don't raise a fuss"—a latent norm tacitly regulating the actions of many wage-laborers; or (2) "I've got the specialized training, and I've seen the lab results and the studies; what do *you* know?"—a claim to normative status differences and thus the deference accruing conventionally to those with expert competence.[16]

In the absence of conditions of democratic discourse and cooperative social organization, those already in power make practical claims and offers about factual conditions, normative rightness, social interests, and particular needs that may be conventionally established but simultaneously removed from criticism—by invoking precedent, incentives, sanctions, exclusion, ostracization, stigma, threat, and so forth. Under such conditions, popular beliefs, consent, trust, and attention are appropriated through conditions of social interaction—influenced by policy initiatives—that discourage critical discourses.[17] The addressees of a critical policy analysis, accordingly, may be all those "taken for a ride" in this way: those made the objects of political claims without recourse to collective and shared criticism. In these ways can cognition, political allegiance, social solidarity, and attention and concern be appropriated when a background consensus is reproduced by policy implementation in a communicative infrastructure that blocks, thwarts, restricts, and constrains the possibilities, the actual avenues, of critical scientific and political discourses of accountability.

Dimensions of Critical Policy Analysis

Public policy can alter the communicative infrastructure of the broader society into which it is introduced. Taken by itself, that claim might be virtually trivial, but its implications for the analysis of changes in structures of social learning and patterns of social action can be substantial. The point of a critical theory of public policy is not to classify each policy proposal into one of two groups, labeled with the summary judgments, "legitimate" or "illegitimate." Instead, a critical theory of public policy ought to fulfill the promise of an historically concrete structural phenomenology by showing us *how* particular policies promise to alter or "impact" (1) the structural conditions of social action and learning, in the dimensions of the rationalization of productive forces and the rationalization of legal-moral and institutional relations; (2) the actual social interactions and lived experiences of affected persons, the concrete policy-influenced management and reproduction of citizens' knowledge and beliefs, allegiance and consent, trust and solidarity, attention and concern; and (3) then, too, the conditions of citizens' recourse to theoretical and practical discourses, the public capacity to challenge, check, question, and noncoercively reestablish claims of truth and justice.

To suggest how such a critical, structural phenomenology of public policy might proceed, we first briefly suggest broad families of the relevant social indicators by which policy alterations of the communicative infrastructure (table 7.2) may be gauged. Second, we consider an example of a significant policy change: Environmental Protection Agency budget reductions as they "impact" the communicative infrastructure of society and thus too the processes of societal learning and social interaction.

Finally, we examine the most difficult problem to which a critical theory of public policy leads: assessing citizens' recourse to scientific and political discourses—and the conditions of power and systematic distortions that influence any effective recourse and voice.

Families of Measures and Social Indicators

If policy implementation alters the communicative infrastructure, we should be able to identify groups of empirically sensitive measures and social indicators of changes in each of the four infrastructural dimensions of table 7.2. We consider first the abstract suggestions and then illustrate these by assessing a specific case: cutbacks of the Environmental Protection Agency's budget.

Changes in those institutions mediating claims of attention will be indicated by shifts in personnel and budgets, resource shifts, allocations of funds, and capital shifts more generally, where capital is recognized here as the generalized capacity to devote attention. Changes in those institutions mediating claims of intentions (subjective expressions of self, desire, will, and interest) may be indicated by shifts in organizational size, membership, structure (role assignment, membership developments), and participation rates. Changes in those institutions mediating claims of legitimacy and rightness will be indicated by shifts in the scope, content, and number of regulations, rules, directives and legal mandates, informal norms, entitlements, eligibility requirements, stipulations, contracts, contract conditions, and so forth. And changes in those institutions that mediate claims of facts and strategic means-ends effectiveness will be indicated by shifts in the scope, content, and number of research studies, experiments, technological innovations, social technologies (administrative and management systems), market and client analyses, published reports and documents, official findings and results. These dimensions of the mediating institutions suggest families of measures and indicators that could be monitored and assessed as a policy is implemented: as health services are cut back or extended, as environmental regulations are changed, or (to consider de facto policies not issued by the state) as industry and labor negotiate "givebacks," as U.S. auto companies and auto workers previously have done. Significantly, a change in a budget—for community health centers or for a wage-benefits package—promises secondary effects in the other three infrastructural dimensions mediating between social action and social reproduction and production.

Policy Illustration: EPA Budget Reductions

Proposing budget reductions at the EPA, the EPA administrator's agenda will of course not simply mean that some people earn less income (perhaps the narrowest economic view), but that profound changes are likely to occur in the practical social infrastructure that the everyday work of this agency's staff reproduced, regulated, investigated, and nurtured. Let us see how the budget cuts can alter each of the infrastructural dimensions discussed above and indicated in table 7.2.

In the arena of *legal-regulatory effects*, budget cuts are likely to lead to rollbacks of regulations and standards, and more certainly still, to reductions of enforcement activities. Regulations may be eliminated in the name of overstringency. Enforcement judgments (fines, suits, or permit restrictions) are likely to dwindle. As *Time* reported in the face of Reagan administration pressures on the EPA a decade ago,

> Enforcement procedures have been disrupted.... The Washington enforcement staff was dispersed into four unconnected subdivisions. Field offices have been told to check with EPA headquarters before pursuing cases against alleged corporate violations of pollution laws. As a result, the number of violations referred for prosecution has dropped from 230 to just 42 in nearly eight months since [EPA administrator] Gorsuch took office. (*Time*, 18 January 1982)

Dismantlers of the EPA attempted to justify this weakening of regulatory effort by arguing that regulations inherited from the previous administration were unworkable: too cumbersome, complex, ambitious, and inflexible. While massive evidence of past EPA effectiveness exists, such appeals nevertheless were made to legitimate agency cuts and so to manage broad-based public consent.

In the arena of *changes in social organization*, the budget reductions promised literal reorganization if not sheer EPA disorganization. Central and field office staff were cut; organizational working relations with state agencies were more ambiguous than ever. Such reorganization meant massive turnover and layoffs for employees. Russell E. Train, EPA administrator under the Nixon and Ford administrations, wrote of the early Reagan administration cutbacks:

> If Gorsuch is allowed to carry out plans that have been circulating within the agency for some time, by this coming June—one year and five months after the Reagan Administration took office—80 percent of EPA's headquarters staff will have quit or been fired, demoted, or downgraded.

It is hard to imagine any business manager consciously undertaking such a personnel policy unless its purpose was to destroy the enterprise. Predictably, the result at EPA has been and will continue to be demoralization and institutional paralysis. Attrition within the agency is running at an extraordinary 2.7 per month or 32 percent a year. (*The Washington Post*, 2 February 1982)

In addition, such organizational changes become public promises not only of diminished activity but of diminished regulatory concern, attitude, and intent: promises of reduced regulatory pressure by the agency. So the expectations of many others can be altered: state and city officials worry that they may be left with regulatory responsibilities without the funds to carry them out; politicians worry that a gutted EPA will represent a political liability in future elections; environmentalists worry that air and water quality will suffer, that toxic wastes will poison the physical and natural environment and human lives; even business may well be worried, Train suggests, about a possible political backlash. *Policy changes alter social expectations:* not only who gets what, but who expects what. Consider the somewhat ironic remark of Dennis Abrams, deputy attorney general of the state of West Virginia, as he commented on EPA budget reductions,

Any cutback in EPA as a viable organization hurts us. Threatening EPA lawsuits is how we mostly get voluntary compliance. We don't have the resources to conduct special investigations. Our hands are totally tied. (*National Journal*, 30 January 1982, 185)

In these organizational changes, then, not only jobs and morale, but stable and trusted relationships are lost, and new ones are yet to replace the old. Businesses no less than potentially affected residents near toxic waste dumps may find the intent of state, local, and federal regulatory organizations unclear, shifting, and ambiguous, however much businesses can better cope with these uncertainties of trusted, stable relationships than unorganized local residents can.

In the area of *scientific-technological and administrative activity*, budget reductions can lead to four initial results. First, actual field inspections can be cut back, and so monitoring activities and problem documentation will suffer. Second, basic research can be slowed, diminishing our understanding of pollution effects and abatement technologies. Third, the publication, issuance, and reporting of findings from field research and basic research alike can be restricted. Fourth, aggressive strategies to fulfill the agency's mandates will likely be undermined. At stake here is the public's potential knowledge and understanding of existing environmental problems and possible remedies. Cutting back these activities weakens the public's capacity to learn about the quality of the water it drinks, the air it breathes, the waste dumps it finds nearby, the materials it uses in industry and home, and so on. Public and environmentalist outcry notwithstanding, such policy changes due to budget reductions reproduce knowledge and belief in a very particular way: here we see the reproduction of public ignorance as information and research is restricted or not gathered in the first place.[18] Noting Administrator Gorsuch's suspicion of some EPA employees who might distribute information inconsistent with her plans, the *Time* report quoted above disclosed,

> Mistrustful of the presumed environmentalist bias of career EPA employees, (Gorsuch) has centralized control. Research scientists now cannot release findings until they have been approved as "appropriate" by four levels of the bureaucracy; public information programs, such as slide shows and computer software dealing with science issues, require seven levels of approval. (*Time*, 18 January 1982)

In the arena of *financial and economic impacts*, the budget reductions mean massive changes in the attention paid, the resources invested, toward the solution of public health and environmental problems. EPA budget cuts are not likely to save tax dollars; these resources are more likely to be spent for weapons than for environmental quality and public health protection. Reduced EPA spending will not only reduce attention paid to research, public information and education, monitoring and inspection activities, but attention to effective enforcement will likely suffer too. This in turn may result in incentives for industry *to pay less attention to, to reduce the resources they invest in*, the prevention and control of myriad air, water, and ground pollution problems.

So another source of public regulation of private capital will be further weakened. Private capital will be further redirected toward ends far less public-protecting than pollution control, and the public at large is again likely to suffer the costs of pollution as a relatively few reap the benefits from such "freed up" capital investments.[19]

Cutting an agency budget, then, is far more than a narrowly economic action, and while this may seem perfectly obvious to some, still it seems equally obvious that we have few systematic ways of mapping the resulting social-political-legal impacts of budgetary changes, cuts or expansions. The suggestion of the communicative or social infrastructure here provides such a preliminary systematic map. That infrastructure is no mere social prop, simply an abstract analytical construction connecting structural learning with social action and interaction. Instead, that communicative infrastructure has meaning only insofar *as it mediates between*, and thus *works institutionally to integrate*, the actual claims-making and claims-taking actions and interactions of workers and citizens, on the one hand, with the development, or the setbacks in the development, of the social relations and forces of production, the general dimensions of social, structural "learning," on the other hand.

Seen structurally, the EPA cutbacks, for example, are likely to advance neither productive relations nor productive forces, neither social arrangements increasingly protecting workers, citizens, and natural environment, nor scientific-technological-administrative arrangements resulting in greater productivity, control, and efficiency. Seen phenomenologically, the EPA cutbacks manage or mismanage information and beliefs, legitimation and consent, trust and expectations, and selective attention and neglect. So policy developments can be assessed as changed elements of the social infrastructure; and these changes can be assessed both with respect to specific phenomenological impacts on personal experience and interaction, and with respect to the social ability to develop not only safer, more efficient, and powerful technologies, but also institutional relations of increasing freedom, justice, and social cooperation.

Policy "Recommendations": Attention to Productive and Reproductive Dimensions—Or Systematic Failure

Because policy "problems" are historically constructed patterns of attention and claims reflecting two dimensions of social learning, the productive and the reproductive, policy strategies (as either official policy implementation efforts or as oppositional movement strategies) ought to address both dimensions—or run the risk of policy failure. Consider, for example, the complex problem of safe disposal of toxic industrial wastes.

First, toxic wastes are immediate threats to social reproduction. Including carcinogens, mutagens, terategens and an array of poisons that stagger the imagination, these wastes are deadly. Second, toxic wastes are generally products of industrial processes, whether generated by chemical factories, hospital test procedures, or heavy industry. Toxic waste generation also involves, then, questions of the organization of production: what is produced and for whom, what functionally equivalent nontoxic chemicals could instead be used, and so on.

Attention to the "toxics" problem has often focused upon health effects, the threats to social reproduction. Public health officials and environmental movement activists alike, it seems, have often been concerned with "proper" containment, shipping, and disposal of toxic waste products. These efforts are essential. Yet the "productive" side of the problem must not be ignored: strategies of waste reduction at the source, i.e., production and its control, must not be neglected, or effective incentives for producers to continue to generate toxics will remain unchanged. Especially when containment technologies remain primitive, attention solely to the reproductive (generally *health* effects) aspects of "toxics" may lead to continual policy failure. As long as toxic waste generation proceeds unabated, virtually any remedial or protective public health strategies designed to minimize risk may be overwhelmed. The agenda for policy makers, public health workers, labor and environmental movement activists alike must include not only reproductive health protection strategies but productive workplace reorganization strategies too.

Conversely, attention paid only to waste generation would obviously avoid the immediate concerns, fears, worries, and experiences of citizens who now face possible dangers from exposure to such waste chemicals. To consider only technical epidemiological issues or the regulation of production can lead to the actual neglect of citizens' demands for timely information, for responsiveness from state health officials, and for counsel that they can trust to be free from conflicts of interest.[20] To neglect health and social concerns in the name of attacking the problem at its productive source may only be another recipe for systematic, and particularly callous, policy failure.

Assessing Recourse to Discourse—And Domination

Altering the social infrastructure of action, policy implementation alters citizens' bases of knowledge, norms, expectations of others, and attention. More profoundly still, policy implementation also alters the very abilities of citizens to check—to find out about, criticize and learn about, test, appeal or file grievances, challenge or debate—claims in these four dimensions of communicative interaction (facts, norms, intentions, attention).

Recall that ordinary communicative action involves a practical structure of four related claims—and the counterfactual possibilities of checking these claims—offered by speakers and potentially accepted or challenged by their listeners. Whether threatening, asserting, offering, challenging, or requesting, for example, ordinary communicative action: (1) establishes or re-creates a normative (claimed to be legitimate) relationship of speaker and hearer (e.g., a county health inspector questions, warns, alerts, tells, promises, or threatens a restaurant owner); (2) refers to some content that may be true or false (e.g., the strike will succeed; the chemical is an organic toxin); (3) expresses the speaker's intentions and feelings (e.g., sincere or joking, ironic or satirical); and (4) calls attention clearly in a language or symbol system shared by speaker and listener (e.g., plain English or technical toxicology).

How such claims are made, when they are made, and which are accepted are all historically contingent, of course. For each of these claims can be challenged by those listening, no less among friends than between politically opposed groups or classes. In a given policy arena, though, can false claims can be publicly distinguished from true ones? Can illegitimate and oppressive claims be publicly recognized and rejected in favor of legitimate ones? How does each policy alternative help or hinder citizens' abilities to check such claims in a generalizable, noncoercive, mutually legitimated manner, rather than allowing claims to be imposed by one dominant group or class (McGuire 1977)?

To what extent are citizens' and workers' attempts to understand the actual conditions affecting their lives blocked by systematically distorting influences of class, power, coercion, or domination? For example, does a newly proposed hazardous waste disposal policy help or hinder affected citizens who wish to learn about the true effects of toxic chemicals? Must those citizens perpetually reduce the results of laboratory studies to the imputed political-economic interests of those who funded the research?

Does the proposed policy help affected citizens establish generalizable political norms (for example, regulating workplace exposure to toxic chemicals by making production decisions accountable to workers)?

These questions point to historically precarious possibilities of institutionally established theoretical-scientific and practical-democratic discourses. A critical theory of public policy leads immediately to ask how relations of class, power, ideology, and policy making may practically and systematically distort such institutionalized discourses.[21]

Only as public discourse free from socially unnecessary constraints and coercion exists can we argue that citizens' beliefs are warranted by scientific standards of withstanding criticism, that the norms and laws regulating public behavior are justified by democratic standards reflecting generalizable interests, that neither are simply instances of unchecked bias, special interests, bureaucratic or class oppression. Yet the actual historical extent of domination-free—or dominated—discourses can never be determined in a theoretical, a priori way.

Distortions of scientific and political discourses must be investigated concretely. Only then can we distinguish between inevitable, "socially necessary," and avoidable, "socially unnecessary," distortions of discourses—to forestall the foolishness of chasing the mirage of any "perfect" and distortionless communication process. A critical policy analysis reveals the historical, scientific, and political importance of domination-free—not distortion-free—discourses. Often unrecognized, this difference is fundamental (Forester 1985, introduction; 1991). Only to the extent that discourses free from socially unnecessary distortions are available to citizens can those citizens scientifically distinguish misrepresentation from factual knowledge and democratically distinguish misinformed consent from informed consent, noncoerced political consent from outright political manipulation.

So a critical theory of public policy leads us first to locate policy implementation in the mediating social infrastructure of action, and second to examine policy-altered social interactions of practical claims-making—with respect to content and beliefs, norms and consent, expressions and trust, and attention or comprehension (Forester 1982, 1989). The analysis leads, third, to empirical and critical questions probing the degree to which these everyday practical claims are institutionally imposed or conversely criticizable (redeemable, legitimated, noncoercively and generalizably established) through processes of democratic and scientific criticism. Thus a critical theory of public policy analysis leads us to examine the systematic, policy institutionalized reproduction of citizens' power and powerlessness: of citizens' knowledge or ignorance, free consent or oppression, cooperation or manipulation, attention to or distraction from pressing social needs, and the corresponding suppression or realization of socially and politically generalizable interests.

Without institutionalized means of checking knowledge and truth claims (about chemical toxicity, administrative efficiency, technological success, energy efficiency, work safety, housing quality, and so on), citizens will remain subject to the opportunistic stories and systematically selective representations of those already in power, without being able to check the misrepresentation, false claims, exaggerations, or unsupportable ideological beliefs that they may actually face. Without institutional means of freely checking and criticizing legitimacy and rightness claims, citizens will be politically disenfranchised, incapable of the autonomous political actions and participation that alone can truly legitimate public policy.[22]

This line of analysis points both to the policy influenced reproduction of social interaction and to the socially necessary or unnecessary distortions of ongoing processes of scientific and political discourses, the bases of structural and societal learning processes. A critical account of policy analysis must address a host of further questions. By what particular processes does the reproduction of belief, consent, trust, and attention take place? How does policy implementation alter these processes? By what means are we to examine the historical justifications for existing distortions of discourse and judge whether they suffice to establish those distortions as "socially necessary"?[23] These questions require further research and attention, and as they are addressed, so will a critical theory of public policy, a critical structural phenomenology of public policy, advance or falter.

Conclusion

A critical theory of public policy analysis, then, is an empirical account of the contingent and variable reproduction—through policy development—of citizens' beliefs, consent, trust, and attention. It may be a "practical" political theory because it can call attention to relations of power, not simply the control of capital but the manipulation of everyday sensibility, credibility, and gullibility as well. It can point to the limits and vulnerabilities of established power by pinpointing how that power itself depends upon background consensuses of taken-for-granted factual beliefs, normative myths of expertise, meritocracy, or authority, social trust and dependency, and selective attention and neglect. It can then identify possible avenues of political opposition and practice: (1) exposing the conditions of dangerous workplaces, declining environmental quality, or economic crisis; (2) questioning and challenging illegitimate "authority" by publicizing the suppression of generalizable interests and citizens' real access to scientific and political discourses; (3) revealing deceit and manipulation by those heretofore trusted; and (4) focusing attention on more substantively democratic policy alternatives and concrete programs for social betterment.[24]

Yet any critical social theory has its own limits. It can be no panacea, no guarantee, no key or gimmick to "social transformation," "major structural changes" (or the euphemism you prefer). A critical pragmatism can reveal, expose, reevaluate, illuminate, encourage, explain, decipher, simplify, inform, educate, challenge, threaten, or support only as it is articulated in practice, including in situated text: article, tract, pamphlet, leaflet, media report, newsletter item, position paper, and so on. Such a critical theory can have little meaning in deed apart from the understanding, the application, the continued articulation as the actual calling of others' attention, that it receives from its bearers. To paraphrase the ordinary language analysts, we can say that it is not properly a "theory" that is confused, but rather theorists. In the same vein, it is likely not to be a "theory" in the abstract that is critical and "practical" but those who articulate that theory in the course of their lives, those human beings who by virtue of being able to anticipate and respond to the exercise of domination are able to organize practically against it, who by virtue of being able to distinguish authority from tyranny are able to articulate critically and move pragmatically toward a vision of a more free and democratic society.

NOTES

Notes to the Preface

1. The chapters that follow have been adapted from the following sources: Chapter 2 from: "Understanding Planning Practice: An Empirical, Practical, and Normative Account," *Journal of Planning Education and Research*, 1(1982):2; Chapter 3 from "Questioning and Organizing Attention: Toward a Critical Theory of Planning," *Administration and Society*, 13(1981):2; Chapter 4 from "Practical Rationality in Planning," in *Rationality in Plan-Making*, ed. Michael Breheny and Alan Hooper. London: Pion, 1985; Chapter 5 from "The Geography of Planning Practice," *Society and Space*, 1(Spring 1983):2; Chapter 6 from "Critical Theory and Public Life—Only Connect," *International Journal of Urban and Regional Research*, 10(1986):2; and Chapter 7 from "A Critical Empirical Framework for the Analysis of Public Policy," *New Political Science*, issue 9–10, 3(Summer 1982):1.

Notes to Chapter One

1. By "critical theory" here, we refer particularly to the more sociological, action-theoretic work of Jürgen Habermas (see bibliography). A theoretical complement to my more practically pitched *Planning in the Face of Power* (University of California, 1989), this book is directly concerned with "theory" as it informs our analyses of practice and policy.

2. In the context of policy analysis, I have argued that critical theory provides us with the basis of a "structural phenomenology," as we explore further below. The recent concern with poststructuralist strategies of textual readings provides a mixed blessing for social research. The good news is that our interpretive powers may be enhanced, as might our sensitivities to the pervasive disciplinary structuring of discourses and thus to the relations of knowledge and power. The bad news is that these advances seem to be purchased at the cost of sweeping away crucial political and

ethical questions of agency and praxis, reflective, politicized, theoretically engaged, practical judgments made in ordinary (but fantastically diverse) contexts. See for example, Dews 1987; Deetz 1992; Fraser 1989.

3. Asked about "the ideal speech situation" in an interview, Habermas responded directly to counter the most typical misunderstanding of this concept: "One should not imagine the ideal speech situation as a utopian model for an emancipated society" (quoted in "Political Experience and the Renewal of Marxist Theory," in Dews 1986, 90). Cf. Forester 1991, 52–55.

4. This analysis also echoes Trent Schroyer's (1973) insight in his *Critique of Domination* that Habermas has transformed the classical critique of ideology into the analysis of systematically distorted communications, the systematically distorted communicative structuring of citizens' attention. This insight makes possible empirical analyses of ideological production because it moves beyond the focus upon disembodied consciousness, the "contents" of ideologies, to the analysis of both ideological claims *and particular practices* (e.g. in administrative, planning, and policy contexts) *of such claims making*. I explore the implications of Schroyer's observation at length in Forester 1989.

5. We might take an organizational level of analysis to mediate between what Habermas has called "system" and "lifeworld," but it may be more useful to understand any social organization as the site at which system and lifeworld intersect. Just how effective organizational socialization is in any given case—replacing the normative influences of the lifeworld altogether (?) at the extreme—must be an empirical question in any particular analysis. For a more agent-centered treatment, see "Three Views of Organizations," in Forester 1989.

6. In the *Theory of Communicative Action,* Habermas (1984) drops the fourfold structure of the "universal pragmatics" of his *Communication and the Evolution of Society* (1979) by putting aside the "comprehensibility claim" speakers make as they employ a shared language of significance. I hope to show that further analysis of this dimension of claims making is needed and, indeed, that it might inform our understanding of basic *economic* transactions. The comprehensibility claim allows us to recognize socially constituted or grammatically structured forms of value. See chapter 7 in this book.

7. For a related analysis of the ways policy initiatives may restructure the worlds of actors, see my "The Critical Theory-Policy Analysis Affair: Habermas and Wildavsky as Bedfellows?" in Forester 1985. That essay argues that if we take policy to reshape patterns of interactions, policy analysis will only be as good as the theory of action on which it relies. Thus, a rich theory of (communicative) action promises insightful results for the analysis of public policy, although few such efforts have yet combined the detailed case analysis with the broader theoretical attention we

need. This account suggests how Giddens's notion of structuration can be developed in the context of policy analysis.

Notes to Chapter Two

1. Research can thus shift from the assessment of more narrow processes of experimentation and testing (social engineering from social science) to the study of the practical means and processes of "articulation" (Marris 1975), argument (Toulmin 1964; Churchman 1971; Fischer 1980; Mason and Mitroff 1980–1981; Webber and Rittel 1973), political discourse (Pitkin 1972), dialogue (Freire 1970), policy or design criticism (Krieger 1981), democratization (Habermas 1975; Dewey 1927) and organizing (Hartman 1975, 1978).

2. Cf. Benhabib 1986; Benhabib and Dallmayr 1990; Rasmussen 1990; McGuire 1977; Van Hooft 1976; Dallmayr 1974; Apel 1977). Furthermore, the shift from the treatment of "information" to "attention" is a shift from a Cartesian, rationalistic and idealistic philosophical tradition to a critical, historical, and phenomenological one. Richard Bernstein's book on the restructuring of social and political theory illuminates these shifts: roughly, from idealism and positivism to a critical pragmatism, which Charles Hoch has also explored (Bernstein 1976; Hoch 1984, 1987). The deeper roots of such an alternative view (Krieger 1974, 1981) are in the traditions of English language philosophy (Pitkin 1972), German phenomenology (Gadamer 1975; Bauman 1978; Schutz 1970; Bolan 1980), American pragmatism (Bernstein 1971), Sir Karl Popper's "critical rationalism" (Popper 1963; Lakatos and Musgrave 1972; Friedmann 1978) and Habermas's "critical communications theory of society" (1968, 1970, 1973, 1975, 1979; McCarthy 1978; Held 1980; Hemmens and Stiftel, 1980).

Notes to Chapter Three

1. The original abstract to this chapter read as follows: To understand what planning and administrative analysts do, and what they can yet do, we need a theory of planning and public administration that combines vision with practice, a theory neither solely utopian nor opportunistic. Jürgen Habermas's "critical communications theory of society" allows us to locate the planning analyst's questioning and shaping of attention, thus organizing and designing, within a political, institutional world of systematically but unnecessarily distorted (and so possibly alterable) communications. A critical theory of administration and planning argues that the planning analysts' organizing of attention can and ought ethically to work to foster true political discourse, dialogue, and the possibilities of genuinely democratic politics.

2. As the text will explain, I will follow several authors, such as Meltsner and Benveniste, in referring to city planners, program evaluators, managers and administrators of public programs, policy analysts, budget analysts, as "planning analysts," "planners," or "policy analysts" (terms I use interchangeably). The similarities among all of these roles far outshadow their differences; thus the critical theory I develop here applies to all of these roles, each deeply faced with problems of assessing possible courses of action.

3. For critiques of instrumental rationality, see Horkheimer 1974; Tribe 1973; Wellmer 1974. For "systems"-perspectives see Etzioni 1968; Friedmann 1973.

4. For work on self-critical systems thinking, see Burton 1981; Truex and Klein 1991.

5. This conception of theory lies at the intersection of work in phenomenology (Taylor 1985), language and analysis (Pitkin 1972), practical judgment (Nussbaum 1984, 1990), pragmatism (Bernstein 1971), and critical theory (e.g. Fay 1987; Bernstein 1983).

6. Empirical support for this proposition is presented in Weiss's "Research for Policy's Sake." Work in social research and social science functions to help policy makers "less to arrive at solutions than to orient (them) to problems...(to) shift the agenda and change the formulation of issues..., bringing new perspectives to attention and formulating issues [N.B.] for resolution.... The major effect of research on policy may be gradual sedimentation of insights, theories, concepts, and ways of looking at the world" (Weiss 1977, 534–535).

7. Cf. here recent work of Martha Nussbaum, for example, *Love's Knowledge*, 1990.

8. Cf. Pitkin 1972; for an account derived from pragmatism, see Schön (1983; for a critical pragmatism, see Forester 1989, 1991.

9. Dekema (1981) has written an extensive philosophical critique of classical rationalistic decision theory (including modern probabilistic versions). Drawing from Wittgensteinian and Heideggerian arguments, Dekema reworks the fundamental concepts of "choice," "alternatives," and "decisions" and thus shows the centrality of interpretation and the constitutive questions of tradition, identity, and direction in any rational decision-making action.

10. The analysis of agenda setting in political science is nothing new; what may be newer is the use of a political speech act analysis, Habermas's claims-making pragmatics of communicative action, to show micropolitically just how subtly and in what dimensions agenda setting really works (cf. Forester 1989; chapter 5 here).

11. Questioning is the true hermeneutic praxis. It is the fundamental mode of shaping attention because it works in language, at once directing and opening, acting and calling forth action, calling forth response and responsibility, caring and calling forth care as well. See Gadamer's "The Logic of Question and Answer" (1975, 333–41).

12. As often as not, illustrations come from case material gathered at a major metropolitan office of environmental review, within the city planning department and staffed by local city planning personnel. Note that the argument here does not assume there are no forbidden questions for administrators and planners, questions they cannot ask for "political" reasons. These are not the only questions whose asking may have significance, though. Indeed, by asking internally, "What might (an external activist organization) have to say about this issue?" to reduce uncertainty, apparently, the planning analyst may work to make it possible for the forbidden questions to be asked by outsiders, nonplanners at least. More importantly, though, the objection that some questions are impossible to ask feasibly misunderstands the actual politics of the broader activities of questioning—by focusing overly on the question's content and ignoring processual aspects of questioning: shifts in involvement, participation, responsibility, channels of information, and so on.

13. This discussion has particular relevance to the work of negotiators and mediators. Cf. here Freire 1970; Forester 1992b)

14. This suggestion comes from Richard L. Meier.

15. Experiences of "whistleblowers" ought to make us look more closely at the successful, but covert, past activities of question spreaders.

16. For earlier applications of the experimental model of scientific inquiry to planning and policy studies, see Weiss 1972; Suchman 1967; Campbell and Stanley 1963.

17. Habermas 1968, 287; cf. Habermas 1973, 38–39: "the theory that creates consciousness can bring about the conditions under which the systematic distortions of communication are dissolved and a practical discourse can then be conducted."

18. As Bernstein (1976, 202) writes in his discussion of Habermas: "Individuals may have only occasional false beliefs about what they are doing, but systematically distorted misconceptions of themselves, the meaning of their actions, and their historical situations." Fred Dallmayr (1976, 77) concurs and goes on, then, to locate our point of departure: "Given the prevalence of distorted or mangled communication patterns, to be sure, actual practice regularly falls short of the norm of ideal speech; yet, because of the consensual thrust, ordinary encounters always proceed on the implicit [though normally counterfactual] presumption that the norm is operative and observed. The distance between actual and pro-

jected patterns, in Habermas's view, involves not so much a logical conflict as a practical challenge and political task: from this challenge, 'The critical theory of society takes its departure.'"

The present chapter may be understood to address Gouldner's (1976) criticism of Habermas "at the level of praxis." Those implications must be worked out at the *level of praxis*, at the level of possible communicative action and *not* the production of the ideal speech situation—a task tantamount to achieving an unreal society (Forester 1991, 52–55). Thus we focus here on the practice of questioning as a speech act in a political world and upon organizing attention and organizing to overcome unnecessary, systematic distortions of information, beliefs, and communications. Readers should note that Habermas has no illusions—nor does he suggest—that perfectly undistorted communication is possible. Rather, he contrasts unnecessary, systematic distortion with what might be called necessary and justifiable, or legitimate, distortion. The former manifests domination; the latter manifests legitimate authority.

19. Dallmayr (1976, 77) explains: "According to Habermas, all speech acts and communicative exchanges are geared toward mutual understanding and agreement and, ultimately, toward a standard of justifiable conduct. Ordinary language, in other words, is permeated by the anticipation of reciprocal consensus, a consensus achievable on the level of nonrepressive discourse or 'ideal speech.' Equally applicable to the validation of propositions and the justification of norms, the anticipatory thrust cannot be questioned or rejected—since such questioning involves the same anticipation of consensus."

20. Habermas (1975, 105) writes (read closely):

We cannot explain the validity claim of norms without recourse to rationally motivated agreement or at least to the conviction that consensus on a recommended norm could be brought about with *reasons*.... The appropriate model is...the communication community of those affected, who as participants in a practical discourse test the validity claims of norms, and *to the extent that* they accept them with reasons, arrive at the conviction that in the given circumstances the proposed norms are "right." The validity claim of norms is grounded *not in the irrational volitional acts of the contracting parties, but in the rationally motivated recognition of norms, which may be questioned* at any time.... The normative-validity claim is itself *cognitive in the sense of the supposition (however counter-factual) that it could be discursively redeemed*—that is, grounded in consensus of the participants through argumentation. (emphases added)

Compare McCarthy's "Translator's Introduction" (Habermas 1975, xiii–xviii): "The very act of participating in a discourse, of attempting to come to an agreement about the truth of a problematic statement or the correctness of a problematic norm, carries with it the supposition that a genuine agreement is possible. If we did not suppose that a justified consensus were possible and could in some way be distinguished from a false consensus, then the very meaning of discourse, indeed of speech, would be called in to question" (1975, xvi).

"It is apparent that the conditions of actual speech are rarely, if ever, those of the ideal speech situation. But this does not of itself make illegitimate the ideal—that can be more or less adequately approximated in actual speech situations—which can serve as a guide for institutionalization of discourse or the critique of systematically distorted communication" (1975, xvii). But cf. Forester 1991 for a more practical interpretation and the difficulties of the notion of an "ideal speech situation." Cf. n.3, chapter 1, above.

21. Habermas (1973, 15, 28) is sensitive to this point but has yet to address it at length. Habermas's more recent system-lifeworld discussion (1983) does little to address this problem.

22. See the discussion of "publicity" in Krumholz and Forester 1990.

23. Recall Schroyer's fundamental insight suggesting that Habermas refines the classical "critique of ideology" into the critique of systematically distorted communications: "In every communicative situation in which a consensus is established under coercion or under distorted conditions, we are confronting instances of illusory discourse. This is the contemporary form of the critique of ideology (Schroyer, 1973, 163)." Yanarella and Reid (1977) argued nevertheless that Habermas still had failed to provide the linkage between "critique" and "emancipation" (Bauman 1978). The present account of the communicative practice of questioning and shaping response though, provides this linkage in the following way. "Emancipation" must be intimately tied to practice overcoming those [needless] distortions of communications shaping our knowledge of one another, ourselves, our possibilities—including feasibilities and strategies. Working to spread responsibility, to foster possibilities of political criticism and discourse, to democratize in actuality, the critical practice of questioning practical possibilities of action links the vision of critique, yet to be embodied in the acts of questioning, to concrete everyday activities of emancipatory practice.

24. To address the meaning of "distorted," see notes above and compare the discussion of systematic and nonsystematic, necessary and unnecessary, types of distortions in chapter 4 and in Forester 1989.

25. See Dallmayr 1974. We might consider the ethics of ordinary discourse to involve a "reciprocal entitlement" (I borrow the phrase from John Friedmann) to intersubjectivity. In the words of Paulo Freire (1970, 73), "Any situation in which some men prevent others from engaging in the process of inquiry is one of violence."

26. See Peter Berger's (1976) discussion of "cognitive respect." Cf. discussions of resistance and counterhegemony (Merry 1990; Ong 1987; Scott 1985, 1990).

Notes to Chapter Four

1. For the functionally rational view, see Faludi 1984 and Reade 1984; cf. Gadamer 1975; Habermas 1970, 1983; Tribe 1972; and Schön 1983.

2. Cf. Vickers 1970. Habermas's 'critical communications theory of society' takes these problems on; it articulates both a theory of universalization and the suppression of generalizable interests, as an account of communicative ethics, and an historical account of social evolution and learning (Habermas 1975, 1979; Benhabib and Dallmayr 1990).

3. Here Habermas's shorthand definition of legitimacy as "worthiness to be recognized" may serve.

4. See Benhabib 1989–1990 here bridging Aristotelian (for example, Wiggins 1978; Nussbaum 1990) and more Kantian (Habermas 1983) accounts. Cf. Forester (1992b).

Notes to Chapter Five

1. The abstract to the following argument reads: "Planning practice is a contingent situated activity. The anatomy of planning practice may be understood as a structure of communicative action involving claims regarding content and context, thus systematically presenting questions and demanding judgments in the face both of uncertainty and of ambiguity. Practical communicative claims are established in the planning process through the ongoing social reproduction of beliefs, consent, trust, and attention. If planners are to be sensitive to these processes of social reproduction, they must be attentive to four dimensions of the geography of their practice: a cognitive geography of knowledge production, a political-legal geography of power and consent, a ritual geography of social identity, and an economic-resource geography of attention. Recognizing this structure and field of practical action, planners may enhance social learning, resisting threats to democratizing movements, in part by distinguishing and protecting learning processes in two dimensions, the technical and the practical. Refusing to reduce issues of normative ambiguity to issues of technical uncertainty, planners may themselves continue to learn about the political and normative aspects of their practice and so foster, rather than render apolitical, democratic social-learning processes."

2. The problem to be addressed here—and neglected in the writing on the theory of the state—is that of a structural-phenomenological analysis of planning practice. As chapter 7 argues in regard to policy analysis,

critical social theory may be able to provide a framework for social studies that are structurally sensitive and phenomenologically compelling as well. Structural Marxists have stressed issues of structure and function to the neglect of actions; Weberians generally have done the opposite (Saunders 1979). The task of a critical theory of planning is to give an account of planners' actions that is at once structurally located and phenomenologically sound—an account that does not decide a priori whose interests, for example, planners effectively serve (if they serve any).

3. I have argued at length elsewhere (Forester 1989) that planning practice may more usefully and appropriately be understood as practical communicative action rather than as a form of instrumental problem solving or of means-ends calculating action. Harold Foster and his colleagues have corroborated these suggestions empirically (Foster et al 1982). Rather than repeating these analyses here, a few summary comments may simply set the stage for the analysis that follows. In particular, we will ask: Upon what reading of the planner's organizational-political environment might effective practice depend?

4. This question has two deep resonances in modern social theory. Giddens (1979, 1981) has suggested a theory of structuration in one interesting, if somewhat forced, attempt to link action and systems levels of analysis. Habermas (1975; 1979) also continues to integrate these analyses, speaking of 'system' and 'lifeworld' and only alluding to a 'communicative infrastructure' that might provide the basis for their integration. Attempting to extend and apply Habermas's theory of communicative action, this chapter seeks to characterize that communicative infrastructure by sketching dimensions of the geography of practice, that is, the geography of practical communicative action.

5. In another project-review context, Susskind and Dunlop (1981, 336) point to seven sources of ambiguity in the environmental impact assessment process: "1) the choice of professional team members; 2) the organization of the work plan; 3) approaches to coping with uncertainty; 4) attitudes toward mitigation; 5) approaches to public participation; 6) the use of data for and the style of forecasting; and 7) attitudes toward the role of the [Environmental Impact Statement] in planning and decision-making."

6. This terrain of resistance will have cognitive, political-legal, ritualized, and economic dimensions. These may be sketched here, but how a planner actually works in these dimensions to counteract abuses of power in each cannot be specified once and for all. An important research problem, then, would be the investigation of a *repertoire* of progressive (democratizing?) and practical actions that might be taken in each dimension of this terrain.

7. Discussing the power of information, Krumholz (1982, 173–174) writes, "Frequently, the successful advocacy of a desirable program or leg-

islative change will rely entirely on the quality of staff work and the ability to present verbal or written recommendations clearly and quickly, remembering always that most politicians do not read much and have short attention spans. The only legitimate power the planner can count on in such matters is the power of information, analysis, and insight, but that power is considerable when harnessed to an authentic conceptualization of the public need." Cf. Wilensky 1967.

8. March and Olsen (1976) suggest the rich texture of those many situations when choices are to be faced (if decisions may not yet be made), perhaps most 'meetings': "choice situations are not simply occasions for making substantive decisions. They are also arenas in which important symbolic meanings are developed. People gain status and exhibit virtue. Problems are accorded significance. Novices are educated into the values of the society and organization. Participation rights are certification of social legitimacy; participation performances are critical presentations of self" (1976, 52). A helpful and politically developed analysis appears in Kertzer 1988.

9. Compare Krumholz (1982, 174) here, "If a planner's work is to be used, he must take it beyond the commission into the political arena, and take his share of risks while arguing on many fronts for the implementation of his recommendations." Krumholz suggests that this should not be construed as an argument against the important function of the planning commission: "The Commission also provides a regular, institutionalized forum which its staff can use to place issues, opinions, and analyses on the public agenda" (1982, 174).

10. Cf. Boyte 1980; Forester 1981d; Pitkin and Shumer 1982; Schaar 1981; Schön 1983; Susskind 1981; Walzer 1980; Burton and Murphy 1980; Pateman 1970 (See also Susskind and Cruickshank 1987; Forester 1992b; Barber 1984; Mansbridge 1983; Cohen and Rogers 1983).

Notes to Chapter Six

1. Habermas's suggestion here is quite falsifiable; citizen conflicts within DVTC or against it would not count as system pressures. Had the administration and industry—the institutionalized embodiments of accumulating/bureaucratizing forces—been mute on these issues and had only other neighborhood groups organized in opposition, Habermas's hypothesis of the systemic penetration of the "lifeworld" would have faced counterevidence in this case.

2. See chapter 7 on the analysis of policy initiatives.

3. This analysis responds to the question, "How can Habermas's recent critical communications theory of society, as reformulated in the

Theory of Communicative Action, be applied concretely to concrete instances of social life?"

Notes to Chapter Seven

1. Here I refer to Habermas (1970; 1973; 1975; 1979). For insightful attempts to distinguish the differences and continuities between Habermas's work and that of the Frankfurt School critical theorists before him, see Honneth 1981; Kellner and Roderick 1981; Held 1980; and White 1988. For secondary works on Habermas, see the comprehensive view in McCarthy 1978.

2. An important analysis of Habermas's relationship to Marx is Wellmer 1976. Cf. Stephen White 1988, Rick Roderick 1986, Thompson and Held 1982, and a virtual Habermas industry of secondary authors. This section presents an emaciated, bare-bones presentation of the conceptual skeleton of Habermas's critical theory essential to frame a critical theory of public policy. For the necessary systematic discussions of his analysis of power, the suppression of generalizable interests, the logic of discourses, legitimation problems, and so on, see the extensive assessments in McCarthy 1978 and Thompson and Held 1982, cited above.

3. For a related argument, see "The Critical Theory-Policy Analysis Affair: Habermas and Wildavsky as Bedfellows?" in Forester 1985. It is worth noting the preliminary nature of the present chapter. Little "middle-range" work has been done integrating the structural and action theories that Habermas has sketched out so far. The present chapter leaves many more questions unanswered than answered, and it only roughly suggests directions for further and far more empirically detailed critical policy studies—assessing in fact infrastructural changes, changes in learning capacity, changes in social interactions, and changes in the institutionalization of discourses.

4. See Habermas 1979, 1, the confusing charts on p. 40 and p. 209 notwithstanding.

5. On the relationship of development of the forces and relations of production to the pragmatic truth and rightness claims made in action, see Habermas 1975, sec. 1 (e.g., pp. 9–10) and Habermas 1979, chaps. 3–4.

6. The characterization of a structural phenomenology is one way of understanding Habermas's reference to the contribution of the theory of communicative action as providing the basis for a "structural analysis of lifeworlds." See Honneth et al 1981. Cf. here the notion of a structural phenomenology with Anthony Giddens's (1984) notion of "structuration," his earlier (1976) hesitations about phenomenology notwithstanding; cf. also the following note.

7. The center of table 7.1 may be largely missing because to date Habermas has considered organizations to be predominately strategic, patterns of purposive-rational action, rather than patterns of routinized social action with productive *and* reproductive aspects corresponding to those organizational actions stressing content or relationship validity claims respectively. Cf. the previous note.

8. Reformulating and broadening Habermas's analysis of "comprehensibility claims" here, the appeal to "attention-focusing" claims makes possible the inclusion and consideration of nonverbal as well as verbal (speech) acts. See notes following, below.

9. This analysis deviates from (but perhaps extends) Habermas's (1979) analysis in his "Reconstruction of Historical Materialism and the Development of Normative Structures" and his account of universal pragmatics. In particular, Habermas has been silent about the character of institutions that might mediate or serve to frame, stage, or set up claims of "sincerity" and "comprehensibility." Here we attempt to specify or suggest the institutional and social conditions that facilitate the ready and routine acceptance of such claims. Just as scientific and engineering laboratories (and the knowledge-producing service sector) routinely provide the institutional infrastructure for the establishment (offering and grounding) of factual and truth claims, so may we understand traditional *and* secular ritual structures—more generally routinized social organization, routinized social relations—to provide the social infrastructure for the ready establishment of sincerity claims, claims to trustworthiness of expressed intention. As we are able to assess another's performance of conventional social rituals, so are we able to judge the consistency between what they say and what they do in deed.

The parallel argument for the infrastructure of the "comprehensibility claim" is more difficult, but equally significant. It is important to remember that the "universal pragmatics" is developed explicitly for verbal speech acts, while the programmatic intention of the argument there includes (in principle) nonverbal action as well, for which Habermas has not yet provided an analysis. First, then, we can generalize the character of the *comprehensibility claim* from the narrow meaning of the claim, producing a well-formed *utterance* in a spoken language, to the broader meaning of *producing a well-formed token in a shared field of conventions* (if not in "forms of life"). Once we make this move, we can render as a claim to the production of meaning (intelligibility, comprehensibility, recognition, uptake) nonverbal actions such as paying for a commodity after asking for it; *writing* someone a *check after* a bribe has been offered and agreed to; *issuing* a check as a *wage* in return for labor; or leaving a "tip," or gratuity, in a restaurant after a meal. Each of these resource movements and economic actions may be nonverbal, but they are actions (for which the actors may be held responsible—as customer, perpetrator of a bribe, employer, patron, or cheapskate), nevertheless, and not only because they are each rule governed (thus *counting* as payment making or tipping), but also because each one produces (generates and here thematizes) a *well-formed, conventionally defined token* (not an utterance), i.e., the payment or the gratuity. Such a meaningful "token" may be as ordinary as a conventional *gesture* (a wave of the hand to greet someone) or as richly economic as the *investment of capital* (presupposing of course the framework of economic institutions *in which* the movement of resources, labor, wealth, and machines may be recognized as capital investment—cf. here Wittgenstein's (1973) *Philosophical Investigations* no. 373, with "economics" as the relevant grammar. If we *then* ask what societal institutions provide the framework in which such nonverbal, conventional tokens may be generated, recognized as meaningful, and emphasized in their very production, the answer appears to point toward the economic institutions and framework of society. Within those institutions, for example, mechanisms such as budgets and accounting procedures are the special "linguistic" (if not ordinarily verbal) means by which the generation, expenditure, and consumption of such "tokens" (resources, staff assignments, debt, credit, and so on) are organized and monitored. If this line of argument can be developed and clarified, we could support the proposal that *the economic institutions of a society provide the social infrastructure for the generation and establishment of actors' "comprehensibility" (or more generally then: attention-directing) claims, as table 7.2 suggests.*

10. Table 7.2 is suggested as a preliminary analysis of the mediating instructions that may fill in the center of table 7.1—suggesting therefore the concrete social forms through which social action and social structure reproduce one another. The identification of mediating institutions may not be very specific for two reasons. First, each actual type of institution itself reflects patterns of action and interaction, and it will therefore (while stressing *one*) involve *each* of the four claims constituting communicative action. A research laboratory and a church congregation will both reproduce norms and rules that their members (ought to) follow: they will both refer to truth claims about the ways that the world is held to be; they will both depend upon the mutually recognized expressive claims of their members, so that cooperation rather than manipulation may be the order of the day; and of course, they will both depend upon these comprehensibility claims ordinarily made so that their members can understand in the most minimal way what they are saying. Each type of mediating institution, then, involves the claims that happen to be oriented toward, stressed, or thematized by the other three types of mediating organization. Second, however, these mediating institutions can only be presented as "families" of institutions and organizations, for their specific forms will vary historically with regional, cultural, urban-rural, industrial-agricultural characteristics, and so forth. What distinguished these organizational forms is only the type of action claim that they may particularly stress, support, and provide the context for: thus research laboratories are directly oriented toward the production of factual knowledge (for whatever

176 NOTES TO CHAPTER 7

subsequent systemic *function*), while legislatures are correspondingly oriented to the production of norms and laws (again for various *functions*), but not vice versa.

11. These mediating institutions are not wholly uncoupled or disjointed, of course. Under a capitalist political economy, we might expect that the legal institutions do not treat questions of the socialization vs. privatization of production equally, i.e., that regulations and incentives will be structured again and again to reproduce capitalist market relations. Likewise, we expect social-cultural institutions to reflect individualistic traditions. Nevertheless, each of these mediating institutions might also provide enclaves for new democratic forms and countermovements (pockets of resistance?) to the continuation of the private appropriation of the social capacity for production.

12. We may expect different policies to alter some dimensions of this "social infrastructure" more than others. Tax policies alter *rules and regulations* of financial management primarily, then obviously resource flows, and then only secondarily do they foster new organizational forms and alterations in public beliefs and knowledge. Welfare policies alter rules, resources, and organizational forms immediately and public beliefs less directly. Symbolic policies (those which are never actually implemented despite rhetoric to the contrary: local resolutions passed without resource commitments for adequate follow-up), for example, are effective, if at all, primarily insofar as they influence public beliefs, while organizational, legal, and economic change may be negligible. Correspondingly, then, we might expect to have different politics associated with them. Where knowledge and belief are at stake (the National Institute for Occupational Health and Safety is threatened, or the National Center for Health Services Research is cut back), the political role of scientific experts will be significantly more important than if social security payments are threatened. This suggests that there might be several clusters of policy politics representing those special cases where a policy does not promise changes in most of the infrastructural dimensions but rather seems to emphasize changes in just one or two of these dimensions.

13. See the concluding full section on assessing the possibilities of "recourse to discourse" below.

14. Cf. Habermas 1983. See also Habermas 1975. I use "background consensus" to elaborate the sociological and political meaning of the term as Habermas uses it in his discussion of the "universal pragmatics," the core of his communications theory. In particular, "consensus" here is taken to refer to a shared position or attitude, not the endpoint of an argumentative process.

15. If social movements and policy problems alike ought to be understood in the context of the interplay or dialectic of forces and relations of

production, of system and lifeworld as Habermas reformulates them, then we must examine the ways in which policies and movements alike alter the communicative infrastructure of society. To date, Habermas has combined and sought to integrate two complementary but different types of analysis: an analysis of social learning understood as structural developments in the reproduction of society and an analysis of social action, and intermediate levels of social organization (factories, firms, hospitals, trade associations, unions, cultural associations, churches, and so forth), perhaps because he has tended to equate "organization" with a pattern of purely purposive-rational, instrumental, or strategic action. Nevertheless, if we seek to integrate action theory and structural systems theory along the lines made possible by the communications account that Habermas has provided, formulation of this intermediate level of social organization, this communicative infrastructure of society, is required. Table 7.2 tentatively suggests one formulation of this infrastructure.

16. These claims are historically contingent, and that is neither to say that they are arbitrary, random, purely ad hoc, and unsystematic, nor to say that they are simply the products of speakers (as the methodological individualists would have it). Speakers and listeners find themselves always already not only in a normative communications community (they share languages together in rule governed ways), but also in an institutional setting of relations of production and power. See also Forester 1989.

17. See Habermas 1975, part 3.

18. Consider this: "...the Federal government is not well equipped to investigate separately all of the tens of thousands of facilities involved in the generation, discharge, transportation, and use of hazardous substances. Federal agencies often have all they can do to issue permits as fast as the applications come in. There is seldom the opportunity to do extensive monitoring or inspecting to double-check the honesty or the accuracy of the permit applicant." *The Toxic Substances Dilemma*, Washington, D.C.: The National Wildlife Federation, 1980, 33.

19. The capital shifts that may be involved here are potentially substantial shifts of attention away from environmental and health protection: "by EPA estimates, business has spent $70 billion or more on pollution control in the eleven years since the agency started bringing lawsuits and unwelcome publicity" (*Time*, 18 January 1982).

20. Residents at Love Canal, New York, for example, feared that state officials were slow to respond for fear of setting precedents of state remedy.

21. On the importance of discourse, see Thomas McCarthy's introduction to Habermas 1975 and McCarthy 1978, 304–10, 314–17. Cf. Habermas 1979, chapters 3 and 5. See also Fischer 1980.

22. Without such discourses, societal learning loses its systematic institutional basis. While processes of learning in the dimensions of the development of productive forces and productive relations are *not* to be *equated* with the processes of noncoercive discourses, still to the extent that the results of the learning processes (local innovation activity, policy demonstration projects, restructuring of production and work processes, new political forms) cannot be checked noncoercively through such discourses, to that extent is domination likely to exist.

23. Notice, of course, that the very phrase "a socially necessary distortion" implies that *generalized* social acceptance or consent, rather than justification by appeal to a particularistic or private interest, ought to distinguish such a distortion from others. How, though, is that generalized acceptance to be judged by a critical political analyst, a critical policy analyst?

24. When we suggest that critical theory can be practical, then, we can hardly mean that *it* unleashes or unlocks the latent forces lying in waiting of a historically suppressed proletariat in the United States. Any such mobilization can only come from the efforts of activists in workplaces, in communities, in ethnic and gender-based social movements whose practical efforts and strategies—if they are not to work divisively at cross purposes—must be informed by a historically based theoretical analysis of established power, emancipatory strategies, and future political-economic possibilities, including both dangers and opportunities.

BIBLIOGRAPHY

Alexander, Christopher. 1964. *Notes on the Synthesis of Form*. Cambridge: Harvard University Press.

Alford, Robert, and Roger Friedland. 1985. *Powers of Theory*. Cambridge: Cambridge University Press.

Alvesson, Mats, and Hugh Wilmott. 1992. *Critical Management Studies*. Los Angeles: Sage Publications.

Amy, Douglas. 1987. *The Politics of Environmental Mediation*. New York: Columbia University Press.

Anderson, Charles. 1985. "The Place of Principles in Policy Analysis," 193–215. In *Ethics in Planning*, ed. M. Wachs, Livingston, N.J.:Center for Urban Policy Research, Rutgers University.

Apel, Karl-Otto. 1972. "Communication and the Foundations of the Humanities." *Acta Sociologica* 15.

———. 1977. "The A Priori of Communication and the Foundation of the Humanities." In *Understanding and Social Inquiry*, ed. F. Dallmayr and T. McCarthy. Notre Dame: University of Notre Dame Press.

Arendt, Hannah. 1959. *The Human Condition*. Chicago: University of Chicago Press.

Argyris, Chris, and Donald Schön. 1978. *Organizational Learning*. Reading, Mass. Addison-Wesley Publishing Company.

———. 1974. *Theory in Practice: Increasing Professional Effectiveness*. San Fransisco, Calif.: Jossey-Bass.

Austin, John. 1961. *Philosophical Papers*. London: Oxford University Press.

———. 1965. *How to Do Things With Words*. New York: Oxford University Press.

——. 1979 (1961). *Philosophical Papers.* London: Oxford University Press.

Bachrach, Peter. 1967. *The Theory of Democratic Elitism.* Boston: Little, Brown & Company.

Barber, Benjamin. 1984. *Strong Democracy: Participatory Politics for a New Age.* Berkeley: University of California Press.

Bateson, Gregory. 1975. *Steps to an Ecology of Mind.* New York: Ballantine.

Baum, Howell. 1980. "Analysts and Planners Must Think Organizationally." *Policy Analysis.* 6(4):480–94.

——. 1983. *Planners and Public Expectations.* Cambridge: Schenkman.

——. 1987. *The Invisible Bureaucracy.* New York: Oxford University Press.

——. 1990. *Organizational Membership.* Albany: State University of New York Press.

Bauman, Zygmunt. 1978. *Hermeneutics and Social Science.* London: Hutchinson.

Beiner, Ronald. 1983. *Political Judgment.* Chicago: University of Chicago Press.

Belnap, Nuel, and T. B. Steel. 1976. *The Logic of Questions and Answers.* New Haven, Conn.: Yale University Press.

Bell, Daniel. 1976. "The Public Household: On 'Fiscal Sociology' and the Liberal Society." In *Cultural Contradictions of Capitalism.* New York: Basic Books.

Bell, Martin. 1975. "Questioning." *The Philosophical Quarterly* 100 (July).

Bellah, Robert. 1982. "Social Science as Practical Reason." *The Hastings Center Report* (October).

Benhabib, Seyla. 1986. *Critique, Norm and Utopia.* New York: Columbia University Press.

——. 1989. "Liberal Dialogue Versus a Critical Theory of Discursive Legitimation." In *Liberalism and the Moral Life,* ed. Nancy Rosenblum. Cambridge: Harvard University Press.

——. 1989–1990. "In the Shadow of Aristotle and Hegel: Communicative Ethics and Current Controversies in Practical Philosophy." *The Philosophical Forum.* 21:1–2 (Fall–Winter).

Benhabib, Seyla, and Fred Dallmayr, eds. 1990. *The Communicative Ethics Controversy.* Cambridge: M.I.T. Press.

Benveniste, Guy. 1977. *The Politics of Expertise*. 2d ed. San Francisco: Boyd and Frazier.

———. 1989. *Mastering the Politics of Planning*. San Francisco: Jossey-Bass.

Berger, Peter. 1976. *Pyramids of Sacrifice*. New York: Anchor.

Berger, Peter, and Thomas Luckmann. 1966. *The Social Construction of Reality*. New York: Anchor.

Berman, Daniel. 1978. *Death on the Job*. New York: Monthly Review Press.

Bernstein, Richard. 1971. *Praxis and Action*. Philadelphia: University of Pennsylvania Press.

———. 1976. *The Restructuring of Social and Political Theory*. Philadelphia: University of Pennsylvania Press.

———. 1983. *Beyond Objectivism and Relativism*. Philadelphia: University of Pennsylvania Press.

Bok, Sissela. 1978. *Lying: Moral Choice in Public and Private Life*. New York: Vintage.

Bolan, Richard S. 1980. "The Practitioner As Theorist: The Phenomenology of the Professional Episode." *Journal of the American Planning Association*. 46:261–74.

Bolan, Richard S., and Ronald L. Nuttal. 1975. *Urban Planning and Politics*. Lexington, Mass.: Lexington Books.

Boyte, Harry C. 1980. *The Backyard Revolution*. Philadelphia: Temple University Press.

Bruner, Jerome. 1990. *Acts of Meaning*. Cambridge: Harvard University Press.

Bryson, John. 1982. "Strategic Planning as the Design of Forums, Arenas, and Courts." Paper presented at the National Conference of the Association of Collegiate Schools of Planning, Chicago.

Burke, John. 1986. *Bureaucratic Responsibility*. Baltimore: Johns Hopkins Press.

Burton, Dudley. 1981. "Methodology for Second Order Cybernetics." *Nature and System*. 3:13–27.

Burton, Dudley, and Brian Murphy. 1980. "Democratic Planning in Austerity: Practice and Theory." In *Urban and Regional Planning in an Age of Austerity*, ed. Pierre Clavel, John Forester, and William Goldsmith. New York: Pergamon Press.

Campbell, Donald, and J. Stanley. 1963. *Experimental and Quasi-Experimental Designs for Research.* Chicago: Rand McNally.

Catron, Bayard. 1977. "Intuition and Rationality in Decision Making." Paper presented at the National Conference of the American Society for Public Administration, Atlanta.

Cavell, Stanley. 1969. *Must We Mean What We Say?* New York: Charles Scribners Sons.

Checkoway, Barry. 1979. "Citizens on Local Health Planning Boards: What Are the Obstacles?" *Journal of the Community Development Society* 10:101–16.

————. 1981. *Citizens and Health Care: Participation and Planning For Social Change.* New York: Pergamon Press.

————. ed. 1986. *Strategic Perspectives on Planning Practice.* Lexington, Mass.: Lexington Books.

Chess, Caron. 1983: *Winning the Right-to-Know: a Handbook for Toxics Activists.* Delaware Valley Toxics Coalition.

Christensen, Karen. 1982. "Planning and Uncertainty." Paper presented at the National Conference of the Association of Collegiate Schools of Planning. Chicago, 22–24 October.

Churchman, C. West. 1962."On Rational Decision-Making." *Management Technology.* 2(2):71–76.

————. 1968. *The Systems Approach.* New York: Delta.

————. 1971. *The Design of Inquiring Systems.* New York: Basic Books.

Clavel, Pierre. 1986. *The Progressive City: Planning and Participation.* New Brunswick: Rutgers University Press.

Clegg, Stewart. 1975. *Power, Rule and Domination.* London: Routledge & Kegan Paul.

————. 1979. *The Theory of Power and Organization.* London: Routledge & Kegan Paul.

Cohen, Joshua, and Joel Rogers. 1983. *On Democracy.* New York: Penguin Books.

Conley, John, and William O'Barr. 1990. *Rules versus Relationships.* Chicago: University of Chicago Press.

Connerton, Paul. 1976. *Critical Sociology.* New York: Penguin Books.

Crozier, Michel. 1969. *The Bureaucratic Phenomenon.* Chicago: University of Chicago Press.

Dallmayr, Fred. 1974. "Toward a Critical Reconstruction of Ethics and Politics." *Journal of Politics.* 36:926–57.

———. 1976. "Beyond Dogma and Despair: Toward a Critical Theory of Politics." *American Political Science Review* (March).

———. 1981. *Beyond Dogma and Despair.* Notre Dame: University of Notre Dame Press.

Dallmayr, Fred, and Thomas McCarthy. 1977. *Understanding and Social Inquiry.* Notre Dame: University of Notre Dame.

Dalton, Linda. 1989. "Emerging Knowledge About Planning Practice." *Journal of Planning Education and Research.* 9:29–44.

Davidoff, Paul. 1965. "Advocacy and Pluralism in Planning." *Journal of the American Institute of Planners,* 31:596–615.

Davis, Kathy. 1988. *Power Under the Microscope.* Providence: Foris.

Deetz, Stanley. 1992. *Democracy in an Age of Corporate Colonization: Developments in Communication and Everyday Life.* Albany: State University of New York Press.

Dekema, Jan D. 1981. "Incommensurability and Judgment." *Theory and Society.* 10:521–46.

DeNeufville, Judith. 1983. "Planning Theory and Practice: Bridging the Gap." *Journal of Planning Education and Research.* 3(1):35–45.

Denhardt, Robert. 1981. *In the Shadow of Organization.* Lawrence: Regents Press of Kansas.

Dewey, John. 1927. *The Public and Its Problems.* New York: Holt, Rinehart & Winston.

———. 1960. *The Quest for Certainty.* New York: Putnam.

Dews, Peter. 1987. *Logics of Disintegration,* London: Verso Press.

———. 1986. *Habermas: Autonomy and Solidarity.* London: Verso Press.

Dreitzel, Hans P. 1972. *Recent Sociology 2: Patterns of Communicative Behavior.* New York: Macmillan.

Dyckman, John. 1978. "Three Crises of American Planning." In *Planning Theory in the 1980's,* ed. George Sternlieb and Robert Burchell. New Brunswick, N.J.: Rutgers Center for Urban Policy Research.

Edelman, Murray. 1971. *Politics as Symbolic Action.* New York: Academic Press.

———. 1964. *The Symbolic Uses of Politics*. Urbana: University of Illinois Press.

———. 1977. *Political Language: Words That Succeed and Policies That Fail*. New York: Academic Press.

Elster, Jon. 1983. *Sour Grapes*. Cambridge: Cambridge University Press.

———. 1986. *Rational Choice*. Washington Square, N.Y.: New York University Press.

Etzioni, Amitai. 1968. *The Active Society*. New York: Macmillan.

Euben, Peter. 1970. "Political science or political silence?" In *Power and Community*, ed. P. Green and S. Levinson. New York: Vintage.

Evans, Sara M., and Harry Boyte. 1986. *Free Spaces*. New York: Harper & Row.

Faludi, Andreas. 1976. *Planning Theory*. Oxford: Pergamon Press.

———. 1984. "The Return of Rationality." In *Rationality in Planning*, ed. M. Breheny and A. Hooper. London: Pion.

———. 1987. "Rationality, Critical Rationalism, and Planning Theory." Paper presented at the Conference on Planning Theory in the 1990's, Washington D.C.

Fay, Brian. 1976. *Social Theory and Political Practice*. London: Allen and Unwin.

———. 1987. *Critical Social Science*. Ithaca: Cornell University Press.

Feldman, Martha. 1989. *Order Without Design: Information Production and Policy*. Stanford: Stanford University Press.

Feyerabend, Paul. 1975. *Against Method*. London: New Left Review Editions.

Fischer, Frank. 1980. *Politics, Values, and Public Policy: The Problem of Methodology*, Boulder, Colo.: Westview Press.

Fischer, Frank, and John Forester, eds. 1993 (forthcoming). *The Argumentative Turn in Policy Analysis and Planning*. Durham, N.C.: Duke University Press.

Fisher, Roger, and William Ury. 1983. *Getting to Yes: Negotiating Agreement Without Giving In*. New York: Viking Penguin, Inc.

Forester, John. 1980. "How Much Does the Environmental Review Planner Do?" *Environmental Impact Assessment Review*. 1:104–7.

———. 1981a. "Questioning and Organizing Attention as Planning Strategy: Toward a Critical Theory of Planning." *Administration and Society* 13(2):161–205.

————. 1981b. "Hannah Arendt and Critical Theory: A Critical Response." *Journal of Politics* (February).

————. 1981c. "Selling You the Brooklyn Bridge and Ideology" A Review of Habermas's *Communication and the Evolution of Society. Theory and Society* 10:745–50.

————. 1981d. "Toward Democratic Health Planning: Political Power, Agenda-setting, and Planning Practice." In *Citizens and Health Care: Participation and Planning for Social Change*, ed. B. Checkoway. New York: Pergamon Press.

————. 1982a. "Critical Reason and Political Power in Project Review Activity." *Policy and Politics* 10(1): 65–83.

————. 1982b. "A Critical Empirical Framework for the Analysis of Public Policy." *New Political Science*. 2:145–64.

————. 1983. "Critical Theory and Organizational Analysis." In *Beyond Method*, ed. Gareth Morgan. Los Angeles: Sage Publications.

————. 1984. "Practical Rationality in Planning." In *Rationality in Plan-Making*, ed. Michael Breheny and Alan Hooper. London: Pion.

————. 1985. *Critical Theory and Public Life*. Cambridge: M.I.T. Press.

————. 1987a. "Anticipating Implementation: Normative Practices in Planning and Policy Analysis." In *Confronting Values in Policy Analysis: The Politics of Criteria*, ed. Frank Fischer and J. Forester. Los Angeles: Sage Publications.

————. 1987b. "How Planners Argue: Rhetorical Strategies and Problems of Substance, Power, and Passion in Planning Practice." In *Planning Theory in the 1990's: New Directions*, ed. Robert Burchell and G. Sternlieb. Washington, D.C.

————. 1989. *Planning in the Face of Power*. Berkeley: University of California Press.

————. 1991. "Reply to My Critics…" *Planning Theory Newsletter*. University of Turin: Dipartimento Interateneo Territorio, viale Mattioli 9 10125 Troino, Italy. 4:43–60.

————. 1992a. "Fieldwork in a Habermasian Way." In *Critical Management Studies*, ed. M. Alvesson and H. Wilmott. Los Angeles: Sage Publications.

————. 1992b. "Envisioning The Politics of Public Sector Dispute Resolution." In *Studies in Law, Politics, and Society*, ed. Austin Sarat and Susan Silbey. Greenwich, Conn.: JAI Press.

———. 1993 (forthcoming). "Learning From Practice Stories: The Priority of Practical Judgment." In *The Argumentative Turn in Policy Analysis and Planning,* ed. Frank Fischer and John Forester. Durham, N.C.: Duke University Press.

Foster, Harold, A. Abramson, and M. Parella. 1982. "Planners' Skills and Planning Schools: A Comparative Study of Alumni." Paper presented at the National Conference of the Association of Collegiate Schools of Planning. Chicago.

Fraser, Nancy. 1989. *Unruly Practices.* Minneapolis: University of Minnesota Press.

Freire, Paulo.1970. *Pedagogy of the Oppressed.* New York: Seabury Press.

———. 1973. *Education for Critical Consciousness.* New York: Seabury Press.

Friedland, Roger., Frances F. Piven, and Robert Alford. 1977. "Political Conflict, Urban Structure, and the Fiscal Crisis." *International Journal of Urban and Regional Research.* 1:447–71.

Friedmann, John. 1973. *Retracking America.* New York: Anchor.

———. 1978. "The Epistemology of Social Practice." *Theory and Society.* 6:75–92.

———. 1979. *The Good Society.* Cambridge: M.I.T. Press.

———. 1980. *On the Theory of Social Construction: An Introduction.* School of Architecture and Urban Planning. Los Angeles: University of California.

———. 1987. *Knowledge and Action: Mapping the Planning Theory Domain.* Princeton, N.J.: Princeton University Press.

Friedson, Eliot. 1970a. *Professional Dominance.* New York: Atherton Press.

———. 1970b. *Profession of Medicine.* New York: Harper & Row.

Gadamer, Hans G. 1975. *Truth and Method.* New York: Seabury Press.

———. 1979. "The Problem of Historical Consciousness." In *Interpretive Social Science: A Reader,* 103–60, ed. Paul Rabinow and William Sullivan. Berkeley: University of California Press.

Gaventa, John. 1980. *Power and Powerlessness: Quiescence and Rebellion in an Appalachian Valley.* Urbana: University of Illinois Press.

Giddens, Anthony. 1976. *New Rules of Sociological Method: A Positive Critique of Interpretive Sociologies.* London: Hutchinson.

———. 1979. *Central Problems in Social Theory: Action, Structure, and*

Contradiction in Social Analysis. Berkeley: University of California Press.

———. 1981. *A Contemporary Critique of Historical Materialism*. Berkeley: University of California Press.

———. 1982. "Reason without revolution." *Praxis International* 318–38.

———. 1984. *The Constitution of Society: Outline of a Theory of Structuration*. Berkeley: University of California Press.

Gilligan, Carol. 1982. *In a Different Voice*. Cambridge: Harvard University Press.

Giroux, Henry. 1983. *Theory and Resistance in Education*. South Hadley, Mass.: Bergin and Garvey.

Goffman, Erving. 1959. *The Presentation of Self in Everyday Life*. Garden City, N.Y.:Doubleday.

———. 1967. "On Deference and Demeanor." In *Interaction Ritual*, ed. E. Goffman. Garden City, N.Y.: Doubleday.

———. 1981. *Forms of Talk*. Philadelphia: University of Pennsylvania Press.

Goodman, Nelson. 1978. *Ways of Worldmaking*. Cambridge, Mass.: Hackett.

Gorz, Andre. 1970. *Strategy for Labor*. Boston: Beacon Press.

Gouldner, Alvin. 1976. *The Dialectic of Ideology and Technology*. New York: Seabury Press.

Gusfield, Joseph. 1981. *The Culture of Public Problems*. Chicago: University of Chicago Press.

———, ed. 1989. *Kenneth Burke: On Symbols and Society*. Chicago: University of Chicago Press.

Habermas, Jürgen. 1968. *Knowledge and Human Interests*. Boston: Beacon Press.

———. 1970. *Toward a Rational Society*. Boston: Beacon Press.

———. 1971. *Knowledge and Human Interests*. Boston: Beacon Press.

———. 1972. "Toward a Theory of Communicative Competence." In Dreitzel, Hans P. (cited above).

———. 1973. *Theory and Practice*. Boston: Beacon Press.

———. 1975. *Legitimation Crisis*. Boston: Beacon Press.

———. 1977a. "A Review of Gadamer's *Truth and Method*," in Dallmayr and McCarthy (cited above), 335–63.

———. 1977b."Hannah Arendt's Communications Concept of Power." *Social Research* 44(1):3–24.

———. 1979. *Communication and the Evolution of Society*. Boston: Beacon Press.

———. 1983. *The Theory of Communicative Action*. Vol. 1, *Reason and the Rationalization of Society*. Boston: Beacon Press.

———. 1987. *The Theory of Communicative Action*. Vol. 2, *Lifeworld and System: A Critique of Functionalist Reason*. Boston: Beacon Press.

Harmon, Michael, and Richard Mayer, eds. 1986. *Organization Theory for Public Administration*. New York: Little, Brown & Company.

Hartman, Chester. 1975. "The Advocate Planner: From Hired Gun to Political Partisan." *The Politics of Turmoil*, eds. R. A. Cloward and F. F. Piven. New York: Vintage.

———. 1978. "Social Planning and the Political Planner." In *Planning Theory in the 1980's*, ed. Robert Burchell and George Sternlieb. New Brunswick, N.J.: Center for Urban Policy Research.

Harvey, David. 1978. "Planning the Ideology of Planning." In *Planning Theory in the 1980's*, eds., Robert Burchell and George Sternlieb. New Brunswick, N.J.: Center for Urban Policy Research.

Healey, Patsy.1990. "Policy Processes in Planning." *Policy and Politics*. 18(1):91-103.

———. 1992. "A Planner's Day: Knowledge and Action in Communicative Practice." *Journal of the American Planning Association*. 58(1):9–20.

Healey, Patsy, and H. Thomas, eds. 1991. *Dilemmas of Practice*, London: Gower Aldershot.

Heidegger, Martin. 1962. *Being and Time*. New York: Harper & Row.

Held, David. 1980. *Introduction to Critical Theory*. Berkeley: University of California Press.

Hemmens, George, and Bruce Stiftel. 1980. "Sources for the Renewal of Planning Theory." *Journal of the American Planning Association*. 46:341–45.

Hirschman, Albert. 1970. *Exit, Voice, and Loyalty*. Cambridge: Harvard University Press.

Hoch, Charles, and A. Cibulskis. 1987. "Planning Threatened: A Prelimi-
    nary Report of Planners and Political Conflict." *Journal of
    Planning Education and Research.* 6(2):99–107.

Hoch, Charles. 1987. "A Pragmatic Inquiry About Planning and Power."
    Paper presented at the Rutgers University Center for Urban
    Policy Research Conference on Planning Theory in the 1990's,
    March 31–April 1.

————. 1984. "Pragmatism, Planning, and Power." *Journal of Planning
    Education and Research* 4(2):86–95.

Honneth, Axel, Eberhard Knodler-Bunte, and Arno Widmann. 1981. "The
    Dialectics of Rationalization: An Interview with Jürgen Haber-
    mas." *Telos* 49 (Fall).

Honneth, Axel. 1981. "Communication and Reconciliation: Habermas' Cri-
    tique of Adorno." *Telos* 39 (Spring).

Horkheimer, Max. 1972. *Critical Theory.* New York: Seabury Press.

————. 1974. *The Eclipse of Reason.* New York: Seabury Press.

Howe, Elizabeth, and Kaufman, Jerome. 1979. "The Ethics of Contempo-
    rary American Planners." *Journal of the American Planning
    Association* 45 (3):243–55.

Hummel, Ralph. 1982. *The Bureaucratic Experience.* 2d ed. New York: St.
    Martins Press.

Innes, Judith. 1990. *Knowledge and Action in Public Policy: The Search for
    Meaningful Indicators.* New Brunswick, N.J.: Transaction Pub-
    lishers.

Jacobs, Allan B. 1978. *Making City Planning Work.* Chicago: American
    Society of Planning Officials.

Kaufman, Jerome. 1974. "Contemporary Planning Practice: State of the
    Art." In *Planning in America: Learning From Turbulence*, ed.
    David Godschalk. Washington, D.C.: American Institute of
    Planners.

————. 1987. "Teaching Planning Students About Strategizing, Boundary
    Spanning and Ethics: Part of the New Planning Theory." *Jour-
    nal of Planning Education and Research* (Winter).

Kellner, Doug, and Rick Roderick. 1981. "Recent Literature on Critical
    Theory." *New German Critique* no. 23 (Spring/Summer).

Kelly, Michael.1990. *Hermeneutics and Critical Theory in Ethics and Poli-
    tics.* Cambridge: M.I.T. Press.

Kemp, Ray. 1980. "Planning, Legitimation, and the Development of Nuclear Energy." *International Journal of Urban and Regional Research* 4:350–71.

———. 1982. "Critical Planning Theory: Review and Critique." In *Planning Theory: Prospects for the 1980's*, ed. Patsy Healey, G. McDougall, M. Thomas, 59-67. Oxford: Pergamon.

———. 1985. "Planning, Public Hearings, and the Politics of Discourse." In *Critical Theory and Public Life*, ed. John Forester. Cambridge: M.I.T. Press.

Kertzer, David. 1988. *Ritual Politics, and Power*. New Haven: Yale University Press.

Kittay, Eva, and Diana Myers, eds. 1987. *Women and Moral Theory*. Philadelphia: Temple University Press.

Klosterman, Richard. 1978. "Foundations of Normative Planning." *Journal of the American Institute of Planners* 44(1):37–46.

Kochman, Robert. 1981. *Black and White Styles in Conflict*. Chicago: University of Chicago Press.

Kraushaar, Robert. 1979. "Pragmatic Radicalism." *International Journal of Urban and Regional Research* 3(1):61–79.

Krieger, Martin. 1974. "Some New Directions for Planning Theories." *Journal of The American Institute of Planners*. 40:156–63.

———. 1973. *Lectures on Design*. Berkeley: University of California. Mimeo.

———. 1981. *Advice and Planning*. Philadelphia: Temple University Press.

Krumholz, Norman. 1978. Cut-back Planning in Cleveland. Mimeo. Cleveland: Ohio State University, College of Urban Affairs.

———. 1982. "A Retrospective View of Equity Planning: Cleveland 1969–1979." *Journal of the American Planning Association*. 48:163–74.

Krumholz, Norman, and John Forester. 1990. *Making Equity Planning Work: Leadership in the Public Sector*, Philadelphia: Temple University Press.

Krumholz, Norman, Janice Cogger, and John Linner. 1975. "The Cleveland Policy Planning Report." *Journal of the American Institute of Planners* 41(5):298–304.

Kuhn, Thomas. 1972. *The Structure of Scientific Revolutions*. Chicago: University of Chicago Press.

Lakatos, I., and Musgrave, A. 1972. *Criticism and the Growth of Knowledge.* Cambridge: Cambridge University Press.

Lakoff, Robin. 1975. *Language and Woman's Place.* New York: Harper/ Colophon.

Lancourt, Joan. 1979. *Developing Implementation Strategies: Community Organization Not Public Relations.* Boston: Boston University, Health Policy Center.

Landau, Martin. 1973. "On the Concept of a Self-Correcting Organization." *Public Administration Review* 533–42.

Lax, David, and James Sebenius. 1986. *The Manager as Negotiator.* New York: Free Press.

Lindblom, Charles. 1959."The Science of Muddling Through." *Public Administration Review* 19:79–88 (Spring).

———. 1977. *Politics and Markets.* New York: Basic Books.

———. 1979. *Usable Knowledge.* New Haven, Conn.: Yale University Press.

Linton, Rhoda, and Michelle Whitham. 1982. "With Mourning, Rage, Empowerment, and Defiance: The 1981 Women's Pentagon Action," *Socialist Review* 12:3–4 (May–August).

Lipsky, Michael. 1980. *Street Level Bureaucracy.* New York: Russell Sage Foundation.

Lukes, Steven.1974. *Power: A Radical View,* New York: Macmillan.

———. 1975. "Political Ritual and Social Integration." *Sociology* 9(2):289–308.

Majone, Giandomenico. 1989. *Evidence, Argument, and Persuasion in the Policy Process.* New Haven, Conn.: Yale University Press.

Mandelbaum, Seymour. 1979. "A Complete General Theory of Planning Is Impossible."*Policy Sciences* 11:59–71.

——— 1991. "Telling Stories." *Journal of Planning Education and Research.* 10(3):209–14.

Mansbridge, Jane. 1983. *Beyond Adversary Democracy.* Chicago: University of Chicago Press.

———. 1988. *Beyond Self Interest.* Chicago: University of Chicago Press.

March, James. 1978. "Bounded Rationality, Ambiguity, and the Engineering of Choice." *Bell Journal of Economics.* 9:587–610.

———. 1982."Theories of Choice and Making Decisions." *Society* 29–39 (November–December).

———. 1988. *Decisions and Organizations*, London: Blackwell.

March, James, and Johann Olsen. 1976. *Ambiguity and Choice in Organizations*. Oslo, Norway: Universitetsforlaget.

March, James, and Herbert Simon. 1958. *Organizations*. New York: Wiley and Sons.

Marcuse, Peter. 1976. "Professional Ethics and Beyond: Values in Planning." *Journal of the American Institute of Planners* 42:264–94.

Marris, Peter, and Martin Rein. 1984 (1974). *Dilemmas of Social Reform*. 2d ed. Chicago: University of Chicago Press.

Marris, Peter. 1975. *Loss and Change*. New York: Anchor. Reprint. London: Routledge & Kegan Paul, 1986.

———. 1987 (1982). *Community Planning and Conceptions of Change* (republished as *Meaning and Action*) London: Routledge & Kegan Paul.

Mason, R., and I. Mitroff. 1980–1981. "Policy Analysis as Argument." *Policy Studies Journal* 9:570–85.

Mayo, James. 1978. "Propaganda with Design: Environmental Dramaturgy in The Political Rally." *Journal of Architectural Education* Special Issue: Politics and Design Symbolism. 32(2):24–27.

———. 1985. "Political Avoidance in Architecture." *Journal of Architectural Education* 38:2 (Winter).

McCarthy, Thomas. 1978. *The Critical Theory of Jürgen Habermas*. Cambridge: M.I.T. Press.

McCloskey, Donald. 1985. *The Rhetoric of Economics*. Madison: University of Wisconsin Press.

McGuire, R. R. 1977. "Speech Acts, Communicative Competence, and the Paradox of Authority." *Philosophy and Rhetoric* 10:30–45.

Mechanic, David. 1976. The Growth of Bureaucratic Medicine. New York: Wiley and Sons.

Meltsner, Arnold. 1972. "Political Feasibility and Policy Analysis." *Public Administration Review* 32 (November–December).

———. 1975. "Bureaucratic Policy Analysts." *Policy Sciences* 1:115–31.

———. 1976. *Policy Analysts in the Bureaucracy*. Berkeley: University of California Press.

———. 1979. "Don't Slight Communication: Some Problems of Analytical Practice." *Policy Analysis* 5(3):367–92.

Merry, Sally.1990. *Getting Justice and Getting Even.* Chicago: University of Chicago Press.

Michael, Donald. 1973. *On Learning to Plan—and Planning to Learn.* San Fransisco: Jossey-Bass.

Mills, C. Wright.1959. *The Sociological Imagination.* New York: Grove Press.

Misgeld, Dieter. 1984: Critical Theory and Sociological Theory. *Philosophy of the Social Sciences* 14:97–105.

———. 1985. "Education and Cultural Invasion: Critical Social Theory, Education as Instruction, and the 'Pedagogy of the Oppressed.'" In *Critical Theory and Public Life*, ed. J. Forester. Cambridge: M.I.T. Press.

Moch, Michael, and Louis Pondy. 1977. "The Structure of Chaos: Organized Anarchy as a Response to Ambiguity" *Administrative Science Quarterly* 22:351–62

Montouri, Joseph. 1984: How Public Employee Unions Are Fighting 'Contracting-Out'. *Labor Notes*, 23:5ff. (February).

Moore, Sally, and Barbara Myerhoff, eds. 1977. *Secular Ritual.* Assen: Van Gorcum.

Mueller, Claus. 1973. *The Politics of Communication.* New York: Oxford University Press.

Myerhoff, Barbara. 1982. "Life History Among the Elderly: Performance, Visibility, Re-Membering." In *A Crack in the Mirror: Reflexive Perspectives in Anthropology*, ed. Jay Ruby. Philadelphia: University of Pennsylvania Press.

Needleman, Carolyn, and Martin Needleman. 1974. *Guerrillas in the Bureaucracy.* New York: Wiley and Sons.

Nelson, John, A. Megill, and D. McCloskey, eds. 1987. *The Rhetoric of the Human Sciences: Language and Argument in Scholarship and Public Affairs.* Madison: University of Wisconsin Press.

New York Community Action Network. 1983: *The Toxics Crisis: A Citizens' Response.* New York Community Action Network.

Nobel, David.1982. "The Selling of the University," *The Nation*, February 6.

Nussbaum, Martha C. 1984. *The Fragility of Goodness.* New York: Cambridge University Press.

———. 1990. *Love's Knowledge.* New York: Oxford University Press.

O'Connor, James. 1973. *The Fiscal Crisis of the State.* New York: St. Martin's Press.

Offe, Claus. 1975. "The Theory of the Capitalist State and the Problem of Policy Formation." In *Stress and Contradiction in Modern Capitalism*. ed. L. Lindberg et al., 125–44. Lexington, Mass.: Lexington Books.

O'Neill, John. 1972. *Sociology as a Skin Trade*. New York: Harper & Row.

———. 1974. *Making Sense Together*. New York: Harper & Row.

———. 1985. "Decolonization and the Ideal Speech Community: Some Issues in the Theory and Practice of Communicative Competence." In *Critical Theory and Public Life*, ed. John Forester. Cambridge: M.I.T. Press.

———. 1989. *The Communicative Body*. Evanston, Ill.: Northwestern University Press.

Ong, Aiwa. 1987. *Spirits of Resistance and Capitalist Discipline*. Albany: State University of New York Press.

Paris, David, and James Reynolds. 1983. *The Logic of Policy Inquiry*. New York: Longman.

Pateman, Carole. 1970. *Participation and Democratic Theory*. Cambridge: Cambridge University Press.

Peattie, Lisa.1987. *Planning: Rethinking Ciudad Guayana*. Ann Arbor: University of Michigan Press.

Perrow, Charles. 1972. *Complex Organizations: A Critical Essay*. New York: Scott, Foresman.

Pitkin, Hanna. 1972. *Wittgenstein and Justice*. Berkeley: University of California Press.

———. 1973. "The Roots of Conservatism: Michael Oakeshott and the Denial of Politics." In *The New Conservatives*, ed. Lewis Coser and Irving Howe. New York: Meridian.

Pitkin, Hanna, and Sara Shumer. 1982. "On Participation." *democracy* 2:43–54.

Piven, Frances F., and Cloward, Richard. 1982. *The New Class War*. New York: Pantheon Books.

———. 1977. *Poor People's Movements*. New York: Pantheon Books.

———. 1975. *Politics of Turmoil*. New York: Vintage.

———. 1971. *Regulating the Poor*. New York: Pantheon Books.

Popper, Sir Karl. 1963. *Conjectures and Refutations*. London: Routledge & Kegan Paul.

Rabinow, Paul, and William Sullivan. 1979. *Interpretive Social Science.* Berkeley: University of California Press.

Rabinowitz, Francine. 1969. *City Politics and Planning.* New York: Atherton Press.

Rasmussen, David.1990. *Universalism vs. Communitarianism: Contemporary Debates in Ethics.* Cambridge: M.I.T. Press.

Reade, Eric. 1984. "An Analysis of the Use of the Concept of Rationality in the Literature of Planning." In *Rationality in Planning,* ed. M. Breheny and A. Hooper. London: Pion.

Reich, Robert.1988. "Policy-Making in a Democracy." In *The Power of Public Ideas.* Cambridge: Ballinger.

Rein, Martin, and Donald Schön. 1977. "Problem Setting in Policy Research." In *Using Social Research in Public Policy Making,* ed. Carol Weiss, 235-251. Lexington, Mass.: Lexington Books.

Roderick, Richard.1986. *Habermas and The Foundations of Critical Theory.* New York: St. Martin's Press.

Rohr, John. 1978. *Ethics for Bureaucrats.* New York: Marcel Dekker.

Roe, Emery. 1994. *Narrative Policy Analysis,* Ithaca: Cornell University Press.

Rorty, Amelie. 1988. *Mind in Action.* Boston: Beacon Press.

Roweis, Shoukry, 1983, "Urban Planning as Professional Mediation of Territorial Politics" *Environment and Planning D: Society and Space* 1:139–62

Sandercock, Leonie, and Ann Forsyth. 1992. "A Gender Agenda: New Directions for Planning Theory," *Journal of the American Planning Association* 58(1):49–59.

Saunders, Peter. 1979. *Urban Politics.* London: Hutchinson.

Schaar, John. 1967. "Equality of Opportunity and Beyond." In *Nomos IX: Equality,* ed. J. R. Pennock and J. Chapman. New York: Atherton Press.

———. 1981. *Legitimacy in the Modern State.* New Brunswick, N.J.: Transaction Publishers.

Schattschneider, E. E. 1960. *The Semi-Sovereign People.* New York: Holt, Rhinehard, Winston.

Schön, Donald. 1971. *Beyond the Stable State.* Random House, New York.

———. 1983. *The Reflective Practitioner: How Professionals Think in Action.* New York: Basic Books.

————. 1991. *The Reflective Turn: Case Studies in and on Educational Practice*. New York: Teachers College Press.

Schroyer, Trent. 1973. *The Critique of Domination*. Boston: Beacon Press.

Schutz, Alfred. 1970. *Phenomenology and Social Relations*, ed. H. Wagner. Chicago: University of Chicago Press.

Scott, James. 1990. *Domination and the Arts of Resistance*. New Haven, Conn.: Yale University Press.

————. 1985. *Weapons of the Weak: Everyday Forms of Peasant Resistance*. New Haven, Conn.: Yale University Press.

Searle, John. 1969. *Speech Acts*. Cambridge: Cambridge University Press.

Seeley, John. 1963. "Social Science? Some Probative Problems." In *Sociology on Trial*, ed. M. Stein and A. Vidich. Englewood Cliffs: Prentice-Hall.

Selznick, Philip. 1966. *TVA and the Grassroots*. New York: Harper & Row.

Shapiro, Jeremy. 1976. "Reply to Miller's Review of Habermas's *Legitimation Crisis*." *Telos* 27:170–76 (Spring).

Silverman, David.1987. *Communication and Medical Practice*. Los Angeles: Sage Publications.

Simon, Herbert. 1957. *Models of Man*. New York: Wiley and Sons.

————. 1969. *The Sciences of the Artificial*. Cambridge: M.I.T. Press.

————. 1979. "From Substantive to Procedural Rationality." In *Philosophy and Economic Theory*, ed. Frank Hahn and Martin Hollis, 65–86. Oxford: Oxford University Press.

Smith, Tony. 1981. "The Scope of the Social Sciences in Weber and Habermas." *Philosophy and Social Criticism*, 8:1 (Spring).

Suchman, E. 1967. *Evaluative Research*. New York: Russell Sage Foundation.

Sunstein, Cass. 1991. "Preferences and Politics," *Philosophy and Public Affairs* 20(1):3–34.

Susskind, Lawrence. 1981. "Environmental Mediation and the Accountability Problem." *Vermont Law Review* 6:1–47.

Susskind, Lawrence, and Connie Ozawa. 1984. "Mediated Negotiation in the Public Sector." *Journal of Planning Education and Research* 4(1):5–15 (August).

————. 1983. "Mediated Negotiation in the Public Sector: Mediator

Accountability and the Public Interest Problem." *American Behavioral Scientist* 27:2.

Susskind, Lawrence, and J. Cruickshank. 1987. *Breaking the Impasse.* New York: Basic Books.

Susskind, Lawrence, and Louise Dunlap. 1981. "The Importance of Non-Objective Judgments in Environmental Impact Assessments." *Environmental Impact Assessment Review* 2:335–66.

Szanton, Peter. 1981. *Not Well Advised.* New York: Russell Sage Foundation.

Taylor, Charles. 1985. *Philosophical Papers.* Cambridge: Cambridge University Press.

Taylor, John. 1977. "Environmentalists in the Bureaucracy: Environmental Impact Analysis in the Forest Service and Army Corps of Engineers." Berkeley: University of California, Political Science Department, Typescript.

Teitz, Michael. 1974. "Toward a Responsive Planning Methodology." In *Planning in America: Learning from Turbulence,* ed. D. Goldschalk. Washington: American Institute of Planners.

Thompson, John. 1983. "Rationality and Social Rationalization: An Assessment of Habermas's Theory of Communicative Action." *Sociology* 17:2.

———. 1984. *Studies in the Theory of Ideology.* Berkeley: University of California Press.

Thompson, John, and D. Held, eds. 1982. *Habermas: Critical Debates.* Cambridge, Massachusetts: M.I.T. Press.

Thompson, James. D. 1967. *Organizations in Action.* New York: McGraw-Hill.

Thompson, James. D., and A. Tuden. 1959. "Strategies, Structures, and Processes of Organizational Decision." In *Comparative Studies in Administration,* ed. J. D. Thompson. Pittsburgh: University of Pittsburgh Press.

Tribe, Laurence. 1972. "Policy Science: Analysis or Ideology?" *Philosophy and Public Affairs.* 2:66–110.

———. 1973. "Technology Assessment and the Fourth Discontinuity: The Limits of Instrumental Rationality." *Southern California Law Review.* 46:617–60.

Thrift, N. J. 1983. "On the Determination of Social Action in Space and Time." *Environment and Planning D: Society and Space* 1:23–58.

Throgmorton, James. 1991. "The Rhetorics of Policy Analysis." *Policy Sciences* 24(2):153–79.

Toulmin, Stephen 1964. *The Uses of Argument*. Cambridge: Cambridge University Press.

———. 1970. *Reason in Ethics*. Cambridge: Cambridge University Press.

Todd, Alexandra, and S. Fisher, eds. 1988. *Gender and Discourse: The Power of Talk*. Norwood, N.J.: Ablex Publishers.

Tronto, Joan. 1987. "Beyond Gender Difference to A Theory of Care." *Signs: Journal of Women in Culture and Society* 12(4):644–63.

Truex, Duane, and H. Klein. 1991. "A Rejection of Structure as a Basis for Information Systems Development." *Collaborative Work, Social Communication, and Information Systems*. 213–36.

Van Hooft, Stan. 1976. "Habermas's Communicative Ethics." *Social Praxis* 4:147–75.

Vickers, Sir G. 1984 (1965). *The Art of Judgment*. New York: Harper & Row.

———. 1970. *Value Systems and Social Processes*. London: Pelican.

———. 1973. "Communication and Ethical Judgement." In *Communication: Ethical and Moral Issues*, ed. L. Thayer. London: Gordon and Breach.

———. 1987. *Policy-Making, Communication, and Social Learning*, ed. Guy Adams, John Forester, and Bayard Catron. New Brunswick, N.J.: Transaction Publishers.

Wachs, Martin. 1985. *Ethics in Planning*. New Livingston, N.J.: Center for Urban Policy Research.

Walzer, Michael. 1980. *Radical Principles*. New York: Basic Books.

Wardhaugh, Ronald. 1985. *How Conversation Works*. New York: Basil Blackwell.

Watzlawick, Paul. 1976. *How Real is Real?* New York: Vintage.

Watzlawick, Paul, Janet Beavin, and Don Jackson. 1967. *Pragmatics of Human Communication*. New York: Norton.

Webber, Melvin. 1963. "Comprehensive Planning and Social Responsibility: Toward an AIP Consensus on the Profession's Roles and Purposes." *Journal of the American Institute of Planners*. 29:232–41.

———. 1978. "A Difference Paradigm for Planning." In *Planning Theory in the 1980s,* ed. R. W. Burchell and G. Sternlieb. New Brunswick, N.J.: Center for Urban Policy Research.

Webber, Melvin, and Horst Rittel. 1973. "Dilemmas in a General Theory of Planning." *Policy Sciences* 4:155–69.

Weber, Max. 1958a. "Religious Rejections of the World and Their Directions." In *From Max Weber,* ed. Hans Gerth and C. Wright Mills. New York: Oxford University Press.

———. 1958b. *The Protestant Ethic and the Spirit of Capitalism.* New York: Charles Scribners Sons.

Weick, Karl. 1969. *The Social Psychology of Organizing.* Addison-Wesley.

Weiss, Carol. 1972. *Evaluation Research.* Englewood Cliffs, N.J.: Prentice-Hall.

———. 1977. "Research for policy's sake." *Policy Analysis* 4 (Fall).

Wellmer, Albrecht. 1974 (1969). *Critical Theory of Society.* New York: Seabury Press.

———. 1976. "Communication and Emancipation: Reflections on the Linguistic Turn in Critical Theory." In *On Critical Theory,* ed. John O'Neill. New York: Seabury Press.

———. 1983. "Reason, Utopia, and the Dialectic of Enlightenment." *Praxis International* 3, 2.

White, James B. 1984. *When Words Lose Their Meaning.* Chicago: University of Chicago Press.

———. 1985. "Rhetoric and Law: The Arts of Cultural and Communal Life." In *Heracles' Bow: Essays on the Rhetoric and Poetics of the Law.* Madison, Wisc.: University of Wisconsin Press. 28–48.

White, Stephen. 1988. *The Recent Work of Jürgen Habermas.* Cambridge: Cambridge University Press.

Wiggins, David. 1978. "Deliberation and Practical Reason." In *Practical Reasoning,* ed. J. Raz. Oxford: Oxford University Press. 144–52.

Wildavsky, Aaron. 1972. "The Self-Evaluating Organization." *Public Administration Review.* 509:20.

———. 1973. "If Planning Is Everything, Maybe It's Nothing." *Policy Sciences* 4(2):127–53.

———. 1979. *Speaking Truth to Power: The Art and Craft of Policy Analysis.* New York: Little, Brown & Company.

Wilensky, Harold. 1967. *Organizational Intelligence.* New York: Basic Books.

Winner, Langdon. 1977. *Autonomous Technology.* Cambridge: M.I.T. Press.

———. 1986. *The Whale and the Reactor.* Chicago: University of Chicago Press.

Wittgenstein, Ludwig. 1973. *Philosophical Investigations.* New York: Macmillan.

———. 1972a. *The Blue and Brown Books.* New York: Harper & Row.

———. 1972b. *On Certainty.* New York: Harper & Row.

———. 1967. *Lectures and Conversations.* Berkeley: University of California Press.

Wolfe, Alan. 1977. *The Limits of Legitimacy.* New York: Free Press.

———. 1974."New Directions in the Marxist Theory of Politics." *Politics and Society* 4(2):131–59 (Winter).

Wolin, Sheldon. 1960. *Politics and Vision.* New York: Little, Brown & Company.

Yanarella, Ernest, and Herbert Reid. 1977. "Critical Political Theory and Moral Development." *Theory and Society* 4.

NAME INDEX

Abrams, D., 154
Adams, G., 22
AFSCME Local 2427, 113–14,
    118–21, 123
  Fight Back Committee, 113–14,
    119
Alford, R., 11, 88
Alvesson, M., 108
Americans for Democratic Action,
    112
Anderson, C., 44
Apel, K. O., 14, 32, 78, 165n2
Argyris, C., 85
Aristotle, 68
Austin, J., x, 14, 25, 33, 41, 49

Bachrach, P., 57
Barber, B., 20, 29, 62, 72, 172n20
Bastille, self-storming and self-
    regulation, 22
Bateson, G., 26
Baum, H., xi, 5, 18, 21, 29, 76,
    84–85
Bauman, Z., 26, 165n2, 165n23,
    165n26
Bell, D., 11
Bell, M., 49
Bellah, R., 68, 71
Benhabib, S., 64, 165n2, 170n2,
    170n4
Benveniste, G., 27–29, 45–47, 76,
    166n2
Berger, P., 25, 169n26

Berman, D., 145
Bernstein, R., 2, 16, 54, 165n2,
    166n5, 167n18
Bolan, R., 17, 84–85, 92, 165n2
Boyte, H., 59, 172n10
Breheny, M., 163n1Preface
Bruner, J., 6, 33, 49
Bryson, J., 85
Burke, J., 19, 62, 78
Burton, D., 29, 85, 172n10

Campbell, D., 167n16
Catron, B., 18
Chess, C., 107, 111–13, 121–23
Christensen, K., 88
Churchman, C. W., 20–21, 44, 69,
    165n1c2
Cibulskis, A., 76
Clavel, P., 76
Cloward, R., 90, 143
Cohen, J., 62, 128, 172n10
Cogger, J., 18
*Communication and the Evolution
    of Society*, 164n6
Community-Labor Coalitions,
    107–33
Conley, J., 50
Critique of Domination, 164n4
Cruickshank, J., 44, 104, 172n10

Dallmayr, F., 28, 64, 165n2,
    167n18–19, 169n25, 170n2
Davis, K., 42, 49

SUBJECT INDEX

Agenda-setting, 6, 102, 166n10
Ambiguity, 9, 171n5. *See also*
    Learning; Practice;
    Rationality
  differs from uncertainty, 9,
    88–89, 96, 104, 170n1C5
  in doubt of legitimacy claims,
    92–96
  and learning, 104
  systematically present in prac-
    tice, 89–90, 92
Analysis, 19–30, 43–66. *See also*
    Practice; Rationality
  and attention organizing, 43–48
  and misinformation, 75–78
  as planning practice, 38
  and slack, 83
  situated, 86–87
Attention. *See also* Communicative
    action; Organization;
    Power; Practice; Reproduc-
    tion; Speech acts
  and agenda-setting, 102, 166n10
  analysis and organizing, 43–48,
    105, 166n6
  and budgets, 101, 152, 155
  and communicative action,
    25–29
  to design approaches, 45
  to effectiveness, 46
  and ideology critique, 62
  and mobilization of bias, 5–6, 8,
    101, 124–25

  organizational, 10, 31–32
  political economy of, 34, 102
  to political positions, 45
  and practical–theorizing, 43, 47,
    161
  pragmatic claim calling, 8, 91
  and problem-framing, 42, 47,
    172n7
  public, ix, 156, 169n22
  and questioning, 43–52, 167n11
  to setting of design, 44
  and social theory, 40–43, 165n2
  to stakes of design, 44
  structural processes, 30–31,
    124–25, 144, 152
  and uncertainty, 47, 60–61
  and vision, 39

Budgets, claims-making analysis
    of, 175n9

Communicative action. *See also*
    Attention; Critical theory;
    Interaction; Learning;
    Practice; Reproduction
  ascribed vs. achieved interac-
    tion, 128, 131, 178n23
  and attention, 25, 158
  claims-making aspects, 4, 27, 90,
    158, 164n6, 174n8–9
  and conflict, 93
  and encouragement, 26
  and ethics, 61–64, 170n4

Communicative action *(continued)*
  infrastructures of, 119, 136,
    140–46, 150–52, 156,
    158–59, 171n4, 173n3,
    174n9
  instrumental and expectation-
    shaping, 25–26
  and planning practice, 24–30,
    90, 171n3
  and rationality, 68–72, 80
  and reproduction, 24–30, 33,
    94–96, 105, 117–18, 126
    128–32
  and staged contra-dictions,
    129–32, 150
  and systematic distortions, 54,
    56–57
  theory of, x, 2
  vs. talk, 24–26
Community-labor coalitions,
  107–33, 148–50
Conflict. *See also* Interaction;
    Learning; Power
  and background consensus,
    148–50
  and claims–making, 120–22,
    126–29
  and contra–dictions, 129–32,
    148–50
  interaction and organizing, 117,
    132–33
  and learning, 93
  and perception of problems, 148
Critical Theory. *See also* Social
    Theory; Pragmatism;
    Structural phenomenology
  addressees of, 150–51
  and communicative action, 5,
    117–18, 138–39, 147
  contradictions as contra-dic-
    tions, 129–32, 139, 148–50
  and critical sociology of policy,
    ix, 135–61
  empirical dimensions, 13, 107,
    126–29, 132–33, 139–46,
    152, 154–61

and ethics, 18–19, 34, 125
Habermasian continuities with
    Marx, 129–32, 173n2
integrating structural and phe-
    nomenological analyses,
    13, 139–46, 151, 156, 160,
    163, 170n2, 173n3, 173n6,
    175n10
lessons for, 124–25, 164n6
methodological problems, 2, 13,
    125, 145, 160–61
with practical intent, limits of,
    125, 160–61
and rationality, 72–73, 128–30,
    170n2
reconstruction of historical
    materialism, 135–39
and reformulation of bounded
    rationality, 6
and research, 30–34, 107,
    126–29, 140–46, 165n2,
    158–60
and social reproduction, 115–25,
    140–46
sources, 163
and systematically distorted
    communication, 53, 55–56
unconventional treatment, ix
and Weber's theory of rational-
    ization, 129

Democratization, 57–60, 62,
    122–24, 127–28, 131–33,
    137–39, 145, 170n1C5. *See
    also* Discourse; Learning;
    Rationality; Power
Discourse. *See also* Communicative
    Action; Democratization;
    Learning; Power; Ratio-
    nality; Speech acts
  counterfactual, 78, 158–59,
    168n19–20
  difficulties of recourse to, 3, 136,
    145, 150–51, 158–61
  and democratization, 57–64,
    122, 127–28, 131–33,

137–39, 145, 150–51,
     159–61, 169n23, 178n22
and foolishness of distortionless
     communication, 159,
     168n18
idealized conditions of "check-
     ing," 3, 138
and political rationality, 99
restricted Habermasian mean-
     ing, 3, 138, 177n21
theoretical and practical, 78,
     138, 159

Economic transactions and claims-
     making, 164n6, 174n9
Empowerment and disempower-
     ment, 4
Ethics. See also Communicative
     Action; Practice; Power;
     Reproduction; Speech acts
and critical theory, 3–4, 18–19, 34
and ideology-critique, 62
of ordinary discourse, 29–30,
     169n25
and questioning, 61–64
and rationality, 18, 69–71,
     73–74, 78, 80, 170n4,
     178n23
and reproduction, 32
and responsibility of analysts,
     26, 28, 63, 64

Gender, 131. See also Reproduction
Goal setting and value formulation,
     18, 21
and background consensus,
     176n14

Hope and counterhegemony, 6

Ideal speech situation, x, 3, 138,
     164n3, 168n18–20. See also
     Communicative Action;
     Discourse; Speech acts
not an ideal model of society,
     164n3

misunderstood counterfactual, 3
not a practical goal, 168n18,
     168n20
no significant role in this book, x
sociological irrelevance, x
Ideology-critique, 56, 62, 73, 164n4,
     167n17–18, 169n23. See
     also Power; Resistance
Incrementalism, 38–40, 53–54, 87
Interaction, social, ix–x. See also
     Communicative Action;
     Learning; Practice; Repro-
     duction; Ritual perfor-
     mance; Speech acts
ascribed agreement vs. achieved
     understanding, 128
and attention-shaping, 46
claims-making structure of, 8,
     159
communicative infrastructure
     of, 12, 126, 135, 140–46,
     159
as derivative from communica-
     tive action, 138
institutionally resisting or main-
     taining, 2, 148–50
and learning, 7–9, 85, 137–39,
     146–51, 156, 159–61
promising vs. tool-using
     metaphors, 26
purposive-rational and commu-
     nicative action, 137
and questioning, 49–53
revealing relations of control,
     149–51
and social identity, 143
and social movements, 148–50
vulnerabilities of, x, 4, 14

Judgment. See also Ethics; Prac-
     tice; Rationality
and ethics, 76, 170n4
and limits of theory, 125, 131
and misinformation, 76
practical, xi, 32
and virtue, 71

Learning. *See also* Communicative
    action; Discourse; Interac-
    tion; Reproduction; Speech
    acts
  and ambiguity, 104
  and conflict, 93, 104
  and democratic processes, 105,
    145–46, 177n22
  and networks, 97
  and planning practice, 85, 103,
    170n1C5
  and policy analysis, 151, 156,
    159–61, 177n15
  and pragmatic structure of
    claims-making, 8
  productive and reproductive, 12,
    85, 103–4, 137–39, 140–46,
    156, 178n22
  purposive-rational vs. commu-
    nicative action, 137
  as rationalization of action,
    137–39, 145–46, 151
  and the reconstruction of histori-
    cal materialism, 136–39,
    145–46

Legitimacy, 56, 160, 170n3, 178n23
Lifeworld
  colonization, 4, 129–30
  and organization, 164n5
  and social reproduction, 115–17
  structural analysis of, 173n6
  and system pressures, 122,
    127–29, 132–33, 172n1
  rationalization, 128, 141

Negotiation, 167n13

Organization, 9–11, 164n5. *See also*
    Background consensus;
    Learning; Public policy
  and community-labor coalitions,
    108–14
  and democratization, 125–26
  and the geography of practice,
    94–126

  Habermas's instrumental view
    of, 174n7
  and learning, 53–54
  mediating systemic relations
    and interactions, 140, 142,
    175n10
  and organizing attention, 5–6,
    27, 31 101–2, 111–13
  productive and reproductive ele-
    ments, 9–10, 94, 140–46
  and ritual performances, 143
  and systematically conflicting
    claims, 129–32

Participation. *See also* Democrati-
    zation; Learning; Repro-
    duction
  and counterhegemonic, democ-
    ratizing roles of planners,
    6, 57–58
  and networks, 59
  and questioning, 51–52, 59
  and rationality, 78, 80
Planning theory, 1–9, 15–35. *See
    also* Pragmatism; Ratio-
    nality; Social theory
  and attention, 40–43
  critical or ethically illuminating,
    18–19
  and discursive model of rational-
    ity, 80
  empirically grounded, 16–17
  irrelevance to practice, 84
  interpretive, 17–18
Policy, public. *See also* Organiza-
    tion; Practice; Rationality;
    Reproduction; Right-to-
    know
  altering social infrastructures,
    12, 136, 140–46, 150–51,
    156, 158–61, 175n10,
    176n12, 177n15
  analysis and theory of action,
    164
  and conditions of discourse,
    150–51, 159–61, 164n7

critical sociology of, ix, 135–61
and implementation, 144–46,
150–51, 154, 158–60
conventional approaches to, 11
and financial and economic
impacts, 155
legal-regulatory effects, 153
mediating system relations and
interactions, 140–46,
150–56, 173n3
micropolitics and microsociology
of, x, 164n7
"problems," 146–49, 156
and right-to-know laws, 111–13
and scientific-technological
activity, 154
and social learning, 12, 136,
140–46, 150, 154, 156, 158
and social organization, 153
and toxic chemical threats,
108–13
Politics, Micro-, xi, 33, 37–66. *See
also* Attention; Practice;
Power; Reproduction;
Resistance
and communicative action, 29,
166n10
and the geography of practice,
86, 105, 122–24
and identity, 123–24
neglected in conventional views
of practice, 19–24
and rationality, 75–77, 79–81
in review committee discussions,
98–99
and right-to-know struggles,
111–13
and social identities, 100
and theory, 40–43
Postmodernism, x
Power. *See also* Attention; Practice;
Politics, micro; Resistance
and agenda-setting, 6, 166n10
and anticipation, 96–105, 148,
160–61
and apparent necessity, 40

and background consensus,
149–51, 161
and conflict, 93, 148–51
and consent, 98–99
and contra-dictions, 150
and cooptation, 48
and ethics, 62–64, 77–78
hegemonic, 11, 122–25, 148–51,
161
and identity, 100, 149
and information management,
48, 54–55, 99, 160, 171n7
and normative communications
community, 177n16
and organization, 93–94
and the organization of attention, 47–53, 146–48
phenomenology of voice, 131,
149
and questioning, 48–53
and rationality, 40, 73–74,
79–81
and reproduction, 118–24,
132–33, 149, 160
and resistance, 11, 14, 58, 60,
83–105, 171n6
and social movements, 148–51
and uncertainty management,
60–61
Practical judgment, xi, 32
Practice, 5–6, 15–35, 37–66,
83–105. *See also* Attention;
Ethics; Planning theory;
Power; Rationality
and background consensus, 148
and claims making, 90–92
cognitive geography of, 95,
97–98, 125, 170n1C5,
171n4
conventional views, 19–24
cybernetic perspectives, 22,
166n3–4
economic resource geography of,
95, 101–2, 124–25,
170n1C5, 171n4
and ethics, 61–64, 69–70, 172n9

Practice *(continued)*
  instrumental and practical-com-
    municative views, 28,
    67–71, 90, 166n3, 171n3
  means-ends models of, 20, 69,
    171n3
  need for grounded theory of, 84
  organizational geography of, 86,
    102–3, 105
  planning, 15, 38, 64–66, 166n2,
    167n12
  political-legal geography of, 95,
    98–99, 125, 170n1C5,
    171n4
  pragmatism and realism in,
    38–40
  problem-solving perspectives,
    21, 86
  requirements of a theory of,
    15–19
  and research, 30–34, 165n1
  and responses to misinforma-
    tion, 76–77, 79–81, 122–24
  ritual geography of, 95, 99–101,
    125, 170n1C5, 171n4
  satisficing perspectives, 23–24,
    80, 87
  and skills, 125
  situated, 86–87, 90–92
  structural-phenomenological
    analysis, 170n2, 173n6
  and theorizing, 43, 47, 85, 165n2
  and timidity, 83
Pragmatism, critical, ix, 1–14,
    38–40, 161, 166n5, 166n8.
  See also Critical theory; Ethics;
    Planning theory; Social
    theory
  and analysis, 65
  and insight, 41
  and naive realism, 40
  and systematic distortion, 54
  and vision, 39, 161, 165n1b

Questioning, 48–53, 167n11,
    167n12, 167n15, 167n17,

    169n23. *See also* Commu-
    nicative action; Discourse;
    Power; Speech acts
  and action, 49
  and democratization, 58–60,
    169n23
  in policy analysis, 64–66
  and the politics of information, 49
  and praxis, 49–52, 167n11
  strategies of, 52–53
  and uncertainty management,
    60–61
  and whistleblowing, 167n15

Rationality. *See also* Attention; Dis-
    course; Power; Practice
  and argument, 57–58, 80
  bounded, 6–7, 38, 67, 74–81,
    166n8
  bounded, Habermasian reformu-
    lation of, 7, 74–81
  forms of, 67–71, 166n3
  and communicative action,
    68–72, 138, 168n20
  and conditions of criticism,
    78–79, 137–39
  and constraints, structural, 7,
    56, 74–81, 159–61, 169n23
  and constraints, unnecessary, 7,
    56, 60–62, 74–81, 159–61,
    169n23
  and ethics, 69–71, 73–74, 78
  and legitimacy, 56–57, 151
  and murder, 69
  and power, 73–74, 79–81
  practical, 32, 39, 72–74
  of production and reproduction,
    115, 128–30, 137–39, 140,
    151
  and rationally motivated agree-
    ment, 128
  and symbolic interaction, 68
  and types of misinformation, 40,
    75
  and unbrotherly aristocracy of
    science, 71

and validity basis of speech, 128,
138, 168n19–20, 170n2
and Weber's iron cage, 70
Reproduction, social. *See also*
Attention; Communicative
action; Critical Theory;
Learning; Power; Policy,
public; Speech acts
and anticipation of power,
122–25
and ascribed vs. achieved outcomes, 128, 131
of attention, 10, 26, 30–31,
94–96, 101, 124–25,
129–32, 136–39, 155,
159–60
of beliefs, 10, 26, 31, 94–96, 118,
120–24, 129–32, 136–39,
149, 155, 159–60
of consent, 10, 26, 31, 94–96,
118, 120–24, 129–32,
136–39, 149, 159–60
and communicative action,
24–30, 94–96, 105, 117–18
and critical theory of policy
analysis, 135–61
and democratization, 128,
137–39
and ethics, 63
infrastructures of interaction,
119–22, 132–33, 140–52,
156, 159
in organizations, 31–32, 121–24
and patriarchy, 131
policy institutionalized, 160
and power, 118
and reputation, 99–101
research questions, 116, 128
and social integration, 115–17,
119–21, 128
and socialization, 115–17,
119–21
systematically conflicting claims
in, 129–32
and toxic chemicals, 157
of trust, 10, 26, 31, 94–96, 100,

118, 122–24, 129–32,
136–39, 149, 159–60
vulnerable processes of, 119,
126–29, 132–33
Reputation, 99, 117, 119, 123, 143
and background consensus,
148–50
and ritual performance, 100,
121–24, 143
and trust, 100, 123
Resistance, 83–105, 169n26, 171n6.
See also Attention; Power;
Pragmatism; Rationality
and communicative action, 94,
122–24
and a critical theory of policy,
145
in organizations, 2, 125–26
and repertoire of action, 171n6
and systematic distortion of
communication, 57–58, 60,
62
Rationalization, 4, 128–30. *See also*
Discourse; Learning;
Reproduction
Ritual performance, 100, 121–22,
143, 170n1C5, 172n8,
174n9. *See also* Reproduction
and identity, 100, 143

Speech acts. *See also* Communicative action; Practice; Structural phenomenology
and context, 91–92, 146–48
and contra-dictions, 129–32,
148–50
double structure of, 8, 90–92,
138–39
doubt and ambiguity in, 9
involving four pragmatic claims,
8, 27, 90–92, 124, 138, 147,
149
and policy "problems," 146–49
and practice, 24, 90–92, 131,
138, 158

Speech act
  and pro
  and que
  shaping
      12
      14
  shaping
      12
      14
  shaping
      12
      14
  shaping
      12
      14
  and socia
  and socia
      12
Social indic
Social move
      mu
  and confl
Social theor
      als
      nal
      Str
  and analy
  and comn